STRESS MANAGEMENT

An Integrated Approach to Therapy

T0347326

STRESS MANAGEMENT

An Integrated Approach to Therapy

by

Dorothy H. G. Cotton, Ph.D.

Routledge
Taylor & Francis Group
New York   London

Library of Congress Cataloging-in-Publication Data
Cotton, Dorothy H. G.
  Stress management : integrated approach to therapy / by Dorothy
H.G. Cotton.
    p.   cm. — (Brunner/Mazel psychosocial stress series ; no. 17)
  Includes bibliographical references.
  ISBN 0-87630-557-5
  1. Stress management.   I. Title.   II. Series.
RA785.C67   1990
616.9'8—dc20   89-38991
                                                                          CIP

This edition by Routledge:

Routledge   Routledge
Taylor and Francis Group   Taylor and Francis Group
711 Third Avenue   2 Park Square, Milton Park
New York, NY 10017   Abingdon, Oxfordshire OX14 4RN

First issued in paperback 2014

Routledge is an imprint of the Taylor and Francis Group, an informa business

Published by
BRUNNER/MAZEL, INC.
19 Union Square
New York, New York 10003

ISBN 13: 978-0-87630-557-7 (hbk)
ISBN 13: 978-1-138-00955-4 (pbk)

To
W. M. C.,
N. G. C.,
&
C. H. (G.) C.

Series Note

As number 17 in the Psychosocial Stress Series, this book by Dr. Dorothy Cotton joins a long and illustrious list of works that focus on the interface between stress research and practice. The first book in this series, published 12 years ago, focused on the long-term psychosocial effects of combat. Subsequent books have provided insights into other types of stressor situations (disasters, family abuse, violence), stressed populations (refugees, hostages, veterans, crime victims), and critical factors in the stressor/stress relationship (stress and addiction, culture, gender, race).

Dr. Cotton's book is the result of well over a decade of research and clinical practice. In addition to working individually with stressed clients, she is also a popular consultant for various public and private organizations. Her approach to stress management evolved as a result of her dissatisfaction with the limitations of standard stress management techniques. Dr. Cotton identified the lack of conceptual framework as the key deficit in current therapies. Her solution is to adapt an integrated approach to stress management as a therapeutic modality. Thus, the mission of this book is to help the reader conceptualize, as well as effectively control, stress in a clinical setting.

Dr. Cotton first clearly defines the concept of stress and stress reactions, and goes on to review thoroughly the scientific and clinical literature. Mid-way through the book she describes her integrative approach to therapy and a novel method of charting the presenting problems and treatment options. The remainder of the book illustrates and clarifies its basic dimensions. An innovative pictorial grid is presented to display graphically the components of various therapies in their interactions. This enables the reader/clinician to identify more precisely the presenting stress-related problem and to draw from the variety of treatment techniques to develop a coherent plan for therapy.

As a cognitive/behaviorist, Dr. Cotton's initial training in social psychology is evident in her approach. Her conceptualization and methods of managing stress are enhanced by her sensitivity to the uniqueness of individual client's needs. Of particular interest is her discussion of gender issues, which includes seven recommendations for therapy with women. Dr. Cotton acknowledges that her experiences as a working mother have provided valuable insights for developing effective stress management techniques for women.

I am happy and proud to welcome this important book to our series. Please contact me with any comments about this book or suggestions for others. I can be reached at the Psychosocial Stress Research Program, Florida State University, Tallahassee Florida 32306-2024. I look forward to hearing from you.

Charles R. Figley, Ph.D., Editor

Contents

Introduction: Stress and Gender

Stress seems to have become the buzzword of the 80s, and will no doubt continue to be a major issue for mental health practitioners for some time to come. Certainly the public has grasped the concept. Clients frequently arrive specifically requesting assistance for dealing with stress-related problems. The popularity of the concept of stress is clearly reflected by the amount of attention that stress has received in both the popular press and in professional literature. In the past few years, this burgeoning field has given rise to many books about causes of stress, physiology of stress, stress in particular target groups, self-help methods for dealing with stress, diets for stress, exercises for stress, stress in children, and particular stress management techniques. The abundance of literature in this field is, at once, exciting, challenging, confusing, intriguing, misleading, contradictory, and informative.

Unfortunately, when all is said and done, the mental health practitioner is still left with the question of where to begin and what to do for the individual stressed client.

This book represents the years of consumption of literature and integration of knowledge that I have experienced in dealing with stressed clients. Like many therapists, I began with knowledge of a few particular techniques useful in stress management. These techniques were indeed helpful, yet always seemed somewhat inadequate in dealing with the "whole" client. Adding additional techniques to my repertoire did not seem to increase significantly my ability to help clients. In fact, it often tended to fragment treatment. What was lacking in my practice was the notion of integration—that is, the possession of a comprehensive and coherent approach to therapy with stressed clients. Over the years, the general approach described in this book has evolved. None of the specific techniques described in this book are new or original. What is new is the presentation of a conceptual framework which allows the therapist

xiii

to employ these techniques in a manner which results in the maximum benefit for the client.

The overriding purpose of this book is to enable the therapist to recognize and treat problems which are attributable to stress. Although employing a stress management perspective in therapy presupposes a basic competence in counseling or psychotherapy, it also requires somewhat of a shift in the focus of the therapist. The foundation of the integrated stress management perspective lies in the conceptualization of stress and the creation of an operational definition of stress. The first goal of this book is to derive from the vast and somewhat contradictory literature on stress a clinically useful operational definition of stress and a description of its effects. The purpose of Chapters 2, 3, and 4 is to derive such a definition of stress for the therapeutic situation and to assess the meaning and implications of stress for the individual client.

The second goal of this book is to propose a model of stress management as a therapeutic modality. How does knowledge of the nature and effects of stress translate into effective psychotherapy or counseling? Chapter 5 examines the interface between assessment and treatment. One of the most problematic aspects of stress management is that of integrating a number of diverse treatment techniques into a meaningful and comprehensive structure. In order to achieve a sense of internal cohesion among the various approaches, a pictorial grid, a graphic display of the various components of therapy and their interactions, is described. Once an understanding of the problem is achieved and a coherent plan is identified, then the actual "work" of therapy begins. Chapters 6 to 9 examine specific therapeutic techniques and discuss their application to stress-related problems.

Aside from the presentation and integration of research findings, the goals of this book will also be achieved through the thorough and systematic presentation of three case studies. None of these cases represents an actual living client, but all represent prototypes of "typical" individuals who may present for treatment. Through the medium of these cases, the principles and techniques described in the text will be expanded and demonstrated. It is hoped that the provision of clinical material and acknowledgment of "real" clinical issues will enable therapists to integrate more easily the stress management approach into their own clinical practice.

The general orientation of this book is cognitive-behavioral, but like most "real" therapists, I find my own approach is eclectic. By training and experience, I am a social psychologist with a feminist bent, who works as a clinician. The cognitive-behavioral techniques are embedded in a supportive and reflective problem-solving relationship, which may need to address the effects of the culture at large on the individual, and which may need also to help the client come to grips with personal needs, defenses, unresolved issues, and interpersonal conflicts. Clearly, the application of purely cognitive-behavioral techniques without a broad context is not enough for most clients.

Nowhere is the need for context more apparent than in dealing with the stressed female client. Women far outnumber men in their use of mental health services. This discrepancy is particularly evident in the relative numbers of men and women experiencing depression and anxiety, common effects of stress. (See Cleary, 1987, for a comprehensive review of this area.) Unfortunately, examination of gender issues in stress and stress management is only in a beginning stage.

DEFINING GENDER ISSUES IN STRESS MANAGEMENT

It is not purely coincidental that two of the three cases examined in this book are women. A therapist is likely to see at least as many women in therapy as men—probably more. Are the issues in stress management the same for women as they are for men? Probably not. This is not to say that the general framework outlined in this book is not as relevant for women as it is for men. Rather, the focus of each component of therapy may be different for female clients as compared to male clients. Since the gender of the client will probably have some implications for the whole process of therapy in general and stress management in particular, it is worth thinking about these implications before embarking on the main body of this book.

It is far beyond the scope of this book to discuss all the gender issues related to stress in any great detail. Those who are particularly interested in this area should refer to the extremely comprehensive volume on this topic by Barnett, Biener, and Baruch (1987). Much of the information following is garnered from this source.

Nevertheless, it would be negligent not to mention briefly the areas within stress management in which gender issues are particularly salient. There are four main areas in which males and females seem to experience the stress process differently:

(1) There may be differences in the frequency with which males and females experience certain stress-related disorders, as well

as differences in the specific physiological reaction accompanying stress.

(2) There may be differences in the types of stressors to which males and females are exposed.

(3) When males and females are exposed to the same stressor, there may be differences in the meaning attached to that stressor by males and females.

(4) There may be differences in the ways in which males and females cope with stress.

Differences in Physiology

Women tend to get sick more often than men, yet they live significantly longer. Conventional wisdom in the past has suggested that women may be hypochondriacal, but that they still live longer because they are exposed to less stress than men. There is no evidence to support either part of this statement. Attempts to demonstrate a lower tolerance for pain or illness on the part of women have been unsuccessful. Furthermore, as measurement of stress has been improved, it becomes evident that women are not under less stress than men, either in the traditional full-time homemaker role or as "working mothers." In addition, women occupying traditionally male roles and occupations do begin to smoke more, exhibit more Type A behavior, and generally acquire other health risk factors much as men do—but the women still live longer. The immediate explanation for this difference is that women tend not to get the same types of illnesses that men do, including those illnesses which occur in response to stress. The differences are most evident in the case of cardiovascular disorder (in which males are overrepresented), and in the case of anxiety and depression (in which women are overrepresented). Much of the responsibility for high rates of anxiety and depression may be attributable to psychosocial causes. The reasons for the differences in physical health problems such as heart disease remain unclear.

There is some evidence that women experience a slightly different physiological response to stress than do men. Studies have indicated that in response to stress, females exhibit smaller elevations in epinephrine levels when compared to males. It has been hypothesized that estrogens and/or progesterone inhibit neuroendocrine reactivity, thus serving somewhat of a prophylactic function for women. Studies comparing premenopausal women, postmenopausal women, and men tend to support this argument (Polefrone & Manuck, 1987). There is also evidence of some variation in the reactivity of norepinephrine and cortisol during the course of the normal menstrual cycle. These findings together suggest that female hormones may provide a level of protection for women, moderating some of the potential ill effects of stress. This line of research remains fairly new and somewhat contradictory, so firm conclusions cannot yet be drawn.

In the case of cardiovascular reactivity, there is also some evidence of gender differences. Males tend to display larger systolic blood pressure responses and smaller heart rate reactions to psychological stress than do women. Again, it seems that female reproductive hormones may account for at least part of the difference.

The evidence in the area remains murky and contradictory. For each study which suggests a gender-related link, there are others which have not found such relationships. Clearly, women do suffer different physiological outcomes from stress as compared to men. Attributing this difference to hormonal effects is an attractive option, but one which remains poorly supported by research.

Differences in Stressors

There are a number of stressors which are generally relevant to members of only one sex or the other. For men, the most obvious example is war and combat. For women, however, there are many gender-specific stressors. Unfortunately, most of these do not find their way onto standardized measures of stress. Being pregnant (or not becoming pregnant when desired), being physically or sexually assaulted, and becoming a homemaker are events which happen exclusively or primarily to women. There are other stressors which more commonly but primarily apply to women: being a single parent, having responsibility for other family members, experiencing financial insecurity, or having a job with no security or benefits.

These stressors, which might be called objectively threatening situations (Barnett, Biener, & Baruch, 1987) are threatening to the individual's well-being, by anyone's standards. The level of stressfulness is a function of the extent to which the stressor limits personal autonomy and blocks access to resources. Given this definition of stressfulness, even stressors which occur with equal frequency in men and women can produce more stress for one or the other. Consider the example of marriage. In a traditional male-female relationship, the female forgoes her identity to support her mate. Her resources are those which the mate chooses to dispense. Clearly, the relative amounts of stress experienced by the two partners are different. Even in more general work situations, women may experience more stress than men. Women's jobs typically involve less control (i.e., nurse versus doctor; secretary versus manager), and provide less in the way of resources (pay, stability, benefits). The maternal role is probably the best example of a stress which is inherently low in control, low in resources, and high in demands. By definition, mothers are expected to look after and care for the needs of others, yet society provides little support (either practically or psychologically) for these activities. This is in striking contrast to the role of father, which is traditionally high in control, and low in demands.

What is stressful for women, then, is not only the specific tasks and responsibilities assigned to them, but also the roles assigned to them.

Differences in Meaning

In some cases, men and women *do* experience the same stressors. Both may be parents, workers, partners, friends, teammates. In spite of the apparent common ground, however, these stressors may differ in their seriousness for women as opposed to men. One determinant of the level of stress inherent in a given role or event is the degree to which it constitutes a threat to sex-linked goals and values.

One of the prime determinants of appropriate behavior in society is gender norms. These norms both prescribe and proscribe certain aspects of behavior—different behavior for different sexes. An obvious example—again—is that of parenting. Both mother and father may be known by the generic label for "parent," but the social and personal expectations are quite different for a male parent and a female parent. The degree of stress engendered by a role will be determined in part by the extent to which the identity of an individual is tied up in that role. Thus, it may be the meaning of the role rather than the role itself which brings about stress. Typically, the identity of a mother is much more strongly tied to her parenting role than is the identity of a father. Given this, a problem with a child may be much more stressful for a mother than for a father.

There are a variety of situations which have a different meaning for a woman than for a man. Being overweight, not being married, being the class valedictorian—each of these events has a different meaning or interpretation, depending upon the gender of the subject.

One of the difficulties with women's sex-linked norms and values is that they tend to be contradictory. It is no longer acceptable for women to subjugate themselves solely to the care and feeding of others, yet it is also not acceptable to enter the work force when one has small children. Women "should be" passive, obedient, trusting, and helpless. Yet being a victim is associated with possessing these traditionally feminine characteristics. Some particularly interesting contradictions arise from studies of adolescence in females, a period in which concerns shift from achievement to popularity. Barnett, Biener, and Baruch (1987) describe the double-bind situation of the adolescent female who aspires to be popular and have dates. In order to do so, she must shift her focus to pleasing others, with a resultant loss of control and autonomy. "Popular" girls actually lose rather than gain self-esteem. But what of unpopular girls, who sit home on Saturday nights? Does their self-esteem increase?

The conclusion that the meaning and interpretation of an event may have more impact than the event itself is not new. This discussion parallels the discussion of life events versus appraisal. What is distressing is the direction in which this discussion takes us. Clearly, expectations and roles put women at increased risk for increased stress.

Differences in Coping

As described in Chapter 5, coping strategies can be loosely categorized as emotion-focused or problem-focused. Emotion-focused strategies are likely to be used when the individual perceives that the stressor itself cannot be altered, but rather, must be tolerated. Problem-focused coping aims at changing the stressor. A number of studies show that women are more likely to use emotion-focused strategies, whereas men are more likely to use problem-focused strategies. Each of these tendencies has advantages and disadvantages. The tendency of men not to release and deal with emotions leads to more acting-out behavior and aggression in men. There is also evidence (Billings & Moos, 1981) that problem-focused coping is less apt to lead to depression than emotion-focused behavior. This is certainly consistent with observations of a greater frequency of depression in women.

However, the relationships are not quite as simple as it might seem. The use of problem-focused strategies in unchangeable situations is not particularly adaptive. The differences in coping strategies between men and women may be partly indicative of the differences in the experience or perception of stress. The relatively low status of women and women's roles in general may lead a woman to conclude that a situation is unchangeable, whereas a man might assess the same situation differently—from a position of power.

There also seem to be some fundamental differences in cognitive style and coping style between men and women. Miller and Kirsch (1987) review evidence that suggests:

- Women tend to be somewhat more negative in their self-evaluations than are men.
- As children, girls tend to be more pessimistic about their performance, and tend to generalize more from past difficulties than do boys—although girls actually tend to perform better.
- Girls are more likely to attribute failure to internal factors (e.g., ability), whereas boys tend to attribute failure to external sources (e.g., the teacher).
- Women, more often than men, tend to use distraction or try to block out stress-relevant information.

In spite of common myths to the contrary, there is not much evidence of consistent differences between men and women in causal attribution or perceptions of control in stressful circumstances. Coping style does tend to be related to appraisal—and appraisal tends to differ in men and women. Research in this area is not conclusive, given the methodological complexities of examining coping styles. Nevertheless, it does seem important to assess the use of coping strategies from within the framework of the individual client, keeping in mind the likely gender biases.

RECOMMENDATIONS

There are a number of points emerging from this discussion which have implications for conducting stress management therapy with women:

(1) Many professional organizations (including the American Psychological Association) have issued guidelines for conducting therapy with women clients. All therapists should read and keep in mind these general guidelines.

(2) In assessing objectively threatening or major life events, the therapist should specifically ask about the "women's issues" which are neither typically included in assessment tools, nor taught in interviewing courses. Histories of physical and sexual abuse, reproductive status, family responsibilities, work versus

family conflict, and the like are all items with clear implications for stress management, yet many therapists do not ask about these items. Clients typically do not volunteer such information unless it is specifically requested.

(3) Consider all situations from the client's standpoint. Particularly when the therapist is male and the client is female, it is important for the therapist to work from the perspective of the meaning that an event or role has for the client rather than for the therapist. The mental health professions have a long history of defining females as a deviation from the male norm. Therapy must derive from the client's own determination of what is meaningful.

(4) Women place more importance and derive more satisfaction from catharsis than do men. In the effort to strengthen problem-focused coping, the need for emotion-focused coping should not be overlooked.

(5) When a woman is truly in a position of little control, some feeling of control or empowerment can come from consciousness-raising, which has been an integral part of the women's movement since the 1800s. Political involvement at some level can help shift the focus of blame or responsibility to an external source, and thus decrease the negative evaluation and self-blame that often lead to anxiety and depression.

(6) Listen. My mother once told me that middle-aged women are invisible. Women are ignored, talked over, and interrupted more often than men. Listen. Hear what female clients say.

Acknowledgment

Nothing important in life ever gets done by a single person. Not even this book. There were many people who helped, by reading, typing, thinking, talking, supporting, smiling, editing, prodding, encouraging. I think these people know who they are, and I thank them all.

STRESS MANAGEMENT

An Integrated Approach to Therapy

1

An Overview

The client settles back in her chair, in apparent relief, having described a litany of problems, including family pressures, work conflict, sleep disturbance, irritability, stomach upset, and crying jags. The therapist silently ponders these problems, attempting to fit them into a straightforward diagnostic category such as anxiety or depression. Such a categorical diagnosis might aid the therapist in establishing a clear direction for treatment. The problem is neither simple nor straightforward, however. As with so many other clients the therapist has seen recently, the problem is stress, and the answer is complex.

As the silence continues, many different therapeutic modalities come to the therapist's mind—relaxation, cognitive therapy, assertiveness, time management. The list is long and all are appropriate interventions. Yet the therapist is torn by the competing demands of the situation. On the one hand, there are immediate practical measures which may offer some degree of relief from the acute aspects of the situation, but which seem stopgap and short-sighted. On the other hand, there are longer term introspective approaches which work toward the eventual goal of maximizing personal strength and awareness, but without providing the immediate relief that the client seems to need.

"I think you have a problem with stress."

STRESS MANAGEMENT: WHAT IS IT?

According to the American Academy of Family Physicians, two-thirds of office visits to family doctors are prompted by stress-related symptoms. The effects of stress on health may be major and life-threatening, or merely annoying and inconvenient. There is little doubt, however, that stress is a significant problem in contemporary society. A number of factors may contribute to the increasing prevalence of stress problems.

3

Television, and the media in general, bring us into daily contact with situations and conflicts which would have been outside of our experience at another time in history. Changes, conflicts, and upheavals in some of society's basic values also contribute to the general experience of stress. Part of the perceived increase in levels of stress may derive simply from the development of a vocabulary and a literature which describe the phenomenon. An increasing number of individuals are actively seeking assistance in dealing with stress-related problems.

The individual seeking help is frequently relieved to find that he or she is not "going crazy" nor is he or she suffering from an elusive (and surely fatal!) medical problem. The simple act of identifying the problem as stress-related opens the door to a wide variety of approaches and techniques subsumed under the heading "stress management techniques."

What is stress management? Everything—and nothing. There are probably few individual psychotherapeutic or counseling techniques which cannot be used to help manage stress. Unfortunately, there are also no magic answers or unique solutions to the problem of stress. Many books and authors zealously advocate the use of one particular technique to manage stress. Perhaps the answer is in a little-known form of Eastern meditation? Perhaps jogging will do the trick? Stress formula vitamins? Maybe—but maybe not. It seems unlikely that any problem as complex and pervasive as stress may be addressed comprehensively by a single technique.

In the present volume, the term "stress management" refers to the identification and analysis of problems related to stress, and the application of a variety of therapeutic tools to alter either the source of stress or the experience of stress. These therapeutic tools are utilized within an integrated and conceptually meaningful framework. The major goal of managing stress is simply to enable the individual to function at his or her optimal level, in a healthy and positive manner.

The first step in this process is to identify and describe stress-related problems. It is easy to ascribe to stress all the perils and misfortunes of life. It may even be likely that most perils and misfortunes do contain a stress-related component. However, if stress management approaches are to be employed, it is essential to assess and clearly delineate the exact role of stress in the individual's current status. The client seeking help with a specific medical problem (e.g. headaches) may not readily perceive or accept that the problem is stress-related. Conversely, a busy working mother may attribute her symptoms to stress when in fact a relatively straightforward medical problem may exist. There is some danger of stress management being viewed as a panacea. In order for stress management techniques and a stress management perspective to be effective, they must be applied to problems which are in fact significantly related to stress.

The source of stress, as will be discussed later, can be internal or external to the individual. What exactly accounts for the individual's symptomatology? Individual pathology? Discrete external events? Systems? Social psychological contradictions? Only with a thorough and comprehensive analysis of the presenting problem can the role of stress as a precipitating factor be identified. Without accurate identification, effective intervention is unlikely.

The goal of intervention is to achieve a balance between the client's individual resistance to stress and the amount of stress in his or her environment. This balance can be achieved in a variety of ways—through change in the individual, through change in specific stressors, or by altering the interaction between the individual and the environment.

Balance is a key concept in an integrated approach to stress management. A common misconception among both therapists and clients is that the goal of stress management is to minimize or eliminate stress. Although this may be appropriate in some instances, a more general concern is that of achieving the proper balance of stress. As mentioned above, one must balance the individual's personal resources against the demands made upon him or her. To do so requires a balance between too little stress—which engenders apathy and boredom—and too much stress—which leads to anxiety and burnout. Even when the desirable amount of stress has been achieved, there is a further need for balance between good or positive stress (sometimes called "eustress") and bad or negative stress ("distress"). If lowering the level of stress further disrupts the balance between the individual's personal resources and the demands made upon him or her, a simpleminded goal of eliminating stress may actually potentiate the problems of a stressed individual. Consider, for example, the plight of a healthy, fit, college-educated individual who, for some reason, is performing a monotonous, sedentary, and repetitive job for eight hours a day. In this case, the level of stress may need to be increased in order to achieve balance. Or consider the middle-aged worker who has been in the same job for many years, but who feels that, at present, family pressures are too great to allow a job change at this time. The absolute amount of stress in this individual's life may be appropriate, but the balance between eustress and distress has not been achieved.

One way of achieving balance is to alter the level and type of stress in the individual's environment. However, this may be difficult, impossible, or undesirable. Balance may also be achieved by altering the individual. Individuals may learn to alter their physiological, cognitive, or behavioral responses to stress. Learning to control or offset the physiological arousal accompanying stress may allow the individual to endure higher levels of stress in an adaptive fashion. Similarly, changes in cognitive interpretation may change a routine task into a challenge, thus allowing the individual to function well in circumstances which may formerly have been regarded as understimulating. Regardless of the specific mechanism of change, the end result is to achieve balance between the individual and his or her environment.

There is, of course, no meaningful "normal" amount of stress or "average" amount of tolerance. The optimal level is that level at which the individual client is able to maintain physiological homeostatis, mental well-being, and behavioral stability.

STRESS MANAGEMENT AS THERAPY

As was mentioned earlier, the practice of stress management requires that the therapist be familiar and experienced with the basic tenets of a psychotherapy or counseling relationship. Like other types of therapy, stress management relies on factors such as the release of tension, through catharsis or through expectancy; cognitive learning and insight; overt or covert operant conditioning; identification or alliance with the therapist; and reality testing (Sloane et al., 1975). What distinguishes stress management from other forms of psychotherapy is the reliance on the dissemination of information. There is a significant didactic component to stress management. The therapist and the client together must "learn" what stress is (for that client), how it is experienced, and how it may be dealt with adaptively. The therapist brings to therapy a knowledge of the literature and research in the area; knowledge based on his or her own personal experience of stress; and knowledge gleaned from others during the experience of being a therapist. The client, on the other hand, comes to therapy with knowledge of his or her own personal experiences of stress; knowledge of previously tried coping methods which may or may not have been successful; and knowledge of the general circumstances and limitations of daily life which may have implications for stress management. Thus, each individual (client and therapist) comes to the relationship with a specific body of knowledge, to be shared and reinterpreted jointly. Occasionally, the client will have labeled his or her problem as a stress problem prior to seeking help, but more often the client enters treatment seeking a remedy for a specific problem, whether it be headaches, insomnia, depression, or poor performance at work. Thus, the initial work of therapy revolves around the development of a common conceptualization for therapy. If the client thinks that he or she has simple headaches, for which a medical cure is indicated, and the therapist thinks that the client has a stress problem, for which "stress management techniques" would be useful, then the therapy is temporarily at a stalemate. No active treatment can be initiated until the client and the therapist agree on the nature of the problem.

Formulation

This first phase of stress management is referred to as the "formulation phase." The Concise Oxford Dictionary defines the verb "to formulate" as meaning "to set forth systematically." Slater and Roth (1977) describe formulation in psychiatry as the "detailed statement of the diagnosis in multidimensional terms. It will contain a classification of the disorder and a specification of the factors, physical, constitutional and psychogenic, which have contributed to its appearance . . . a short plan for further investigation and for treatment" (p. 35).

In the case of stress management, the tasks of the formulation phase are to define the problems and to set forth systematically the goals, procedures, and mechanisms of change which are to be employed in therapy. The definition provided by Slater and Roth (1977) is perhaps too reminiscent of the medical model to be employed literally. The term "diagnosis" might better be replaced by "problem identification," and along with the physical, constitutional, and psychogenic factors are interpersonal, behavioral, cognitive, and social factors. Nevertheless, the intent of the process is the same: to describe and to plan.

Formulation is, of course, an integral part of any therapeutic process. In the stress management process, however, the role of formulation is particularly significant for several reasons. First, and most importantly, in stress management (unlike in psychiatry in general, as described by Slater & Roth), formulation is a joint effort of the therapist and the client. Each attempts to consider and evaluate the information presented by the other, in order to incorporate that evidence into his or her own schema. Rather than the therapist formulating a diagnosis which is then superimposed upon the client, client and therapist jointly reach an agreement as to the nature of the problem. The therapist may surmise that the client has trouble coping with stress; the client considers that he or she has a headache. In order for the client to establish the legitimacy of the "headache" as a problem, he or she must explain, collect data, and otherwise describe such features as intensity, duration, frequency, situational determinants, adverse effects, and impact on functioning (for example). In order for the therapist to establish the legitimacy of "stress" as a problem, he or she must explain, collect data, and otherwise describe such factors as the physical, cognitive, and behavioral aspects of stress, and its relation to illnesses such as headaches. Through this exchange of information, a mutually satisfactory formulation of the problem may be attained (e.g., stress-related headaches).

Models of Helping

The presence of a didactic exchange between the therapist and the client suggests that stress management requires both therapist and client to adopt the same model of helping or coping behavior.

The therapist and the client may each come to the therapy situation with different expectations of his or her own role and that of the other. As Shulman (1979) points out, one of the first tasks to be accomplished in any therapeutic relationship is that of clarifying roles. When the client and the therapist are both operating from the medical model (which is often the case, particularly in clients with physical problems), roles tend to be relatively clear. In the medical model, the client is not seen as responsible either for his or her problem or for the solution to the problem. The therapist, on the other hand, is seen as responsible for providing a treatment, which is specific to the disorder.

Application of the medical model to stress problems would therefore yield the kind of "packaged" stress management program that has become popular in many circles (viz. *Newsweek*, Oct. 12, 1987, p. 64, for example). Such programs prescribe identical treatments for all participants, and leave responsibility for success or failure largely in the hands of the program leader, rather than in the hands of the participant. However, stress management programs which are geared to groups of people rather than tailored to individual needs do not take into account the personal vulnerabilities and coping deficiencies which may have initiated the problem originally (Turk et al. 1980; Lazarus & Folkman, 1984).

Several alternative models of helping have been proposed by Brickman et al. (1982). In addition to the medical model, these authors describe the moral model, which states that individuals are responsible both for creating their own problems and for finding solutions; the compensatory model, which does not hold individuals responsible for problems but does hold them responsible for solutions; and the enlightenment model, which holds individuals responsible for problems but not for solutions. Brickman et al. hypothesize that the model from which the therapist and client operate (i.e., the pattern of attribution of responsibility) will affect both the way in which help is offered and the way in which it is received. They further suggest that models such as the moral and compensatory models, in which the client has responsibility for solutions, are more likely to increase the client's personal competence than are models which do not confer responsibility (e.g., the medical model and the enlightenment model). Certainly, the assumption of personal responsibility for solutions is essential to the success of stress management procedures. The latter are largely cognitive and behavioral self-control procedures which must be carried out in the context of a model which stipulates that the client assumes responsibility for his or her own outcome.

Brickman et al. conclude that only the compensatory model is consistent with the idea of helping. If the client is responsible for both the problem and the solution, as in the moral model, there is no room for the "helper." Similarly if the client is not responsible for the solution, as in the medical and enlightenment models, then there is no room for the client in the helping relationship.

The issue of responsibility for the problem is particularly significant in the case of stress management. One of the dangers of stress management is that of labeling the client as deficient, and of operating from the perspective that stress problems are attributable to some failure or inability on the part of the client to cope adequately with stress (i.e., "a moral" point of view). However, in the case of stress problems, the source of the problem may be external to the client, and outside of his or her control. To hold clients responsible for problems which are engendered by unrealistic and demoralizing workplace expectations (as in the case of employees whose rate of work in carrying out monotonous, repetitious tasks is monitored by computer) or which are attributable to socially sanctioned impossibilities (i.e., single working parents with no external supports) is inappropriate and potentially damaging to both the individual client and the society at large.

This discussion of abstract models may seem on the surface to be somewhat removed from the actual therapy situation. On the contrary, the resolution of this dilemma is an essential part of the formulation phase of stress management. The roles of the therapist and the client and the responsibilities of each are defined through the exchange of information as described above. That is, the therapist presents information about the nature and effects of stress, and thus defines the responsibility for the problems as external to the client. The client presents information about his or her experiences of stress and works with the therapist to identify the relationships between his or her behavior and symptoms—and thus defines the responsibility for the solution as being internal.

(The factual information necessary to create the proper orientation to therapy is contained in Chapters 2 and 3.)

The formulation of problems will begin in the first interview, but will continue to evolve over the course of several sessions. Although it may be evident early in therapy that the client has headaches and that the headaches are attributable (at least in part) to stress, the client and the therapist need to pose some specific hypotheses about the exact nature of the relationship between stress and symptoms. A further task of the formulation phase is to collect data in regard to these hypotheses and test them accordingly.

Stress problems are rarely simple, and given that there are behavioral, cognitive, and physiological aspects of stress, treatments are rarely unidimensional. The formulation phase of treatment concludes with the determination of a plan for treatment, a plan which usually encompasses a number of different interventions, carefully arranged in order of priority, each addressing a different aspect of the problem. The purpose of setting out a clear plan for therapy is twofold.

First, as mentioned earlier, the complex nature of stress and stress management can easily lead to a chronic crisis-intervention situation in therapy. Clients typically need assistance in a variety of areas, the relative importance of which may vary from one week to the next. It may be clear to both the therapist and the client that relaxation training, time management, and assertiveness are all desirable interventions, but it may be difficult to carry out all three procedures simultaneously. One can easily fall into the trap of drifting between the various treatments without focusing sufficiently enough on any one of them to ensure its success. Consider, for example, Rosenthal and Rosenthal's (1983) chapter in which they describe their multifaceted stress management program. The many potential stress management techniques discussed include going for walks, relocating the family's television sets, and holding a garage sale—as well as more mundane strategies such as relaxation training and assertiveness. The breadth and comprehensiveness of their approach is commendable. The question, however, is how to systematize and order these strategies so that they form a comprehensive whole. A structure for identifying and organizing treatment strategies is spelled out in some detail in Chapter 5. The essential procedure, and the culmination of the formulation process, is the identification and ranking of these strategies, in order of their importance to the client. Thus, the first goal of planning is to lend coherence and structure to therapy.

The second goal of the planning process is to begin to address the issue of values and priorities for the individual client. This procedure is also double-barreled, in that identification of priorities is not only part of the planning process, but is also one of the most important stress management techniques to be developed in the application phase of treatment. A key component of managing stress is to be fully aware of what is important and what is not. For the over-stressed client, "don't sweat the small stuff" is an important phrase to remember. Many clients have a difficult time sorting out their own priorities. It is not uncommon for clients to choose to address a small and relatively insignificant aspect of their total stress problem, while ignoring much more major issues. Although there are many potential explanations for such behavior, one possibility is that the client has failed to consider the relative importance of the various facets of stress impinging upon him or her. The importance and complexity of assigning priorities will be discussed at length in Chapter 5. Certainly, there are a number of factors which influence decisions about when to address which problem. These include the relative importance of the problem; the ease and likelihood of change; the relationship of this problem to others; and the psychological readiness of the client to address the problem. Nevertheless, the exercise of assigning priorities to problems and solutions is an essential and enlightening exercise.

Application

Once the plan has been established and the priorities assigned, the application phase of therapy begins. If the formulation has been completed thoroughly and properly, the learning and application of new skills—whether cognitive, behavioral, or physiological—follows easily. This part of therapy corresponds to what is sometimes called the "work" of helping (Shulman, 1979). Here, specific new skills are presented, taught, discussed, rehearsed, and analyzed within the therapy situation. The new skills are applied in situations outside of therapy, usually in a prescribed and limited fashion initially, then in a more general context. Progress in the performance of the new skills is monitored from week to week and effectiveness evaluated.

The application phase of therapy, although quicker to describe, forms the bulk of therapy. Its length is obviously variable, depending upon the goals of the individual client. The learning and application of skills is not different in stress management compared to other types of therapy; the skill of relaxation is the same whether it is learned as part of stress management or in conjunction with systematic desensitization. What differs is the context within which it is learned.

As mentioned earlier, stress management has essentially a self-control orientation. Thus, skills are taught in a broad context, then applied to specific problems. The teaching of skills in this fashion enables the client to develop a repertoire of coping skills which he or she can then access as needed outside the therapy situation.

Rosenthal and Rosenthal (1983) point out (somewhat apologetically it seems) that they have "no brand new stress reduction techniques to offer" (pp. 19–20). Again, it seems that to some extent, there is no such thing as a "pure" stress management technique (here we will assume that stress reduction a la Rosenthal and Rosenthal is a subtype of stress management). Stress management techniques are those techniques which enable us to manage stress in a healthy and adaptive fashion. They may be loosely grouped according to the target system (i.e., cognitions, behavior, physiology), but they acquire the designation "stress management technique" only when applied in the context of stress management. This argument may appear circular; indeed, it is.

Unfortunately, both therapists and clients often approach stress management in the hope of finding a magic cure—a treatment specific to the disorder "stress." This is a hope reminiscent of the medical model, which postulates a treatment specific to diagnosis. (The plethora of untested and unscientific miracle cures aimed at stress which have appeared on the market in the past few years is similarly reminiscent of the dubious tonics which appeared on the market in days of yore.) Alas, there are no proven treatments specific to stress. The wide variety of interventions which may be appropriate in the application phase of therapy are not "new" treatments created only to deal with stress. Rather, they are general supportive, psychotherapeutic, cognitive, and/or behavioral measures which have been shown to be effective and which may contribute toward moderating stress and its effects.

Perhaps the closest to a pure stress management technique is relaxation training. It is clearly oriented toward decreasing arousal and presents itself as a credible method by which to address the effects of stress. The necessity of finding something which "looks like" a stress management technique is probably as important a reason for the popularity of relaxation training as is its demonstrated effectiveness (see Chapter 6). However, even relaxation training had its origins outside of the realm of stress management (viz. Wolpe, 1959).

The discovery that there are no stress management techniques per se is often disappointing to the client, who may have entered therapy in the hope that learning to "manage stress" would allow him or her to avoid dealing with marital strife, job dissatisfaction, or role conflict. Alas, it is not so. Again, the need for thorough formulation is clear.

It should be noted that the fact that are no stress management techniques does not suggest that stress cannot be managed. In fact, relatively small material or practical changes in the client's life may effect a significant alteration in his or her experience of stress. In the application phase of therapy, these changes evolve and are realized, with a (it is hoped) measurable impact on the client's life. Thus, the "work" reaches fruition through the acquisition and application of new skills and behaviors.

The above progression, from intake through formulation to learning and applying new skills, describes stress management in an ideal situation with an ideal client. However, ideal clients who are in ideal circumstances never seem to seek (or need) help! The conceptualization of stress management as a two-tiered logical and ordered procedure is somewhat artificial. The bruised female client who presents for immediate help in dealing with her abusing partner cannot be told to hold on until formulation is complete. The employee who is about to be passed over for promotion because his supervisor does not know that he is interested in the job should not be told to wait, since assertiveness is #4 on the priority list and the therapist is still on #2! The described model of stress management should serve as a conceptual framework, a basis from which to derive satisfactory individual courses of therapy. Without flexibility, this approach falls prey to the same criticisms as the "packages" described earlier.

Formats for Therapy

The manner in which stress management is carried out will, of course, be determined largely by the individual client's needs, in combination with the orientation and skills of the therapist. There are essentially four options:

Individual Therapy. The therapist is probably in the best position to assess thoroughly the needs of the individual client and to tailor treatment to the client's needs in a one-to-one situation. There are clear advantages to individual therapy, particularly in the case of difficult clients or those with quite idiosyncratic problems. However, one drawback to this approach is that it can be difficult to present the necessary amount of factual material to the client without the therapist appearing to be somewhat dogmatic and without turning the therapy hour into a lecture. There are obviously time and expense constraints as well. The learning of new skills is not likely to be completed very effectively if therapy sessions are held infrequently. Nevertheless, the proposed model of stress management is well suited to individual therapy, which facilitates the necessary collusion between therapist and client. This format is probably the most desirable for stress management, all factors considered.

Group Psychotherapy. There are many reasons for considering the option of group therapy, as opposed to individual therapy. Some of these reasons are not related to the specific type of therapy at all, but have to do with more practical concerns. Group therapy is often less expensive for the participants, less time-consuming for the therapist, and enables the therapist to serve more clients than he or she would be able to see individually. In the case of stress management therapy specifically, groups have the added advantage of enabling the therapist to provide the factual information base to more than one client at a time. Because there is such a pronounced didactic component to stress management, it seems an ideal type of therapy to be carried out in groups.

There are two types of therapeutic groups which can easily incorporate a stress management perspective. The first of these is the psychoeducational group. This particular type of group emphasizes the educational component of therapy. In a psychoeducational group, the primary interaction is between therapist (or group leader) and client, rather than between clients. Group sessions are usually fairly structured, with a predetermined amount of material to be presented. Although there is some group interaction, it tends to be around prescribed subjects and structured exercises. This type of group generally meets for a limited number of sessions, the number and content of each one being determined ahead of time. Logically, the psychoeducational group is ideal for the dissemination of information, but is less useful for identifying a comprehensive and personalized treatment plan for each individual group member. This type of group may be most useful for fundamentally healthy individuals who are well motivated, and able to generalize well from the information presented. It is also useful as an introductory measure; clients may participate in a six or eight session series of psychoeducational meetings, then progress to individual therapy, to build upon the new knowledge. In this context, the first phase of therapy (formulation) may occur in a group setting, whereas the actual learning and application of skills would be accomplished on an individual basis.

A psychoeducational group would probably not be ideal for clients who are uncomfortable in a "learning" situation, or who are extremely distressed, unless the group were supplemented by individual therapy. The outline for a typical psychoeducational group on stress management is presented in Table 1–1.

The second type of group which might accommodate a stress management perspective is the mutual aid group, as described by Shulman (1979). In a mutual aid group, individuals with a common problem (i.e., stress) are brought together in a group, to help each other. In this type of group, the primary interaction is between the clients, with the therapist helping group members to help each other. Although this type of group is more difficult to orchestrate, it has the potential for providing greater individual attention and development. The pool of past information and experience is greater than could be provided by the therapist alone. Shulman (1979) describes the process in a mutual aid group as a dialectical process: group members present their tentative ideas, and in response receive challenges from other group members. In essence, one group member presents the "thesis," the others the "antithesis," with the hope of eventually obtaining a synthesis of material. Into this process, the group leader may need to inject factual material, in the case of the stress management group. Although the information is not presented in as organized a manner as in a psychoeducational group, a careful group leader can monitor the group process to ensure that all necessary information is illuminated at some point. Mutual aid groups are not typically time-limited, and are generally closed groups, so there may be more latitude within which the group leader can present the necessary material.

The mutual aid group also has the potential for evolving into a situation of the blind leading the blind; in the absence of skilled leadership, group members may indeed present many theses, but without any synthesis.

Whether a group is psychoeducational or of the mutual aid variety, one of the primary advantages of groups over individual therapy is that the group members can derive social support from each other. Even in the absence of any other benefit from therapy, such support can help to ameliorate the effects of stress.

Workshops. A workshop is not, strictly speaking, a form of therapy. However, the popularity of stress management workshops makes their inclusion here relevant.

A workshop is, in many ways, similar to a psychoeducational group, but is conducted within a condensed period of time. Typically, an "ex-

TABLE 1–1
Stress Management: An Eight-Session
Psychoeducational Program

Session	Content
1	What Is Stress? -defining stress -stress and illness -how stress affects the individual
2	What Is Stressful? -types of stressors -life events versus hassles -identifying individual stressors
3	Dealing with Stress -where to start -planning and priorities -setting goals
4	Changing How You Feel -how to relax -when to relax -why to relax
5	Changing How You Think -identifying cognitive distortions -changing cognitions -effective problem solving
6	Changing How You Behave -identifying problem behaviors -self-monitoring -life-style behaviors -assertive behavior
7	Time Management -getting organized -setting time priorities -doing more with less time
8	Putting It All Together -where to go from here -making personal plans -rehearsing skills

pert" in the area is asked to address a group of varying size for a period of time (from one half day to several days). A workshop is an ideal place in which to teach the necessary factual information about stress and its effects. This is easily done in a lecture format.

The difficulty with the workshop format is that it encourages the "cookbook" approach to stress management, alluded to earlier. Stress management is a highly individual matter; it is impossible to address the needs of many different people simultaneously without appearing to prescribe particular approaches. Although some approaches (i.e., life-style management) are broadly applicable, others are highly individualized. It is simply not possible to provide any more than an overview of stress management in a workshop format.

Unfortunately, many "experts" choose to concentrate on their own pet approaches in the course of a workshop. Some, for example, try to conduct relaxation sessions for a hundred people in straight-backed chairs! Although it may be presumed that the idea is to give participants some idea of what relaxation might be like, this approach may have significantly negative results as well. People are not likely to feel relaxed in this context. In addition, any one particular relaxation technique is not likely to be appropriate for more than a small portion of the audience. The result of this practice may be to discredit what would otherwise be an effective technique.

What is probably most important in carrying out stress management workshops is to be realistic and honest about the goals of such an endeavor, and to focus on factual content rather than on making prescriptions for individual change.

The overall organization of a workshop is likely to parallel that of the psychoeducation group. Depending upon the length of time available, and the specific concerns of the audience, individual topics may be emphasized to a greater or lesser degree. Frequently, workshops are sponsored by a group with a particular concern (e.g., stress in women, stress in mental health practitioners, stress in the workplace). Obviously, it is desirable to include a segment which addresses these concerns in particular. In general, the lecture portions of a workshop are best broken down into segments of an hour or less, since adult attention spans rarely last longer than that. Small group discussion and use of paper-and-pencil measures help to change the pace and maintain attention over the day.

Bibliotherapy. It is appealing to think that one can learn to manage stress by reading a book. This has not yet been proven. One would suspect that a relatively intelligent and essentially healthy person could gain some benefit from reading some of the self-help books on stress management which are currently on the market (there are a great many of these currently available). In the absence of any concrete evidence that any of these books does in fact evoke significant change, one cannot recommend books as a means of therapy by themselves. However, one is not usually put in the position of having to make this recommendation, since people who choose to help themselves rather than seeking professional help do not usually ask a professional opinion on this matter! However, if one is asked one's professional opinion on this matter, it would be wise to err on the side of caution. Many individuals seeking assistance with stress have medical problems; self-prescribed treatment could be ill advised.

However, bibliotherapy can be a useful adjunct to individual therapy. For a motivated and literate client, outside reading can cut down therapy time significantly, by eliminating the need for the therapist to provide all the necessary factual information. If the information is reviewed outside the therapy situation, then therapy time can be spent integrating and analyzing information, rather than disseminating it. Therapists are well advised to review the self-help section at the local popular bookstore. Not only will this provide the therapist with potential sources for clients, but it will also keep the therapist aware of the books that his or her clients may be reading.

Who Needs it?

There seem to be essentially three categories of individuals who seek assistance with stress management. First are those people who are not experiencing any particular difficulty with stress, but are generally health conscious and who have become interested in the topic in a preventive way. They are not as likely to seek out individual therapy as they are to join groups or attend workshops. Often, they are individuals who are aware that they live high-stress lifestyles, and are interested in avoiding any potential health problems before they begin.

The second type are the distressed clients—clients who find it difficult to get through each day, clients who may present as being chronically anxious or depressed. This type of client does not usually have a specific and clear-cut symptom of stress which precipitates involvement in therapy, but may be generally miserable or unhappy. The distressed client may think that there is something wrong with him or herself individually, either medically or emotionally, which is responsible for his or her distress. This type of client is often unaware of the relationship between his or her symptoms and stress, since he or she may not perceive his or her life as overly stressful. The distressed client is often a person who is facing many ongoing small stresses or hassles, and who feels that he or she "should" be able to cope. Within the formulation phase, knowledge about the importance of balance, and the nature of various sources of stress is most important for this client.

Third are clients with a specific medical problem, which is felt to be related to stress. This client also may be unaware of the relationship between his or her specific illness and stress. Often, such a client is referred by a physician. The "sick" client may resent seeing a mental health practitioner at all, balking at the suggestion that the illness is "all in your head." Many clients with specific medical disorders do not perceive themselves to be stressed; businesspeople who exhibit the Type A behavior pattern, for example, may deny that their heart problems have anything to do with their stress levels. This type of client is apt to require a great deal of education about the physiological relationship between stress and illness.

These three types of clients are not mutually exclusive, nor are they exhaustive. Some clients with medical problems are distressed; some clients seek assistance with stress management for other reasons altogether. The utility in the above classification is in helping to identify the varying needs of different types of clients, and to enable the therapist to focus on the most important aspects of therapy for each type of client. The three case studies in this book represent each of the three described types.

Stress management is in essence a two-stage therapy, emphasizing first the development of a common conceptualization of the problem between therapist and client, and then the acquisition and application of specific stress management techniques. Although the practice of stress management employs the same basic components as any other type of therapy, there is a very significant didactic component as well. The experienced therapist may be able to incorporate the principles of stress management into his or her repertoire with a minimum of change in approach. What is essential in this process is the development of a cooperative approach to therapy, an approach in which the client and the therapist together derive a definition and a solution for the problems. The actual techniques to be employed in therapy will vary, depending upon the nature of the presenting problem, the type of client, and the format that therapy is to follow. These factors notwithstanding, a sound understanding of the mechanisms of stress—cognitive, physiological and behavioral—is essential to carrying out the therapy. These mechanisms are explored and developed over the course of the next three chapters.

Below, three case studies which are to be followed throughout the book are introduced. Each of these represents different yet fairly typical problems in stress management. The information presented in this first chapter is that which might be obtained in a typical 50-minute initial interview session with any new client. (A suggested framework for an intake interview is presented in Table 1-2.) This information is clearly not exhaustive, as most initial interviews are not exhaustive. However, in order to parallel the actual therapy situation as realistically as possible, information will be presented throughout the book, much as it emerges throughout therapy.

CASE STUDIES

Cathy

Cathy is a 25-year-old university graduate student who applied to participate in an eight-week stress management program offered by the university's student counseling center. At the time she applied, Cathy was asked to provide a thumbnail sketch of herself to share with other group members. She provided the following information.

Cathy is currently enrolled in the second year of a master's program in business administration. She is living alone, but has a steady boyfriend, with whom she spends a great deal of time. Cathy's health is good, and she denies any particular problems with her lifestyle at present. She stated that her reason for enrolling in the course was to prepare her to deal with the stresses she expects to encounter in the next few years, including entering the work force, and considering a permanent relationship and children.

In describing her past, Cathy stated that she was born in a rural community about 200 miles from the university. She is the middle child in a family of three daughters. Her father is an insurance broker, and her mother, after many years at home, has recently returned to work as a nursery school teacher. Cathy describes her relationship with her family as good, and does not report any particular conflicts. Cathy is the only one of the daughters who does not reside in their hometown; this is a source of concern to her parents, but seems unavoidable in view of her chosen field of endeavor. Cathy enjoys living in the city where she now resides, but finds that her rural upbringing is a bit of a disadvantage at times, in that she feels more vulnerable than some of her "big city" friends.

TABLE 1–2
Case History Format: Obtaining Initial Information

I. Demographic Data
   -sex
   -age
   -marital status
   -occupation
   -education
   -religion

II. Presentation
   -referral reason and source
   -mental status—memory, affect, language, insight, psychotic symptoms, orientation, etc.
   -physical status—visible handicaps, health problems, etc.

III. Personal History
   -infancy and childhood
   -educational history (including interpersonal aspects)
   -sexual history
   -occupational history
   -recreation and use of leisure time (hobbies, etc.)

IV. Family History
   -parents and grandparents
   -siblings
   -children
   -other significant relatives

V. Psychiatric History (if any)

VI. Medical History
   -chronic and acute conditions
   -medication history
   -unexplained symptoms

VII. Current Profile
   -"typical" day
   -identified hassles
   -life-style (eating, smoking, exercise, and drug habits)
   -significant relationships
   -personal goals

VIII. Summary and Formulation
   -problem identification
   -treatment formulation
   -goal setting

Adapted and reproduced courtesy of J. S. Lawson, Ph.D., Queens' University, Kingston, Canada.

Prior to beginning the group, Cathy was asked privately about her physical and mental health; she described both as good. Cathy denies any emotional or psychiatric problems in the past. The only medication she takes on a regular basis is the oral contraceptive.

Comments. Cathy presents as a relatively normal university student who is interested in maintaining a good level of functioning. As would often be the case in such a situation, we do not know a great deal about Cathy, but have made certain that her mental and physical health are at a level such that her involvement in the stress management course does not seem to present a risk to her. Based upon the information given, she has been accepted into the stress management program.

Jean

Jean is a 42-year-old single mother of twin 12-year-old boys. She has been separated from her husband for six years, and works fulltime as a legal secretary in a small law firm. At the time of the initial interview, Jean arrived slightly late because of a last minute hassle at the office. She was well groomed and neat, but seemed somewhat harried.

Jean stated that she had been referred by her family physician; however, she was not sure exactly why. She stated that she had been having a number of minor health problems over the past year, including headaches, insomnia, and intermittent gastrointestinal problems. Although none of these problems appeared to be serious, she had expressed concern that some larger problem loomed in the background. At her insistence, her family doctor had completed a battery of screening tests, but all had come back with normal results. Jean did mention that her doctor had then suggested that some of her complaints might be stress-related, but she was reluctant to accept this verdict. However, at the encouragement of the doctor, she had agreed to see a therapist on a trial basis to determine if there was a stress component to her illness. Jean made a point of telling the therapist in the initial session that she was convinced that her complaints were "real," and not "all in my head."

At the time of the initial interview, Jean was most concerned with the frequent headaches that she experienced. Although her headaches were described as only moderately uncomfortable, she reported experiencing them about twice a week, which she found bothersome. She was also concerned with her sleeping habits; she described her trouble in getting to sleep. Often, she would experience a series of three to five nights in which she was unable to get to sleep for several hours after going to bed. On these occasions, she would experience a great deal of diffuse muscle aches, in her back, in her legs, and in her neck. Once asleep, she did not usually have difficulty staying asleep.

Jean is the second of two daughters of a steel worker and his wife. She described her childhood as relatively "normal." She got along reasonably well with her other family members, and was an average student at school. Jean reports that she did feel some pressure to perform at school, in that her parents both were poorly educated and were determined that their children should do better. However, she felt that her parents had been reasonably pleased with her performance. In her teenage years, Jean had not been particularly outgoing, although she had several close friends and generally had a boyfriend. Much of her time was spent on homework, as she did not find schoolwork to be easy. Although Jean's parents live in the same town that she does, and she sees her parents once every two weeks, their relations are cordial but not close. Jean expressed the concern that her parents tend to overreact if she is having any difficulty, so she feels it necessary to edit information she gives them. Her sister is married to a man in the military and thus moves frequently, which makes it difficult to maintain a close friendship.

Jean was married to her high school sweetheart at age 20, after dating for four years. She worked as a legal secretary for several years, before giving birth to her sons. She remained at home with the children until they entered school. At that time, she began to become aware of difficulties in her marriage. Jean declined to elaborate on these problems in the interview, but merely stated that they seemed to be "growing apart." The children are described as normal 12-year-olds. Jean does express concern about what the teenage years will bring.

Jean has no psychiatric history, and has not seen a therapist in the past. Aside from the above-mentioned somatic complaints, she has no ongoing medical problems. The only medication she takes is a small dose of a mild tranquilizer, when needed.

Jean describes a typical day in her life as beginning at 5:30 A.M. when she arises to make lunches for herself and her sons. (She does this daily to save money.) Generally, she has time to do a load of laundry and tidy the living room before the twins rise. After she prepares their breakfast, assembles their school equipment, and gets them off to school, she leaves for work herself. As her old car is somewhat unreliable, she generally takes the bus.

Jean begins work at 9:00 A.M. She works in a small law firm with four lawyers. Jean enjoys her job, but finds it somewhat monotonous at times. She has held the same position, with little change in job duties, for several years. There is one other woman in the office, the receptionist, who is a 55-year-old single woman. She and Jean get along well, although they do not socialize outside of work.

On her lunch hour, Jean generally runs errands or does shopping. She returns home by 5:45 P.M. and immediately puts supper on so that the family can eat by 6:30. After supper, she clears the dishes and cleans the kitchen while the boys do homework. The evenings are generally taken up with helping her sons with their work, more cleaning, and budgeting. Jean also does some typing at home to earn extra money. She does not have any active hobbies at present, but does make a point of doing something special with her children on Sundays. (Although her husband had formerly taken the boys on alternate weekends and paid regular child support, he had recently returned to school, so that both the checks and the children's visits with him had become somewhat erratic.)

Comments. Jean seems totally unaware of the amount of stress in her life, and does not interpret her medical problems as being related to stress. Although she seems to be coping fairly well with her everyday demands, she feels chronically unwell, and does not present as a happy person. At the conclusion of the initial interview, the therapist expressed admiration for Jean's ability to tolerate an extremely demanding lifestyle. It was pointed out to her that it was not uncommon for people as busy as she was to experience some physical problems as a result of their hectic life-styles. When she was reassured that the therapist did not feel that her problems were imaginary, Jean was able to acknowledge that she found it trying to keep up her current pace. She stated that she might appreciate some assistance in altering her ways—but she still remained unclear as to what this had to do with her headaches. She was agreeable to scheduling another meeting to discuss this further.

J. B.

J. B. is a 50-year-old industrial sales representative who has had a peptic ulcer for about five years. J. B. is well aware that ulcers may be exacerbated by stress and thus asked to be referred to a therapist for stress management. His internist suggested that he contact the mental health clinic, and an appointment was scheduled.

J. B. is a large, overweight man who looks older than his stated age. At the initial interview, he explained at some length the intricacies of his present job, and why he finds it to be stressful. He is on the road several days a week, works on a commission, and has some difficulty dealing with his immediate supervisor. As part of his employment, he has attended some stress management workshops, but reported that although they helped him understand the problem, he still was unsure as to how to deal with it.

During the initial interview, the client spoke quickly and with some pressure, almost answering questions before they were asked. His mood was jovial, which was somewhat inconsistent with the content of his speech. It was difficult to ask him specific questions, since he seemed to have thought out exactly what he wanted to tell the therapist.

J. B. was the oldest of four sons of a mother who was a lawyer and a father who ran a small newspaper. Although it was expected that, as oldest son, he would take over the family newspaper, J. B. had no interest in this area and pursued a university degree in engineering. This choice precipitated many arguments with his parents. J. B. felt that his relationship with his parents had never recovered from that disagreement. Their relationship was now civil but distant.

J. B. is married to a teacher. They have a 16-year-old son—"but that's another story," he reported, before bringing the conversation back to his own health.

J. B. has no psychiatric history. He has not personally sought therapy in the past, although he acknowledged that his family had seen a therapist together—about his son's problems.

Other than his ulcer, his health is good, although the doctor has suggested that he alter his diet and try to lose weight. J. B. does not exercise, and winces at the mention of the subject.

A typical day in J. B.'s life sees him rising at 6:30 A.M. and on the road by 7:00. He does not eat breakfast, but usually grabs coffee and a danish en route to his first appointment. Because of his concern about his weight, he usually skips lunch and works straight through the day. If he is home in the evening, he has dinner with the family, then works on his accounts for a while after dinner. He likes to watch a couple of hours of television before going to bed. If he is out of town, he generally follows the same pattern, but with a few drinks with dinner.

On weekends, J. B. usually works on Saturday morning, then does some work around the house for the rest of the day. He sometimes accompanies his wife to church on Sunday, but usually sleeps until noon, then relaxes in the afternoon.

Comments. J. B. is clearly aware that he has a stress problem, but obviously is not aware of the full implications of that conclusion. He is able to recognize the role of work stress in his life, but does not appreciate the role of life-style, nor the role of his family. In fact, he seemed to regard them as irrelevant to the present problem. Nevertheless, he seemed responsive to the need to take a broader approach to the problem, and agreed to meet again to set some specific goals for therapy.

2

Formulation and Definition in Stress Management

A primary goal of the formulation phase of therapy is to create a working definition of stress, mutually acceptable to client and therapist. Although the term "stress" is widely recognized and acknowledged, there are a variety of definitions in use, both in common parlance and in the professional literature. Thus, the therapist and client may both realize that a stress problem exists, but each may have a different idea about what that means.

In order for the working definition to actually serve its desired function in therapy, it must have several important characteristics.

First, it must be face-valid to the client. In order for an operational definition to be valid, it must reflect the conceptually defined property which it is intended to measure (Runkel & McGrath, 1972). In the case of a stress-related disorder, the "conceptually defined property" is stress. In therapy, the most important type of validity is face validity—which concerns the extent to which the definition "looks like" it represents what it is intended to represent (Nunnally, 1967).

The therapist must define the concept of stress in such a way as to make it look to the client as if there is a reasonable and believable connection between his or her complaint and the concept of stress. For some disorders, the connection is obvious and easily believable, as in the case of anxiety. The client who is experiencing anxiety in anticipation of a clearly defined event may need little explanation or discussion in order to be convinced of the relationship between stress and anxiety. For other disorders, however, the connection is less clear and a more detailed analysis may be necessary. The client who experiences frequent and persistent bouts of the flu, for example, may need to be acquainted with the physiology of stress and its effects on the immune system before the attribution of the problem as "stress" is accepted. If the therapist and the client together cannot develop a face-valid description of the connection, then it may be that the problem is not primarily stress-related and another approach to therapy may be more appropriate.

A second characteristic of a useful definition is that it is flexible. Since anxiety and flu may both be indications of stress, a working definition must be flexible enough to explain the connection between either of these problems and stress. A definition which requires a rigid interpretation of symptoms and behaviors would not readily account for the wide range of manifestations of stress which present in therapy. Similarly, a definition must be broad in scope, so that physical, cognitive, and behavioral symptoms can all be accommodated. It may be that "anxiety" and "flu" will be manifest in the same client—along with cognitive distortions and avoidant behavior. The definition must be of sufficient breadth to encompass all of these items.

Finally, a definition must provide a direction for therapy. A thorough examination of the key components of the concept "stress" should indicate which areas may need attention in general, as well as pinpoint specific problem areas for the individual client. Thus, although the definition of stress needs to be flexible and broad, it should not be over-inclusive. If it appears to the client that all of his or her actions cause stress, and that all of his or her experiences are a result of stress, then effective intervention may seem overwhelming. The definition must indicate a clear direction to both the therapist and the client.

These four characteristics suggest that the concept of stress should be broadly defined, to accommodate a variety of interpretations. However, the specific content and emphasis will vary from one client to another.

The issue of definition may be addressed at two levels. First, what are the words or terms that will be used to define the process? Secondly, how is the process described? The former issue is one of semantics; the latter, of empirical knowledge.

DEFINING STRESS: THE TERMS

Part of the work of describing stress involves the development of a vocabulary to employ in the description. Although the word "stress" is familiar to almost everyone, it is used in a variety of different ways. "Stress" may refer to a stimulus, to a response, or to a combination of the two. For the sake of clarity, the following definitions will be used in this book:

Stressor. Any stimulus which the individual perceives as a threat. Stressors may be physical, psychological, or psychosocial (Asterita,

1985). Physical stressors include such conditions as environmental pollutants, environmental pressures such as extreme changes in temperature, electric shock, prolonged exercise, injuries and other trauma to the body, and exposure to disease.

Psychological stressors are those threats which are attributable to the individual's internal reactivity—thoughts, feelings, and concerns about perceived threats. Psychological stressors are somewhat more subjective in that the threat occurs because of the individual's interpretation of an event, rather than as a result of the event itself.

Psychosocial stressors are a result of social interrelationships. They may derive from intense social interactions—such as with family members—or from social isolation. Psychosocial stressors are often role-related.

Stress Response. The integrated and nonspecific reaction of the body to demands or stressors. The stress response is comprised of cognitive, behavioral, and physiological components. It is an integrated response, in that a variety of symptoms, in several systems, coexist. It is nonspecific in that the response is the same, regardless of the stressor. (The response *is* specific in that the pattern of the response is consistent and dependable, and affects certain organs in a reliable way.) The stress response is referred to as "stress reactivity" by some authors (viz. Greenberg, 1987).

Stress. The term "stress" is sometimes used to mean stressful stimulus or stressor. In other contexts, it refers to the effect, or the stress response. In the literature, the term stress has come to preempt a field previously shared by a number of other concepts, including anxiety, conflict, and trauma. (Confer & Appley, 1964).

No definition of the term "stress" has been universally accepted, even among a majority of stress researchers (Elliot & Eisdorfer, 1982). For the purpose of the current book, stress may best be regarded in relational terms, as the interaction between the stressor and the stress response. Lazarus (1984) summarizes this relationship by describing stress as "a relationship between the person and the environment that is appraised as taxing or exceeding his or her resources and endangering his or her well-being" (p. 21).

The phenomenon of "stress" must also be differentiated from "anxiety" and "burnout."

Anxiety. The syndrome of "apprehension, tension or uneasiness from the anticipation of danger, the source of which is largely unknown or unrecognized" (Stone, 1988, pp. 16–17). Thus, anxiety may be a sign of stress, or a part of the stress response. Anxiety is often viewed as a trait or individual personality characteristic, whereas stress is a function of a particular set of circumstances. From the medical and pharmacological standpoint, one can treat anxiety but not stress. (Lazarus, 1984, acknowledges a great deal of overlap between the two concepts, and suggests that one should not quibble about which term to use.)

Burnout: The result of failing to cope successfully with stress. Freudenberger (1985) suggests that burnout may be manifest as "waning enthusiasm, irritability and feelings of disengagement caused by stress, pressure, and exhaustion" (p. 1).

Putting these terms into context, one can conceptualize an individual as experiencing stress if he or she is exposed to a stressor, and exhibits a stress response, of which anxiety may be a part. If the individual does not resolve the stress in some way, he or she may experience burnout.

DEFINING STRESS: THE FACTS

What Is Stressful?

If a stressor is defined as any stimulus perceived as a threat, then a great variety of events are potentially stressful. Stressors may be loosely grouped into four categories, which range on a continuum from global, nonspecific, and impersonal factors, completely external to the individual, through to idiosyncratic and subjective interpretations of events. At one extreme are environmental events and phenonena which impinge equally on all individuals. There is no element of specificity; everyone is affected. Somewhat more specific are life stress events, which are measured objectively and are believed to be stressful to all who experience them. However, the individual must have actually encountered the particular event in order for it to have an effect. A third type of stressor is the minor life event or "hassle." Hassles are the smaller, perhaps ongoing events which are perceived by the individual as being stressful but which may or may not be perceived as stressful by others. Finally, the most idiosyncratic and subjective group of stressors are those personal tendencies, quirks, and vulnerabilities which engender stress attributable to one's own interpretation of events.

Environmental Stressors. The 1980s have sometimes been referred to as the Decade of Stress. This title may be largely attributable to the increasing amount of general environmental stress which impinges on all individuals. For individuals who live in the city, for example, noise, crowding, commuting time, high real estate costs, worry about crime, traffic congestion, pollution, and lack of a sense of community are ongoing stressors. Individuals living in rural areas also experience environmental pressures particular to their habitat. Economic problems, social isolation, job insecurity, and lack of community resources are problems typical of rural existence (Coleman, 1978).

A major part of the general climate of stress today may be attributable to the increased presence of the media. Airplane disasters, famines, and revolutions in any part of the world become part of the general atmosphere of stress. Until recently (the past few decades) individuals were unaware of issues or situations outside of their personal lives. However, in contemporary society, one is expected to be familiar with and have an informed opinion on such diverse issues as abortion, trade relations, nuclear disarmament, child care, pollution control, and the sex lives of international figures. Political crises in far-flung and previously unheard-of countries are brought to us in glowing technicolor on the six o'clock news daily.

Even more basic are some of the changing views and expectations in relation to the family and sex roles. The nuclear family, hailed by some as the hallmark of our culture, is under attack and is disintegrating rapidly. Both men and women are under continual assault in regard to their family roles. There are no longer any correct answers to questions about women's roles in particular—whether or not to have children, to be employed outside the home, to become or remain married. Along with the increased freedom is the increased stress of decisionmaking. Similarly, men may find that the traditional male role is no longer totally acceptable. Behavior which may once have been labelled unmasculine may now be seen as desirable, whereas behaviors formerly accepted may now be seen as chauvinistic.

It is unusual for an individual to seek out help with stress management solely because of general environmental pressures. At the same time, it is an unusual individual who is not affected by at least some of these issues. Unfortunately, it is difficult to quantify this type of stressor or to assess its specific impact on health and well-being. Nevertheless, environmental stressors create a general underlying foundation of stress, upon which the other, more specific stressors, build.

Life Stress Events. Life stress events are those major life events, discrete and measurable, which require adaptation on the part of the individual. Typically, items such as deaths, marriage, divorce, financial changes, and changes in life-style are included. The pioneering work in this area was carried out by Holmes and Rahe (1967), who itemized 43 specific life events in their Social Readjustment Rating Scale and assigned each event a weight, in "life change units." Events which require a greater amount of adaptation incur a higher number of life change units. Stressful life events, as Dohrenwend and Dohrenwend (1981a) point out, tend to be those events which are proximate to the onset of a disorder, rather than removed from it. Thus, for example, the recent death of a close relative is a life stress event, whereas the fact that one's father died when one was a child is not. Life stress events are typically measured over a specific and limited period of time (often one year). As one acquires increasing numbers of life change units, the risk of illness or accident attributable to stress also increases. Those individuals who obtained between 150 and 299 points of the Social Readjustment Rating Scale in Holmes and Rahe's (1967) original work, for example, showed a 37% chance of becoming ill, as opposed to a 79% chance for those obtaining over 300 points.

In determining which life events are stressful, and how stressful each is, Holmes and colleagues have emphasized two considerations. First, stressfulness was defined in terms of the need for readjustment by the individual, following the event. Since both positive events (e.g., personal achievement, marriage) and negative events (e.g., trouble with the boss, divorce) may require adjustment, both types are included in the list. Secondly, ratings of stressfulness were derived from the objective opinions of outside judges, rather than from judgments made by the persons experiencing the events (Holmes & Masuda, 1974).

An impressive literature demonstrates the connections between life stress events and both physical and mental illness. Much of this literature is summarized by Bloom (1985) and Creed (1985). It seems likely that life stress events do contribute to the occurrence of schizophrenia, affective disorders, heart disease, accidents, tuberculosis, and a host of other physical conditions. The effect of a life stress event is not thought to be specific (as the effects of stress are not thought to be specific). Rather, the effect is to precipitate the occurrence or flare-up of a preexisting condition or vulnerability.

Unfortunately, although findings of associations between events and illnesses apppear to be consistent, the magnitude of the association is typically low (Monroe, 1983). In addition, the theoretical mechanism by which major life events attain their adverse effects has not yet been delineated. There seems to be general agreement in the recent literature that life stress events must be interpreted within a model which also takes into account personal predispositions and social situations. Dohrenwend and Dohrenwend (1981b) provide five possible hypotheses about the manner in which these factors may interact; these are presented in Figure 2–1.

Life stress events are typically easy for both the client and the therapist to identify. They are generally perceived and accepted as stressors. This is particularly the case for negative events. No one would argue, for example, that the death of a spouse is not stressful. However, it can be somewhat more difficult to establish the nature of the link between these events and actual organic illnesses.

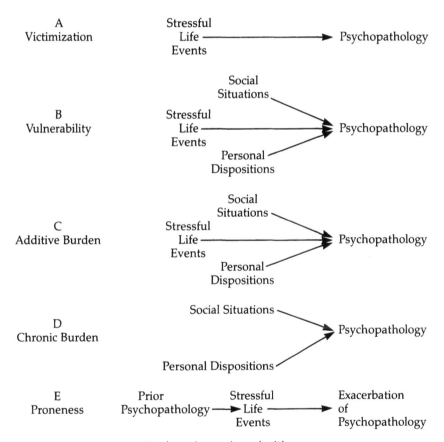

Figure 2–1. Five hypotheses about the life stress process.

Reprinted with permission from B. S. Dohrenwend and B. P. Dohrenwend (1981b), Life stress and psychopathology. In D. A. Regier & G. Allen (Eds.), *Risk factor analysis in the major mental health disorders*. Washington, D. C.: U.S. Government Printing Office, pp 131–141.

Hassles. In contrast to the major life events approach, Lazarus and colleagues have suggested that it is the adaptation to the relatively minor stressors and pleasures (or hassles and uplifts) which has the most significance for health outcome (Kanner et al., 1981). Hassles are described as the "irritating, frustrating, distressing demands and troubled relationships that plague us day in and day out" (Lazarus & DeLongis, 1983, p. 247). A typical listing of hassles (i.e., the Hassles Scale, Kanner et al., 1981) includes items in the area of work ("too many meetings"), health ("concerns about weight"), family ("not enough time for family"), friends ("unexpected company"), and the environment ("neighborhood deterioration").

Since it is unlikely that any individual lives a hassle-free existence, the impact of hassles on health depends upon such factors as a chronically high frequency of hassles, a critical period of heightened hassles, or the repetition of psychologically significant hassles.

The assessment of the experience of hassles is obviously more subjective and idiosyncratic than is the determination of major life events. It is not difficult for an outsider to deduce objectively whether or not one's spouse has died, but it may be impossible for an outsider to assess "fear of rejection," "being exploited," or "too many things to do." In the latter three cases, for example, the salient consideration is not whether the individual has eight or 15 or 37 tasks to accomplish, but whether he or she feels overloaded.

Obviously, hassles and major life events are not totally separate phenomena. If, as Hinkle (1974) suggests, the impact of major life events is attributable to their disruption of social relations, habits, and patterns of activity, then major life events may exert their impact by altering the individual's experience of daily hassles. Thus a major life event such as divorce may result in an increase in hassles such as housework, child care, and finding companionship (Kanner et al., 1981). However, Kanner et al. (1981) also maintain that separate from major life events, hassles may originate in the individual's personal style or routine environment.

Generally, hassles have been found to be better predictors of health status than major life events (Kanner et al., 1981; Weinberger, Hiner & Tierney, 1987; Holahan et al., 1984; Monroe, 1983). There is some statistical evidence from these studies that the effect of major life events is in fact indirect, and operates through an increase in hassles. This point of view is essentially consistent with the vulnerability hypothesis proposed by Dohrenwend and Dohrenwend (1981b), represented as Hypothesis B in Figure 2–1. This hypothesis stipulates that preexisting personal dispositions and social conditions mediate the causal relation between stressful life events and health outcome (Dohrenwend & Shrout, 1985). To make this relationship clearer graphically, one could insert the term "hassles" as is done in Figure 2–2. Hassles may represent the behavioral and cognitive manifestations of the adaptation engendered by the interaction among stressful life events, social conditions, and personal dispositions.

Proponents of the life stress events approach disagree with proponents of the "hassles" approach in several significant ways. One of these is in regard to the role of positive or pleasant experiences.

As was mentioned above, Holmes and his colleagues view any change which requires adaptation as being stressful. Thus, marriage and divorce are both seen as being stressful, as are financial changes in either direction. This point of view is essentially consistent with that of Selye, who emphasizes that stress may arise as a reaction to *any* demand made upon the system.

Lazarus and colleagues, however, argue that "uplifts" or positive minor events are not stressful but rather serve a protective function, as an emotional buffer against stress disorders (Kanner et al., 1981). Lazarus et al. (1980) suggest, for example, that positive experiences may act as "breathers" from ongoing stress, or as aids in sustaining coping activity. Kanner et al. (1981) define uplifts as "events that make you feel good" (p. 30). They include items such as being rested, solving an ongoing practical problem, sex, shopping, and socializing as potential uplifts. Since little work has been done looking at either negative major life events alone, or at the differential impact of hassles versus uplifts, this question remains largely unanswered.

A second area of dispute involves the relationships among major life events, hassles, and symptoms. As noted above, when major life events and hassles are both entered into the equation, they tend to account for much of the same variance. They also overlap considerably with symptoms. Monroe (1983) contends that daily hassles are a better predictor of

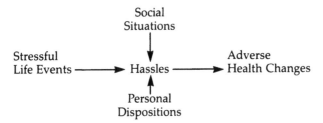

Figure 2–2. An expanded vulnerability model of the relation between stressful life events and health outcome.

symptoms than are major life events, and that the relationship holds up even when the initial symptom levels are taken into account. He does, however, concede that such findings are tentative, given the large amount of overlapping variance among events, hassles, and symptoms. Lazarus (1984) also points out that many hassles are independent of life events, and that measures of hassles do add unique variance to the relationship to symptoms, whereas life events do not.

Dohrenwend et al. (1984), generally proponents of the life stress events approach, have expressed concern about the circularity of the relationship between hassles and symptoms, particularly symptoms of psychological disorder. They maintain that stress measures such as Kanner et al.'s (1981) Hassles Scale are seriously confounded with measures of psychological distress. That is, the items identified as hassles may actually be symptoms of stress rather than causes. This problem was also evident in the Holmes and Rahe (1967) scale, but to a much lesser degree. They conclude that "some life events, some hassles . . . are consequences of personal dispositions in general and psychopathology in particular, whereas others are independent of such characteristics" (Dohrenwend et al., 1984, p. 229).

The arguments about the relationship among symptoms, hassles, and major life events are evident in a stimulating exchange of articles and letters (Deutsch, 1986; Green, 1986; Lazarus & Folkman, 1986a, 1986b; Dohrenwend & Shrout, 1986; Cohen, 1986; Lazarus et al., 1985; Dohrenwend & Shrout, 1985). The issue remains largely unresolved.

Personality and Appraised Stress. Any event, including nonspecific environmental situations, major life stress events, and hassles, can be made more or less stressful depending upon the individual's appraisal of that event. It may be that particular personality types are apt to appraise circumstances in such a way as to increase the likelihood that stress will be encountered, and thus illness will ensue. Friedman and Booth-Kewley (1987) have addressed this issue in a meta-analysis of demonstrated relationships between illness and personality factors. They observe that although there does not appear to be much evidence that different diseases have different personality traits linked with them, there may well exist a generic disease-prone personality. They suggest that "Personality may function like diet: Imbalances can predispose one to all sorts of diseases" (Friedman & Booth-Kewley, 1987, p. 552). The personality traits which they question involve depression, anger/hostility, and anxiety.

In a similar view, Kobasa (1979) has proposed that the personality characteristic "hardiness" may act as a source of positive resistance to the debilitating effects of stressful life events. Hardiness is conceptualized as a constellation of three personality characteristics—commitment, control, and challenge. The "hardy" person will tend to make optimistic cognitive appraisals, take decisive action, and thus transform stressful events into less stressful forms (Kobasa, Maddi, & Puccetti, 1982).

However intriguing such suggestions may be, there remains a great need for further investigation and refinement before the specific role of temperament and personality in disease is clarified. In particular, the interactions between personality factors and other known precursors of stress-related illness, including social factors and health-related life-style factors (such as smoking) require illumination.

One of the difficulties with this line of research is, of course, the inherent difficulty in both conceptualizing and measuring personality styles. Tennant, Langeluddecke, and Byrne (1985) point out that methods for assessing personality are generally poor. In addition, they note that the role of personality is probably complex, and may operate at a variety of stages in the stress process. Personality may influence the way in which individuals perceive their environment, including the stressful impact of events which they encounter. Personality variables may also influence the way in which individuals cope with stressors. Personality may affect vulnerability to physical and psychological illness, independently of stressors. Finally, personality may contribute to the experience of certain stressful life events, such as divorce.

Perhaps in response to the difficulties in measuring the nature and effects of personality, the issue of personal appraisal of stress has more commonly been looked at from other perspectives. (This may also reflect the clinical concern that personality—regardless of its role in the stress process—is largely not amenable to change through psychotherapy, so the question of its exact role may be somewhat academic.) The other perspectives which have been considered are the investigation of subjective appraisal of objectively stressful events; and the assessment of personal coping styles.

Lazarus and Folkman (1984) have formulated and described an extensive model of the relations among stress, appraisal, and coping. They define appraisal as an evaluative cognitive process that intervenes between the encounter and reaction, and have identified three types of cognitive appraisal. Primary appraisal refers to the judgment that an encounter is either irrelevant, benign (or positive), or stressful. Stressful appraisals can further take the form of harm/loss (in which the damage is already sustained); threat (in which the harm is anticipated); or challenge (which presupposes the possibility for mastery).

Secondary appraisal refers to the appraisal of coping options. It includes the evaluation of what coping options are available; whether or not they will be effective; and whether or not the individual is capable of applying the particular coping strategy effectively. Secondary appraisal may well affect and interact with primary appraisal. If the individual is confident that he or she can cope with a given event, that event's potential as a stressor may be reduced.

The third type of appraisal is reappraisal, which refers to a changed appraisal, usually based on new information from the environment and/ or from the person. Reappraisal may also be the result of cognitive coping efforts.

There are a number of personal factors and characteristics which influence the individual's appraisal of any event or situation as stressful. These include commitments (what is important to the individual), and beliefs (particularly beliefs about personal control, and existential beliefs). These factors interact with situational factors such as novelty, predictability, uncertainty, imminence, duration, and ambiguity, to determine to what extent an event will be appraised as stressful. (All of these factors are discussed at length in Lazarus & Folkman, 1984.)

Coping, as it is defined by Lazarus and Folkman (1984), represents "the constantly changing cognitive and behavioral efforts to manage specific external and/or internal demands that are appraised as taxing or exceeding the resources of the person" (p. 178). Coping is therefore a process, not a trait. Coping is part of the process of appraisal (i.e., secondary appraisal), yet it is also part of the process of managing stress. Coping may be directed toward lessening emotional distress which is the result of a stressful encounter (called emotion-focused coping by Lazarus & Folkman), or it may be directed toward altering the definition of the problem itself by redefining the stressor (problem-focused coping).

Although attempts have been made to classify and categorize coping styles which may be typical of specific individuals, it appears that on the whole, people are more variable than consistent in their use of coping strategies (Folkman & Lazarus, 1980), and that the selection of coping strategies is as much a reflection of differing contexts as it is of differing personalities.

Comments. When one considers all the varying events and situations which might be construed as stressful, it is easy to conclude that everything is stressful. Yet this is clearly not the case (for most people). In spite of the disagreements and disputes evident in the above discussion, there seems to be at least one fundamental conclusion which can be drawn.

Stressful events are those events which are seen to tax the capabilities of the individual. Regardless of the nature and magnitude of the event, it must be recognized and acknowledged by the individual in order for it to act as a stressor. In some cases, the role of appraisal may be minor in comparison to the role of the event itself, whereas in other cases, appraisal is the primary "cause" of stress.

What Is the Stress Response?

As noted above, the stress response has cognitive, behavioral and physiological components, which are summarized in Figure 2–3. Because the cognitive and behavioral components are most easily understood in the context of the physiology, it is important for both the client and the therapist to become familiar with the physiological mechanisms involved in the stress response.

It is far beyond the scope and intent of the present volume to provide a detailed and up-to-date analysis of the literature on the physiology of stress. Readers who are interested in such an analysis may refer to Asterita (1985). The information presented here is intended to provide the client and therapist with a functional basis for therapy.

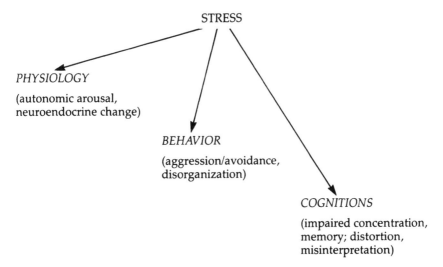

Figure 2–3. The stress response.

The study of the physiology of stress typically begins with discussion of Cannon's "fight or flight" response, a concept which is both historically significant and clinically meaningful. In the early 1900s, Walter Cannon (1929), a physiologist, described an emergency reaction which is displayed by an organism when it is confronted with a threat or danger. The intent of this reaction is to prepare the organism to deal with the threat, either by facing the threat (fighting) or avoiding it (fleeing). Thus, the reaction has been named the "fight or flight" response. Cannon argued that arousal of the autonomic nervous system (ANS), mediated by the secretion of adrenaline, was a basic expression of stress (Krantz, Grunberg, & Baum, 1985). Most pronounced are changes in the sympathetic aspects of the ANS; these are summarized in Table 2–1. Many of these changes are obvious, such as increased muscle tension and sweat-

TABLE 2–1

Examples of the Effects of Autonomic (Sympathetic) Arousal on Organs

Organ	Effect
eye	pupil dilates, ciliary muscle relaxes
glands—including	vasoconstriction, and slight secretion
nasal	
lacrimal	
parotid	
submaxillary	
gastric	
pancreatic	
sweat glands	copious sweating
heart muscle	increased rate, increased force of contraction
lungs:	
bronchi	dilated
blood vessels	mildly constricted
gut	decreased peristalsis and tone in lumen; increased sphincter tone
liver	glucose released
kidney	decreased output
blood	coagulation increased
	glucose increased
basal metabolism	increased up to 100%
adrenal cortical	
secretion	increased
skeletal muscle	increased strength
piloerector muscles	excited

Adapted with permission from A. C. Guyton (1981), *Textbook of Medical Physiology*, p. 715. Philadelphia: Saunders.

ing. Some are less obvious, including increased blood coagulation and relaxation of gallbladder and bile ducts. All of these changes serve to prepare the organism to act upon a challenge or threat. Muscles are readied for action; energy is diverted from the gastrointestinal system; the cardiovascular system is prepared for exertion; adrenaline is pumped to provide a general surge of energy.

The General Adaptation Syndrome. The fight or flight response is essentially the first stage of a complex series of physiological changes which occur in response to stress. Hans Selye (1956) incorporated some of Cannon's ideas into a more complex description of the response to stress, which he labeled the "General Adaptation Syndrome." Rather than being a simple all-or-nothing response to threat, the General Adaptation Syndrome (GAS) is a process which enables the body to deal with stress in an effective manner. The GAS comprises three phases:

(1) The Alarm Reaction (generally considered to be equivalent to the fight or flight response): This stage is characterized as an initial motivation of the body's defense mechanisms. Sympathetic arousal occurs, along with the release of adrenaline (also called epinephrine), due to adrenal medullary activation.

(2) The Stage of Resistance (the stage at which coping and adaptation occurs): This stage is characterized by the reversal of most of the changes which occurred during the alarm reaction. There is increased cortisol secretion, yielding heightened metabolism, increased muscle strength, decreases in swelling and inflammation and decreased immunity. Thus, although the body provides maximum resistance to the identified stressor, it is at risk to other stressors. In addition, this stage acts to deplete the body's resources; the body's defense mechanisms will weaken unless the stress is resolved.

(3) The Stage of Exhaustion: At this point, adaptation no longer prevails, and the effects of high levels of cortisol begin to have pronounced negative effects. Shock and lowered resistance to infection are evident. In the most extreme cases, the organism dies.

The General Adaptation Syndrome is represented graphically in Figure 2–4.

Physiological Changes. There are two primary aspects of the physiological stress response; these are the neural and the neuroendocrine (Asterita, 1985).

Neural mechanisms. The term "neural" refers to actions occurring through the autonomic nervous system (ANS). The ANS can be stimu-

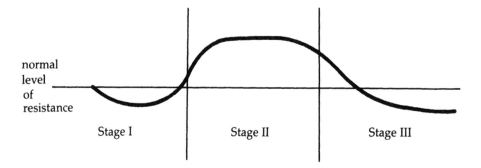

Stage I: The Alarm Reaction

Stage II: The Stage of Resistance

Stage III: The Stage of Exhaustion

Figure 2–4. The general adaptation syndrome.

lated either by action within the central nervous system (CNS) (e.g., thoughts, feelings); or by actions external to the individual, which are processed through sensory receptors (e.g., optic, tactile, acoustic) to the CNS. The sympathetic portion of the ANS (already described in Table 2–1) is triggered by the hypothalamus, resulting ultimately in innervation of the specific end-organs. This sequence is summarized in Figure 2–5.

Neuroendocrine mechanisms. In his work on the fight or flight response, Cannon (1929) stressed the important role of the adrenal medulla. Neural stimulation of the adrenal medulla (part of the reaction of sympathetic arousal) results in the release of epinephrine and norepinephrine. These substances essentially mimic (and therefore heighten) the activity of the sympathetic nervous system. In addition, chronic excitation of the stress response results in endocrine activation. Under the influence of the hypothalamus, the pituitary is stimulated, which in turn stimulates target endocrine organs. Although the exact mechanism of these changes is not relevant here, the effects of activation are important, since it is these changes which allow the individual to adapt to heightened arousal. Some of the changes which are most important clinically are briefly summarized below (from Asterita, 1985).

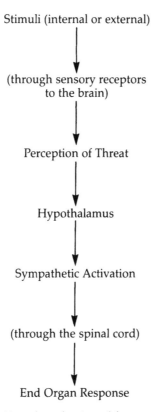

Stimuli (internal or external)

(through sensory receptors
to the brain)

Perception of Threat

Hypothalamus

Sympathetic Activation

(through the spinal cord)

End Organ Response

Figure 2–5. Neural mechanism of the stress response.

(1) *Pituitary.* This gland influences metabolic activity both directly and indirectly by influencing the activity of other glands, such as the thyroid and the adrenal cortex.

(2) *Adrenal Gland.* The adrenal produces epinephrine and norepinephrine, which excite the CNS, causing anxiety, and stimulating breathing. Its effects also slow down digestion, increase and strengthen heart rate, may increase blood pressure, increase basal metabolism rate, raise blood sugar level, and decrease overall level of immune function.

(3) *Thyroid.* It is not clear under what conditions thyroid activity is increased or suppressed; either may occur under stress. There may be differences attributable to age, sex, or nutritional status.

(4) *Reproductive Glands.* Stress precipitates lower testosterone (male

sex hormone) levels. Prolactin levels in women may be increased, but implications of this are not clear. The menstrual cycle may be irregular or halted temporarily under stress.

(5) *Immune System.* Generally, as mentioned, stress yields decreased immunity. There may be greater likelihood of the development of autoimmune diseases. There is also some evidence that stress promotes tumor growth through the effects of catecholamine interference.

(There remain many questions about the exact mechanisms of change in the above-mentioned systems. In spite of the contention of Selye and others that the response is nonspecific, there do seem to be some differences in the stress reaction, depending upon the nature of the stressor, and other factors. However, these fine points are not generally relevant in the treatment of the individual client. What is important is for the client and therapist to develop an understanding within the limits of current knowledge as to how stress is related to that client's own experience of the stress response.)

Cognitive Changes. Keeping in mind the physiological basis of the stress reaction, the cognitive changes which accompany increased arousal are predictable. Generally, neither fighting nor fleeing require a great deal of cognitive input, or are the result of a systematic problem-solving approach. Since the energy of the body is directed to more basic survival needs when stressed (at least during the initial Alarm Reaction Stage) cognitive functioning tends to be inefficient and disorganized. Although low levels of stress will improve cognitive functioning and problem-solving ability to some extent, the relationship eventually reverses itself. An extremely stressed individual or a chronically stressed individual will typically demonstrate a general depression of intellectual functioning, including distortions and misinterpretations of situations, unproductive and ruminative patterns of thinking, and indecisiveness. The stressed individual will display the apprehensive expectation that is typical of anxious individuals, including worrying, anticipation of "something bad" (such as losing control, dying, danger to others). According to the Diagnostic and Statistical Manual of Mental Disorders, Third Edition-Revised, the individual may be distractible, have difficulty concentrating, be impatient and easily irritated (DSM- III-R, 1987). On formal assessment, memory and concentration may be impaired.

There is some circularity in the relationship between cognitions and stress. It may be difficult to delineate which cognitive symptoms are a result of stress and which are part of the stress response. Beck (1976) observed that stress-prone individuals seem prone to making judgments which are one-sided, categorical, and extreme. It may be that such tendencies are personality characteristics inherent in individuals who are sensitive to stress, or it may be that stress engenders such a cognitive style in the affected individual. Whatever the origin, these cognitive styles do generally accompany the stress response.

Behavioral Changes. The basic behavioral symptoms accompanying the stress response also fall in line with the expectations of the fight or flight response. A stressed individual will typically display a pattern of either aggressive behavior or of avoidance. The aggressive individual, in keeping with cognitive irritability, may actually strike out, or (more frequently) be argumentative, stubborn, or confrontational. Often, such a response is not consistent with the seriousness of the matter at hand. The individual may overreact to relatively minor situations. Anger and hostility may be evident.

Conversely, the individual may become passive, avoiding stressful situations, whether minor or significant. He or she may be unable to take required actions, sometimes to the point of becoming immobilized.

The "normal" degree of aggression or avoidance of course varies with the individual and his or her own personality style. Regardless of the individual's own baseline of behavior, deviations in one direction or the other may be symptomatic of stress.

From the above descriptions, it is probably clear that much more is known about the physiology of the stress response than about the resultant cognitions or behavior. It is also more difficult to describe and quantify behaviors and cognitions as opposed to changes in physiology, which can often be evaluated by way of laboratory tests. There are, however, some measures which help to further delineate the exact nature of the changes in cognitions and behavior; these are presented in Chapter 4.

DEFINING STRESS: THE PROCESS

The process of defining stress occurs during the early sessions of therapy. The purpose of the above presentation of information is to provide the therapist with a framework within which to integrate information elicited from the client. This framework is presented in Figure 2–6. At this point, the therapist is aware that there are generally four levels of

Individual Characteristics +	*Stressors* =	*Stress Reaction*
-personality	-environmental	-physiology
-medical history	-life stresses	-behavior
-personal history	-hassles	-cognitions
-coping efforts	-appraisal	

Figure 2–6. A framework for assessing individual stress-related problems.

stressors which may be investigated, and that there are three components of the stress reaction which should be assessed. Much of this assessment will take place formally—through the use of rating scales, observations, and the like. These tools are described in some detail in Chapter 4. However, sometime in the first one or two meetings with the client, the question of whether or not a stress problem exists will arise. Through the general interview, already described in Chapter 1, much information which fits into the stress framework will already have been gleaned. It is the job of the therapist to begin to structure the questions asked of the client, to assess the suitability of the stress model for therapy. Whereas earlier, the therapist had probably conducted a fairly open and nondirective interview, he or she must now begin to structure the interview somewhat more, to obtain information about areas which have not yet been addressed. If the client has volunteered information only about physiological symptoms, he or she should be asked about behavior and cognitions. If he or she attributes problems to major life events which have occurred recently, he or she needs to be questioned about the impact of these events on everyday life, and the meaning of these events to him or her. In essence, the therapist is now beginning to pose some specific hypotheses about the existence of a stress problem. The general framework states that four types of stressors may lead to a three-component stress reaction. It is unlikely that all four types of stressors and all components of the stress reaction will be present in the individual client. Therefore, the client-specific hypotheses will have to be tailored to suit the individual client. The hypothesis may become "when client a is exposed to stressors b, c, and d then symptoms x, y, and z occur." The postulates underlying this hypothesis are the facts which are known about stress (i.e., the factual information presented above). The therapist may propose, for example, that when Mrs. Jones gets overwhelmed by having her in-laws visit over the Christmas holidays—because money is short, she has to work, she feels guilty about leaving her children, and she feels time pressure—she gets headaches. In this example, one can readily identify stressors which fit into several of the identified categories, as well as physiological symptoms which are consistent with the mechanism of the stress reaction. It is likely that in this case, one might pursue the issue of stress management.

However, consider the case of Mr. Smith, who experiences asthma attacks around Christmastime but only when poinsettas are in the room. Further questioning does not suggest any particular appraisal of Christmas as being stressful. On the one hand, asthma attacks may be stress-related, and Christmas is a stressful time for many people. However, in this example there seems to be a significant relationship between only one "stressor" (poinsettas) and one symptom (asthma). Thus, a framework as broad as "stress" may be less appropriate than a more narrow or specific interpretation (such as "he has allergies" or "he has learned to react to poinsettas and might benefit from desensitization").

It is worth noting again that almost any stimulus/response connection could fit, very generally, into the proposed stress framework. However, it is not necessarily desirable to fit every such connection into this framework. Trying to accommodate cases in which one specific stressor leads to one specific response is probably not an efficient use of the framework—nor of the time spent in therapy. The advantage of utilizing a stress framework is that it enables the client and therapist to organize and interpret a complex interaction of situations, thoughts, and symptoms into a coherent whole which serves as a basis for a broad-based and multidimensional approach to therapy. If this type of therapy is not indicated, then the framework is probably not appropriate.

Once the therapist has formulated an initial hypothesis in his or her own mind, this hypothesis is shared with the client. Obviously, if this is to be done, the client must also be aware of some of the factual information presented above. The amount of information which needs to be presented will vary, as will the manner in which it is presented. The client will need to understand how the body reacts to stress, and how that reaction relates to his or her own experience. The client also needs to be aware of what types of experiences are stressful in general, so that he or she can analyze and categorize his or her own experience within that framework. The presentation of factual information to the client also permits disclosure of additional information by the client, who now has an idea of which areas in his or her life to examine. Thus, additional hypotheses are proposed by the client. (Mrs. Jones may suggest, for example, that normally she can handle her in-laws and her concern about working, but that the interaction of the two is too much, since she becomes very aware of her in-laws' disapproval of her life-style. She may not have mentioned this fact earlier, since she was looking for "outside" causes for her distress.)

The definition portion of formulation concludes with the statement of various hypotheses about the nature of the problem, and questions about the exact relationships between stressor and stress reaction for that client. This is not, however, the end of formulation. The next task is to test and reevaluate systematically the hypotheses in light of evidence, and then to propose a course of treatment. These issues are discussed in Chapters 4 and 5.

Below, these principles are applied to the three case studies introduced in Chapter 1.

CASE STUDIES

Cathy

The first session of the stress management group began by having each group member identify his or her reasons for enrolling in the group. Cathy stated, as she had earlier, that she was not aware of a major stress problem at present, but that she anticipated encountering a number of major stresses within the next few years. She was quite interested to see that several other group members presented similar information. She was also surprised to note that one other group member mentioned that she tended to have a great deal of difficulty with insomnia, and that she wondered if it could be related to stress. Cathy also wondered that, because she had had similar experiences occasionally.

Once the initial introduction of group members had been accomplished, the group leader presented an outline of the eight sessions of the group, then began to give some background information about the nature of stress. Briefly, he described the fight or flight response, a concept with which most of the participants were familiar. In response to specific questions about how they personally experienced stress, the group members were able to generate a fairly lengthy list of symptoms and experiences which they had attributed to stress. These included headaches, stomach problems, depression, increased smoking and alcohol consumption, irritability, aggression, sleep problems (both too much and not enough sleep), anxiety, and loss of self-confidence (as well as a host of others). The group leader pointed out that these symptoms tended generally to fall into the three categories of physiological, cognitive, and behavioral symptoms.

In addition, he asked group members to identify the types of stressors that they were currently experiencing. Many participants had concerns related to student life—too much work, erratic hours, worries about grades, interpersonal and dating problems, anxieties about living away from home. Two members of the group had recently had major deaths in the family. Cathy and one other member pointed out that they could not identify any particular things that they could not handle, but that they felt a lot of pressure around expectations for the future, particularly from their families.

Again, once a list had been generated, the leader pointed out that there were clearly a variety of things that could be conceived as stressful, some of which were outside the individual, some of which were inside. He posed a question to group members as to why it might be that although all group members were students and therefore subject to the same anticipated changes as Cathy, others might not perceive such a situation as stressful. A discussion of personal goals and values ensued, in which the issue of personal viewpoints emerged. The group leader further described the role of appraisal.

Once the initial information about the various sources of stress and the types of reactions had been presented, each student was asked to keep a diary over the course of the next week. In this diary, each participant was asked to identify any stressful situations which occurred, and to describe his or her response to it, addressing physiological, cognitive, and behavioral aspects. In addition, each participant was to analyze the identified stressor, pinpointing those aspects which were external to the individual, and which were internal, as well as deciding which stressors could be changed, and which required adaptation.

Jean

Since Jean ended the initial interview by commenting that she was still unclear about the relationship of her health to stress, the therapist began the session by bringing up this topic. She began by describing to Jean the assumed nature of the stress response, and briefly mentioned the effects of stress on the body. The therapist also drew an analogy between the fight or flight response as animals experience it, and Jean's symptoms. Jean was able to see that her physiological response was "normal," but not adaptive. This information put Jean considerably more at ease than she had been previously. She acknowledged that in coming to see a therapist she had expected to be told that her symptoms were imaginary, and that she was relieved to receive a "legitimate" explanation for the discomfort.

At this point, Jean was eager to begin working on a treatment for the headaches in particular, but was cautioned that more information was needed before effective treatment could be started.

Jean was asked to describe the last time that she had had what she considered to be a "bad" day. She mentioned a time two weeks ago, when her ex-husband's check had been late, and her parents dropped by unexpectedly. When asked to describe how she felt at that time, Jean mentioned getting a headache after her parents had left. However, she also described feelings of extreme anger toward her parents. In retrospect, she commented, her reaction seemed somewhat out of proportion to the circumstances of their visit, as they do sometimes drop in and usually she does not mind. At the time, however, she did not want to talk to them, and was extremely quiet throughout their visit. At the conclusion of the visit, she sent her children outside to play, as she wanted to be left alone.

The therapist asked Jean if she remembered what was on her mind during this episode. Jean laughed and commented that that was easy to answer, as she frequently has the same thoughts. They center around three areas: (1) that her parents must think she is awful because she is not a good hostess when they drop in; besides, they do not think that she is a good parent because she works; (2) that she probably is a lousy mother because she should be spending time with her kids but instead sends them out; (3) that her husband will probably never send her any more money, and they will end up bankrupt.

At this point, the therapist interrupted to point out to Jean that when she is feeling stressed, she seems to be experiencing more than just physical changes. She pointed out to Jean the changes in her behavior, and in her thought patterns. Jean acknowledged that these changes were fairly typical of her.

At the same time, the therapist asked Jean to try to list the stressors in the above situation. Jean readily identified the ongoing hassles of worrying about money, and about being a single parent. She seemed puzzled about why the visit to her parents had been such a problem that day. The therapist suggested two possible explanations: first, that it had simply been "the straw that broke the camel's back"; second, that it was not as much the situation itself as her appraisal of its meaning to her (i.e., a comment on her ability as a parent or society's expectations of her).

At this point, the therapist pointed out to Jean that many different types of things can be stressful, and that most people have a definite limit to the amount they can tolerate at any time.

The remainder of the session was spent discussing other problematic situations, in less detail, but with the goal of elucidating how Jean responds to stress, and what makes her respond.

At the conclusion of the session, Jean was able to summarize fairly well how she thought all the presented information applied to her. She expressed frustration that they had not yet "done" anything in therapy. She was given several brief rating scales to complete at home before the next session (see discussion at the end of Chapter 4) and was assured that at the next session, they would set some concrete goals and plan intervention strategies.

J. B.

J. B. was well versed in the academic aspects of the relationship between stress and his ulcer. When the therapist began to explain how his life-style might make him prone to such a problem, he quickly interrupted to say, "Yes, yes—I know that! But how can I learn to get rid of the symptoms?" Thus, it was necessary for the therapist to emphasize the shortsighted view of stress that was engendered by such thinking, and the inevitability of either failure or relapse unless a broader interpretation of the problem was made.

J. B. was quickly able to identify both the cognitive and behavioral symptoms which he manifests under stress. However, he expressed reluctance to change his aggressive behavior or his impulsive cognitive style, stating that these characteristics were essential in his line of work, and that in fact they were responsible for getting him where he is professionally.

Similarly, he was readily able to identify any number of stressors in his life. Interestingly, he did not mention his family or any interpersonal situations as causes of stress. Once again, he tried to deny the utility of addressing any of these issues, pressing instead for a way to simply control the physical symptoms.

At this point, the therapist pointed out to J. B. that she and he seemed to disagree about the nature of his problem, and thus also disagreed over the course of action. She asked for five minutes of uninterrupted time to present her point of view. Reluctantly, J. B. agreed.

The therapist began by reiterating the tripartite nature of the stress response, and by pointing out that although the ulcer was the most obvious aspect of the problem, there were clearly other symptoms. Similarly, she pointed out that of the many sources of stress in his life, J. B.

was not claiming responsibility for any; rather he viewed them as outside influences. She concluded by suggesting that there were two items which needed further investigation. First, she suggested that they monitor the factors which contribute to ulcer flare-ups, in order to assess the validity of her proposal, as well as to provide a basis for intervention. Second, she indicated some concern about his generally "driven" nature, and expressed interest in discussing J.B.'s specific priorities and goals in life, to see whether or not his fast pace was indeed getting him to where he wanted to be in life.

J. B. reluctantly acceded to the first request, stating that it did seem a necessary step toward setting up a treatment program. However, he was not convinced that the second issue was relevant to his current problem. The therapist pointed out that from his discussion thus far, it appeared to her that his job was extremely important, but that his family was not of much concern to him. J. B. was shocked by this statement, and denied it emphatically. However, when asked what his family thought of his life-style, he acknowledged that it had been the source of a major rift between himself and his wife in the past. He was unable to say what his son thought, since "we don't talk much—you know, I'm not at home much." At this, J. B. mumbled that the hour was up, and that he would think about these things before next week.

The therapist concluded by pointing out that they had not yet agreed on the exact problem to be dealt with in therapy. She suggested to J. B. that for next time, he should make a list of the things that he thinks cause his ulcer to flare up. In addition, he should make a list of those things that his ulcer prevents him from doing (i.e., how it interferes with his life). They agreed to try to decide on an agreeable course of action at the next meeting.

3

Stress and Illness

The notion that stress (or other emotional factors) might precipitate somatic illness is by no means new. Many years ago Plato remarked:

> For this is the great error of our day in the treatment of the human body, that physicians separate the soul from the body.
>
> (O'Neill, 1955)

For much of the history of medicine, psychological or spiritual causes for illnesses have been invoked whenever physicians have been unable to determine an organic cause. Hippocrates, for example, believed that epilepsy was the result of a visitation from the devil (Murray, 1983).

PSYCHOLOGICAL MODELS OF STRESS AND ILLNESS

There are basically two different ways in which psychological factors may precipitate disease, and each of these ways is represented in a number of different theories. First, personality factors may predispose the individual to experience certain emotional reactions, which may exaggerate stressful experiences, or which may lead to inadequate coping strategies, and therefore result in feelings or behaviors which are damaging to health (e.g., anxiety, smoking, drinking). Secondly, stressful life situations may demand increased coping mechanisms, and thus create strain. Although these two types of theoretical explanation tend to be examined separately in the literature, the separation is somewhat artificial; there is some degree of overlap between them. Below, one major example of each approach is summarized. It is the latter approach, the diathesis-stress approach, which is derived from Selye's General Adaptation Syndrome Model, which most closely represents the approach taken in this book.

The Psychosomatic Model

Traditionally, the field which has addressed the interface between mind (psyche) and body (soma) is referred to as psychosomatic medicine, a field which reached its height in the 1950s—and has since waned. One of the most well-known proponents of the psychosomatic approach to medicine was Franz Alexander, whose beliefs about the relationship between psychological factors and illness were derived from Freud's psychoanalytic teachings. Alexander (1950) proposed that if a specific stimulus were to occur, then it would express itself in a specific physiological response in a predetermined organ. His conceptual model may be summarized as follows:

(1) All healthy and sick human functions are psychosomatic in nature.
(2) Emotions are always associated with action patterns expressed through a portion of the autonomic nervous system and its innervated organs.
(3) For specific emotions, there are appropriate vegetative patterns.
(4) Emotions suppressed from overt expression lead to chronic tension, thus intensifying in degree and prolonging in time the concomitant vegetative innervation.
(5) The resulting excessive organ innervation leads to disturbance of function, ending eventually in morphological changes in the tissues.

Alexander maintained that a specific psychosomatic disorder would therefore occur in an individual with a specific character structure, which would be illuminated by psychoanalytic techniques.

Although the details of other psychosomatic theorists' models differed in various ways from Alexander's, these models tended to have in common the notion of response specificity; that is, a particular type of conflict in a particular personality type would lead to dysfunction in a specific organ.

In spite of Alexander's contention that all functions are psychosomatic to some extent, a number of diseases which were generally considered to be "psychosomatic" in origin were identified. Some of these diseases, and the (alleged) personality characteristics associated with them are described in Table 3–1.

The notion of specificity of response attributable to personality style has largely been refuted, and the field of psychosomatic medicine has

TABLE 3–1

Examples of Psychosomatic Specificity

Disorder	Expected Personal Characteristics
Bronchial asthma	Excessive unresolved dependence upon the mother; fear of abandonment.
Neurodermatitis	Showing the body (exhibitionism) in order to obtain love and favor, combined with guilt and masochism.
Rheumatoid arthritis	Repression of rebellious tendencies; difficulty handling hostile impulses.
Ulcerative colitis	Frustrated hope of carrying out an obligation; frustrated hope in accomplishing some task.
Duodenal ulcer	Frustration of dependency needs.
Essential hypertension	Conflict over expressing aggressive impulses; difficulty in asserting oneself.
Hyperthyroidism	Fear of death; development of phobias related to this fear.

Adapted from F. Alexander, T. French, and C. Pollack (Eds.), *Psychosomatic specificity.* Chicago: University of Chicago Press, 1968.

gone through a period of decline, until its recent resurgence in association with the field of behavioral medicine, of which the study of stress-related diseases is part. However, the idea of specific personality types engendering specific diseases is not unknown to the general public. It is not unusual to hear references to the "typical" ulcer candidate, or the "usual" migraine personality. In addition, the medical profession still propagates such beliefs. For example, in Wyngaarden and Smith's (1985) *Cecil Textbook of Medicine*, the description of migraine headache includes the statement, "Characteristically, the headache affects individuals with perfectionistic and 'driven' personalities." The tendency to label individuals according to their somatic complaints may be responsible in part for the resentment and resistance that some clients display when they are referred to mental health practitioners for assistance with physical problems. This difficulty is compounded by the general misconception that "psychosomatic" means "imaginary" or "fabricated." The therapist needs to be aware of the general evolution of these concepts in order to identify and correct them in clients.

It should be noted that although response specificity does not seem to occur as a result of personality, there is a great deal of individual variation in response to stress. Some individuals seem to consistently respond more strongly in the cardiovascular system, whereas others respond in the gastrointestinal system. These individual differences probably combine with medical predispositions to result in specific stress-related disorders. However, it should be pointed out that individual response specificity is difficult to establish. Although some individuals are very consistent across physiological symptoms and sources of stress, others react differentially to different forms of stress, or to the same stressor at different times. It may be that those individuals who respond consistently in one organ system are those most likely to exhibit a "psychosomatic" disorder in that system (Bakal, 1979).

The Diathesis-Stress Model

The demise of the traditional psychoanalytically based models of psychosomatic illness does not suggest that psychosocial variables play an unimportant role in the development of illness. The above models have been replaced by models such as the diathesis-stress model of illness, an interactionist model. This model suggests that biochemical vulnerability, although necessary, is not sufficient to explain disease onset. At a physiological level, it is assumed that the individual possesses a predisposition to develop a particular disorder. The predisposition may be congenital, hereditary, learned, or a result of previous illness or injury. It is when this predisposition interacts with the stress response (as described in Chapter 2) that a "psychosomatic" disorder occurs. The exact manifestation of disease is therefore a result of personal physiology rather than of personality. In a physically robust individual, illness may take the form of vague feelings of unwellness; in an individual with a strong family history of migraines, it may take the form of a headache.

Given the breadth of the diathesis-stress model and the diffuse nature of the stress response, it is conceivable that almost any ailment may be psychosomatic in nature (as, in fact, Alexander suggested). The DSM-III-R (1987) suggests that there are many examples of physical conditions which might fall into this category; some of the more common ones are listed in Table 3–2. (It is interesting to note that most of the entries from Table 3–1 are contained in this list.)

STRESS-RELATED DISORDERS IN GENERAL MEDICAL PRACTICE

When stress is manifest through physical symptoms or illness, it will generally first come to the attention of the general practitioner, family

TABLE 3–2
Common Examples of Disorders Which May Be
Attributable to Psychological Factors

obesity	tachycardia
tension headache	arrhythmia
migraine headache	gastric ulcer
angina pectoris	duodenal ulcer
painful menstruation	cardiospasm
sacroiliac pain	pylorospasm
neurodermatitis	nausea and vomiting
acne	regional enteritis
rheumatoid arthritis	ulcerative colitis
asthma	frequency of micturition

physician, or other primary care physician. Certainly such physicians do see many stress-related disorders in their practices. Charlesworth and Nathan (1984) estimate that up to 75% of all visits to physicians are made by people with stress-related disorders. Among the disorders that they cite as being stress-related are hypertension, coronary heart disease, headaches, asthma, various skin disorders, and gastrointestinal disorders.

There is a small but significant percentage of individuals who present to the primary care physician with purely psychological problems, although the individual's presenting complaint is often some form of physical discomfort. Spaulding (1976) has reviewed studies that suggest that 12 to 30% of patients seen in primary care present with illnesses which were considered to have no physical cause but rather, were attributable to psychological factors. In many cases, these individuals will receive some form of counseling or reassurance from the primary care physician or they will be referred for psychiatric assistance.

Of interest to the practitioner of stress management are those individuals who do in fact demonstrate a "bona fide" medical disorder, demonstrable through medical and laboratory tests, but whose disorders are related to stress. Disorders such as hypertension or asthma may be viewed as falling into the realms of both the primary care physician and the mental health practitioner, which provides an opportunity for teamwork and cooperation—as well as for conflict.

The Medical Model

It may be useful to the nonmedical therapist to digress here and review the basic tenets of the medical model, and how this model manifests itself in the care of individuals with stress-related disorders.

The traditional medical model of disease suggests that:

(1) each constellation of symptoms is definable as a particular disease entity;
(2) each disease entity has a specific etiology;
(3) this etiology indicates a specific treatment, which will be medical or surgical in nature.

Therefore, the role of the physician is to diagnose a specific ailment according to the presenting symptomatology, and to prescribe treatment, based on what is known about the etiology of the disease. The medical model, however, largely fails to address the fact that many different illnesses can share the same symptoms (e.g., increased autonomic arousal), the same etiological factors (e.g., stress) and the same treatment (e.g., stress management). In the general practice of medicine, psychological factors tend to be viewed as default factors, useful primarily when organic factors are insufficient to account for the symptoms. This summary is, of course, somewhat of an oversimplification of the situation, but it serves to highlight some of the basic inconsistencies between the approach of the medical practitioner and that of the stress therapist.

Reasons for Referral

Physicians are therefore most apt to refer stress-related disorders to mental health practitioners under several circumstances:

(1) when the physician operates from a more "psychosomatic" or holistic model, rather than from the medical model in its narrowest sense;
(2) when the disease in question is one of the "recognized" psychosomatic illnesses;
(3) when there is obvious evidence of psychological disturbance in the patient;
(4) when the disease has failed to respond to the usual medical interventions;
(5) when the symptoms do not fit the description of any known medical disorder, or the symptoms are not supported by objective laboratory data.

In the first instance, the work of the stress therapist may be considerably easier if the referral has come from such a physician. Some of the initial formulation may already have been done with the client. In addition, the approach of the therapist is less apt to clash with or contradict that of the physician.

The second category accounts for a significant proportion of referrals for stress management; much of the work on the treatment of stress-related disorders involves illnesses in this category. Thus, even a physician who is not particularly holistic in his general orientation may well refer patients with illnesses such as headaches and asthma. Similarly, patients with obvious indications of psychological disturbance are apt to be referred regardless of the presenting complaint.

Frequently, however, referrals may originate for the fourth or fifth reason. The physician may have been treating a patient with a known disorder for some time, but with limited or no success; or the physician may have been unable to diagnose a specific disorder, but nevertheless has attempted to treat the individual symptomatically. In either case, these individuals can bring two types of unique problems into therapy.

Client Expectations

Many individuals exhibit an inherent reluctance to seek or acknowledge a need for psychological or other mental health assistance. In the case of an individual with a diagnosed medical complaint, this reluctance may be compounded by surprise and a feeling of betrayal when the physician makes the referral. If such a referral follows unsuccessful medical treatment, the individual may interpret the referral as an indication either that he or she has failed by not responding appropriately, or that the fact that he or she did not respond indicates that the illness is in some way fraudulent. It is worth remembering that most individuals seeking medical treatment are themselves operating from the medical model. The individual assumes that he or she has a diagnosable medical problem (a disease or disorder) which is attributable to a germ, injury, or biological predisposition, and which will abate or be controlled by means of a medical or surgical procedure. The physician's act of referring the patient to a mental health practitioner challenges these beliefs. Most individuals do not come into therapy with sufficient factual knowledge about stress to reinterpret symptoms within a stress model. They are therefore left to conclude that either (1) they are a problem case and the physician does not want to see them any more, or (2) the physician thinks that they are "crazy."

The situation is even worse for individuals who do not have a diagnosable illness. They may conclude that either of the above statements apply, or that (3) the physician thinks that they made it all up and that the symptoms are imaginary.

Regardless of which of these five reasons for referral applies in a given situation, the first task of the therapist is to reinterpret the situation for the client. In the course of the first one or two sessions, the therapist obtains information about the client's specific problem and tries to determine if the identified symptoms fit into a stress conceptualization. At the same time, the client becomes familiar with the mechanisms of stress, and attempts to determine whether or not the therapist has anything to offer to him or her. This process has already been described.

Medication Usage

Many clients with either diagnosable medical disorders or other physical complaints will have been exposed to the possibility of taking medication to deal with the symptoms. There are two types of problems which can emerge from the use of medication for stress-related disorders. The client may become overly dependent upon the prescribed medication, making the physician want to discontinue it. Conversely, the client may be reluctant to rely on medication at all, and may not comply with treatment.

In the first case, the client may begin to abuse the prescribed medication, or to self-medicate with over-the-counter drugs. The problem seems to occur most frequently with the use of minor tranquilizers, and with pain medication. A typical scenario involves the client seeking help for a problem such as a headache. The physician may conclude that the headache is a migraine, and he or she therefore treats it accordingly, providing strong pain medication. The client is pleased to receive relief from the drug, so he or she asks for it again the next time that a headache occurs. The more relief that is obtained from the medication, the more apt the client is to request it. The problem is compounded with some drugs by the fact of increasing tolerance, so that a larger dose becomes necessary to achieve the same results. Eventually, the physician fears that the client is addicted or is otherwise abusing the drug, and so attempts to discontinue it. There are a number of actions that the physician may take at this point, most of which are outside the scope of this discussion. One alternative, however, is to refer the client for other-than-medical help for the original problem. Thus, the headache sufferer, for example, may be referred at this point for biofeedback training.

Well intentioned as this action may appear, it presents some difficulties for the therapist who receives the referral. Most clients who become dependent upon drugs do so for the simple reason that the drug helps—it makes the pain go away, or it makes him or her relax. The client is usually not entirely pleased with the prospect of having the drug withdrawn. This may have a contradictory effect on therapy. If the client agrees to seek help from a mental health practitioner, then his or her main source of relief (i.e., the drug) is withheld. In order for such a referral to be effective, there must be a temporal separation between the referral and the drug withdrawal. Consider the following options. In all cases, the physician has first decided that the client's problem has a significant stress component, that the client is abusing medication for this problem, and that the medication should be decreased or withdrawn.

(1) The physician may stop the drug, then refer the client to a therapist;
(2) The physician may set up the referral, then discontinue the drug upon learning that a successful contact has been made and the therapist and client intend to pursue the matter;
(3) The physician may refer the client to the therapist, and not alter the medication until such time as the therapist and client feel that the client has acquired sufficient stress management skills so as to offset the effects of decreasing the medication.

Obviously, the first two of these options create a high risk of therapeutic failure. If the client is faced with the option of losing a "sure thing" (the drug) by virtue of his or her having agreed to participate in therapy (an unsure thing), the logical action for the client to take is either to refuse the referral or sabotage the therapy, so that his or her drug treatment must be reinstated. In contrast, if the matter of drug withdrawal is left until skills are developed, the client then possesses a viable alternative to drug usage.

For every client with a problem of drug dependency, however, there is probably one who prefers not to take any drugs, and thus does not comply with medical treatment. In some cases, of course, this is harmless, or even admirable. But in other cases, there is risk of harm to the client, as well as the possibility of worsening the medical condition. In this case, the responsibility falls (to some extent) on the shoulders of the therapist, who must ensure that the participation in therapy is not interpreted as license to discontinue medication.

In either of these situations, the key to successful and comprehensive treatment is a close liaison with the client's physician. It is generally not sufficient simply to receive a written referral from a physician and then embark on a course of therapy. There must be continuing contact with the physician, so that matters of medical status, medication usage, and disease progression can be monitored. (It is easy to forget that therapy can make things worse as well as better.)

In either case, it is also necessary for the therapist to gradually educate the physician about his or her approach to the treatment of medical complaints related to stress. Reasonable goals for the use of medication, whether the client is an abuser or a reluctant user, can only be derived through the joint efforts of the therapist, the physician, and the client. It behooves the therapist to proceed with extreme caution (if at all) in cases in which the client denies permission to consult with his or her physician.

STRESS-RELATED DISORDERS

Below, some of the more common stress-related illnesses are described in more detail. It is not intended that these descriptions be used for diagnostic purposes. Diagnosis of any medical disorder, stress-related or otherwise, should be undertaken only by a qualified medical practitioner. The purpose of delineating the nature and mechanism of these disorders is to aid the therapist in formulating a definition of stress and a suitable treatment plan for the individual client. It is assumed that the client arrives at the therapeutic situation with a diagnosis. The role of the therapist is to interpret that diagnosis within the stress perspective.

The disorders described below are grouped according to the biological system which they affect. Those disorders which are discussed at some length are those which the therapist is most likely to encounter, as well as those to which significant attention has been paid in the stress research literature. These include tension and migraine headaches, hypertension, asthma, irritable bowel syndrome, ulcers, and anxiety. Other less common or less well-researched (in the context of stress) disorders are mentioned briefly. These particular disorders are, of course, not the only "stress-related diseases." It should be clear from the earlier discussion of the physiology of stress that prolonged exposure to stress may have an adverse effect on virtually any disease process.

Disorders of the Muscular Skeletal System

Much of the body mass is comprised of muscle, and muscle plays a major role in preparing the body to fight or flee. Chronically tense muscles may result in a number of disorders, the most notable of which are general anxiety and tension headaches. Disorders of the joints (such as rheumatoid arthritis) are implicated as well.

Anxiety.

Description. Anxiety is, of course, a common symptom—one which can be adaptive when mild. At times, however, anxiety becomes extreme and pervasive, to the extent that it may interfere with daily functioning. There are a number of abnormal anxiety states which can be diagnosed from the medical standpoint. These are listed in Table 3–3. However, most clients who experience anxiety symptoms will not meet the formal criteria for diagnosis of an anxiety state, nor will they warrant such a diagnosis. In general, formal psychiatric assessment and diagnosis of an anxiety state is not particularly useful, either in defining a problem or in establishing a treatment plan. What is useful for the anxious client is a thorough assessment of symptoms, as well as assurance that the identified symptoms are in fact attributable to anxiety.

The symptoms of severe anxiety are many and varied; they are summarized in Table 3–4. Although most individuals will not display the full range of symptoms, many will experience symptoms of such a severity as to raise the question of other somatic illness. Because of the pervasive nature of the symptoms, individuals experiencing anxiety are often apprehensive about having another, more serious medical condition. Symptoms similar to anxiety can occur with coronary heart disease, thyroid problems, and other diseases. The possibility of other illness should, of course, be ruled out medically.

TABLE 3–3
Classification of Anxiety Disorders

Anxiety States
Panic Disorder—with or without agoraphobia
Generalized Anxiety Disorder
Obsessive-Compulsive Disorder
Post-traumatic Stress Disorder
Phobic Disorders
Agoraphobia—without panic disorder
Social Phobia
Simple Phobia

Adapted with permission from the *Diagnostic and statistical manual of mental disorders* (3rd ed.-revised, 1987, p. 235). Washington, D. C.: American Psychiatric Press.

TABLE 3–4

Symptoms Which May Be Part of An Anxiety Disorder

1. *Apprehensive Expectation*

   Anxiety; worry; fear; rumination; and anticipation of misfortune to self or others.

2. *Motor Tension*

   Shakiness; jitteriness; jumpiness; trembling; tension; muscle aches; fatigability; inability to relax; eyelid twitch; furrowed brow; strained face; fidgeting; restlessness; easy startle.

3. *Autonomic Hyperactivity*

   Sweating; heart pounding or racing; cold, clammy hands; dry mouth; dizziness; light-headedness; paresthesias (tingling in hands or feet); upset stomach; hot or cold spells; frequent urination; diarrhea; discomfort in the pit of the stomach; lump in the throat; flushing; pallor; high resting pulse and respiration rate.

4. *Vigilance and Scanning*

   Hyperattentiveness resulting in distractibility; difficulty in concentrating; insomnia; feeling "on edge"; irritability; impatience.

Adapted with permission from the *Diagnostic and statistical manual of mental disorders* (3rd ed.-revised, 1987., pp. 252–253). Washington, D.C.: American Psychiatric Press.

Anxiety can occur in several ways:

(1) as an affective response of an individual under circumstances of threat or danger;

(2) as a symptom of another psychiatric disorder (e.g., depression, dementia);

(3) as a prominent feature of a psychopathologic state;

(4) as a symptom of another illness or disorder (e.g., hyperthyroidism, or a head injury).

It is generally the first of these manifestations which will bring the anxiety sufferer to seek assistance with stress management.

Mechanism. The mechanism by which anxiety occurs under stress is relatively self-explanatory. The general arousal of a variety of systems is evident, but symptoms are often vague and diffuse. Many organs may be affected, but none to the extent that specific impairment in that organ is evident. Although there does appear to be evidence of a familial tendency toward clinical anxiety, it is most often a direct manifestation of heightened autonomic arousal. As was discussed in Chapter 2, stress and anxiety are similar and somewhat interchangeable phenomena. Depending upon the specific symptoms manifested by the individual, any of the various cognitive, behavioral, and physiological interventions may be appropriate.

Tension Headache.

Description. Tension headaches (also called muscle contraction headaches) are probably the most common type of headache in adults. Tension headaches are recurrent and may be present as often as every day. They may begin in the afternoon or evening, and often become progressively worse over the course of the day. They are characterized by a steady, nonthrobbing, aching pain, which may be unilateral but is more often bilateral. Patients complain of feelings of tightness and pressure around the head, as if the head were in a vise. The pain often starts in the back of the head and neck, and expands to the frontal and temporal areas. The pain may be mild or severe, but it is not usually accompanied by nausea or vomiting, although dizziness, blurring of vision, and ringing in the ears may occur.

There is much overlap between the symptoms of common migraine and tension headaches, and many patients suffer from both. The distinguishing features of tension headache are the tightness in the back of the head and neck and the increasing pain over the course of the day.

Mechanism. Tension headaches are often directly associated with stress and anxiety-provoking situations. The exact nature of this relationship is not clear. Conventional wisdom is that the pain is attributable to increases in muscle tension in the region of the neck (trapezius), face, and jaw. This viewpoint is supported by the success with which these headaches are treated by methods which decrease muscle tension. These include massage, antianxiety drugs, rest, relaxation, and biofeedback. However, physiological monitoring of muscle tension does not support this belief (see Chapter 6 for further discussion of this issue).

Tension headaches may also be the result of sustained contraction of head and neck muscles secondary to structural diseases or abnormalities of the head and neck area, or postural problems (Wyngaarden & Smith, 1985).

Rheumatoid Arthritis. Rheumatoid arthritis is a chronic inflammatory condition of the joints. It is characterized by persistent pain and stiffness, usually starting in the hands and feet, although its effects may progress to include involvement of all joints, as well as interference in the functioning of the heart, lungs, spleen, and eyes. At first, symptoms may be intermittent, but gradually they become constant and affect almost all joints in the body. The inflammatory process affects cartilage and the surrounding joint capsule, tendons, and ligaments, often resulting in either contraction or overextension of the joint, and thus deformity.

Rheumatoid arthritis is thought to be an autoimmune disease, and thus represents a deficiency in the functioning of the immune system. The effects of stress on the immune system may contribute to the etiology of rheumatoid arthritis.

Disorders of the Gastrointestinal System

It is somewhat puzzling that the gastrointestinal (GI) tract is as responsive to stress and emotional demands as it is, given that it plays no significant role in the fight or flight response. However, it is generally accepted that almost all areas of the gastrointestinal tract are intricately tied into the emotional and psychological components of the individual. Functional gastrointestinal disorders are common, and almost no one experiences stress without encountering some GI complaints. Among the more minor of these are dry mouth, loss of appetite, mild nausea, heartburn, and alterations in bowel habits. Two common disorders in which stress plays a significant part are irritable bowel syndrome and peptic ulcer. Less common but more serious are the inflammatory bowel diseases, ulcerative colitis and Crohn's Disease.

Irritable Bowel Syndrome (IBS).

Description. Irritable bowel syndrome is the most common functional digestive disorder. The predominant feature is a history of chronic constipation or diarrhea, or both, sometimes accompanied by abdominal discomfort. There is frequently excessive flatulence as well. The symptoms tend to occur intermittently, and may last for weeks or months, then disappear for some period of time (Braunwald et al., 1987).

Although the disorder is not life-threatening, it is unpleasant. Apprehension about possible episodes often restricts the individual's mobility, as does fear of being embarrassed by uncontrolled flatulence.

The diagnosis of IBS is most common in young and middle-aged adults; females are twice as apt to experience this disorder as males. Affected individuals typically report symptom exacerbation in response to stress, ingestion of food or medication, or following acute gastroenteritis (Mitchell & Drossman, 1987). Individuals with IBS are also apt to report an increased number of medical complaints unrelated to gastrointestinal function.

Mechanism. The basic abnormality in IBS is an alteration in bowel motility. IBS sufferers, relative to controls, are described as having a hyperactive gut which overreacts to a variety of stimuli, including hormones produced in response to eating. Some IBS sufferers also experience food intolerances.

Various explanations for the increased reactivity have been proposed, including a reduction in pain threshold and abnormal myoelectric activity in the colon or in the entire gastrointestinal tract, but evidence is contradictory (Mitchell & Drossman, 1987). One of the defining features of IBS remains the lack of abnormalities determined by physical examination, sigmoidoscopy, blood work, barium contrast x-rays and other objective measures.

Diarrhea and other gut-related stress responses are commonly reported by healthy adults (with or without IBS). Strong emotions are typically associated with changes in colonic contractions and vascularity in the area. Thus, there is significant evidence that stress affects the bowel functioning of normal as well as IBS patients. In addition, there is some evidence (cf. Mitchell & Drossman, 1987) that IBS sufferers report significantly more stress prior to the onset of symptoms. The stressors do not appear to be unique.

IBS should not be confused with the inflammatory bowel diseases (Crohn's Disease and ulcerative colitis). Although the presenting symptoms may be similar, the latter diseases are diagnosed by identifiable organic abnormalities.

Peptic Ulcer.

Description. Ulcers are "miniature excavations in the mucus membrane (of the gastrointestinal tract). They resemble the divot a Sunday golfer carves in the fairway" (Kiester, 1982, p. 477). Ulcers occur most often in the stomach (gastric ulcers) or in the duodenum (duodenal ulcers), although they may occur anywhere in the gastrointestinal tract. Duodenal ulcers account for about 80% of diagnosed ulcers.

Peptic ulcer usually represents itself as a painful conglomeration of abdominal symptoms known as "dyspepsia," a poorly defined feeling of nausea, anorexia, bloating, and abdominal discomfort. These symptoms are often present in conditions other than ulcer; conversely, many ulcer patients have no symptoms, until the ulcer perforates or hemorrhages.

The pain accompanying ulcers is usually episodic and short-lived, lasting minutes rather than hours, and is often relieved by ingestion of food or antacids. Episodes of pain are generally clustered in periods of days or weeks, interspersed with long symptom-free periods.

It is difficult to estimate the frequency with which ulcers occur. Signs of peptic ulcer are evident on autopsy in about one-quarter of men and one-sixth of women. However, only 5 to 10% of the population actually develop symptomatic ulcers. Men are twice as likely to develop duodenal ulcers as women, but equally likely to develop gastric ulcers. Duodenal ulcers usually first produce symptoms between the ages of 25 and 55, whereas gastric ulcers tend to appear later in life, between ages 40 and 70. Ulcers are rarely a cause of death. They do, however, tend to be chronic and recurrent. Sixty percent of healed duodenal ulcers recur within one year; and 80 to 90% do so within two years. The poor correlation between symptoms and the presence of ulcers is problematic in determining whether or not ulcers have healed, as well as whether they have recurred.

Mechanism. Originally all ulcers in the upper gastrointestinal tract were thought to be caused by the action of hydrochloric acid and the enzyme pepsin on the mucosa. This belief is the source of the name "peptic" ulcer. However, this viewpoint is probably an oversimplification of the mechanism involved. On the averge, patients with duodenal ulcer do produce more acid than most people, but patients with gastric ulcers produce less acid. The ulcer seems to be produced when the aggressive effects of acid and pepsin override the protective effects of gastric or duodenal mucosal resistance.

There is evidence of a genetic predisposition to ulcers. In addition, cigarette smoking, use of anti-inflammatory drugs, adrenocorticosteroid therapy, and consumption of alcohol or caffeine-containing beverages are thought to exacerbate ulcer symptoms, although it is doubtful that they have a causal role.

Induction of emotional stress has been demonstrated to increase basal acid secretion in both ulcer patients and normal subjects. There is some suspicion that stress may also alter factors which maintain mucosal integrity in the gastrointestinal tract, and thus predispose toward ulcer flare-ups. Contrary to popular belief, there is no significant empirical evidence of a particular ulcer personality type.

Inflammatory Bowel Disease. Inflammatory bowel disease is a general term for a group of chronic inflammatory disorders of unknown etiology, involving the gastrointestinal tract. The two major groups are ulcerative colitis and Crohn's Disease. The clinical manifestations of these diseases are diverse and may include bloody diarrhea and abdominal pain, with fever and weight loss. Anemia, dehydration, and stools containing pus may be evident in severe cases. Onset is usually in adolescence or early adulthood, but may occur in any age group.

The clinical course is variable. Many patients suffer relapses within a year but there may also be prolonged periods of remission, with only minimal symptoms. However, the long-term course of these diseases is relentless, with a significant number of patients eventually requiring surgical intervention.

While the cause of inflammatory bowel disease remains unknown, it appears that genetic factors, infection, immune response, and psychological factors may all be involved. As is the case with any gastrointestinal disorder, stress appears to precipitate or exacerbate symptoms (Braunwald et al., 1987).

Previously, there was considered to be a specific personality type associated with inflammatory bowel disease, but current evidence refutes this.

Disorders of the Cardiovascular System

The cardiovascular system as a whole has been considered a major end-organ for the stress response. Disorders of this system include those that affect the heart itself, blood pressure, and systematic blood flow. Although the exact mechanism by which the cardiovascular system is affected remains unclear, there is no doubt that heightened psychophysiological arousal plays a major role in hypertension, heart disease, migraine, and other disorders such as arrhythmias and Raynaud's Disease. Of recent interest in this area is the Type A behavior pattern, a coronary-prone pattern of behavior which has been the subject of much interest. Although this is not a disease or disorder per se, it is discussed below, as it appears to be a significant risk factor.

Type A Behavior Pattern. The Type A behavior pattern, first described by Friedman and Rosenman (1974), is considered to be a constellation of behaviors which render the individual vulnerable to coronary heart disease. Rather than displaying a particular personality style, the Type A person is identified by particular behavioral traits, including a sense of time urgency, a chronic struggle to achieve more, excessive competitive drive, aggressiveness, impatience, and hostility. Type A individuals tend to act quickly—they walk faster, talk faster, and interrupt others often.

Type A individuals have, in fact, been demonstrated to have increased incidence and prevalence of heart disease (Cohen, 1980). Although the original research in this area linked Type A behavior to coronary heart disease, there is evidence that some aspects of Type A behavior may also predispose to angina pectoris, and myocardial infarction.

In spite of the widespread popularity of the concept of Type A behavior, there remain many questions about its exact nature and mechanism. Reliable measurement remains a problem. It may be that Type A behavior is part of the more general disease-prone personality identified by Friedman and Booth-Kewley (1987). Regardless of whether individuals with heart disease exhibit a distinct pattern of behavior, the evidence is strong that stress is a problem for these individuals. However, Type A individuals are often reluctant to change their behaviors, since they attribute their level of personal success to the very hard-driving and competitive nature which is also the focus of change in therapy.

Essential Hypertension.

Description. The term "hypertension" refers to chronically or intermittently elevated blood pressure. Hypertension is one of the most prevalent chronic conditions in North America, affecting about one in six persons. The incidence rises with age, primarily affecting men over 35 and women over 45. Blacks are affected almost twice as often as whites (Marcinek, 1980).

Hypertension is labeled "essential" or primary in cases in which the elevation in blood pressure does not appear to be secondary to a disease state (such as kidney disease). In essential hypertension, therefore, there is no identifiable cause for the increase in blood pressure. Most cases of hypertension fall into this category; in over 90% of individuals with high blood pressure, the etiology of the disorder is unknown. In the early stages, it appears that the effects of hypertension are reversible and that normal functioning can be restored. However, the consequences of long-standing high blood pressure can be quite serious; arteriosclerosis can occur, eventually leading to heart disease, kidney problems, and cerebral hemorrhage (Lachman, 1972).

There is no precise line between normal and high blood pressure. Generally, a diastolic pressure below 85 is considered to be normal, as is a systolic pressure below 140 (Braunwald et al., 1987). Current evidence suggests that treatment is beneficial for pressures above 160/95 (Wyngaarden & Smith, 1985).

The main clinical importance of hypertension is not so much that it is a disease in itself, but rather that it predicts future risk of vascular disease—risk which can be decreased by lowering blood pressure.

Many cases of hypertension are asymptomatic and are determined only through routine assessment. Individuals with systolic pressures over 170 and diastolic over 110 may show symptoms such as morning headache, weakness, tachycardia, or palpitations. More problematic is the sudden and apparently unpredictable appearance of major medical crises such as myocardial infarction and cerebrovascular accident.

The measurement of blood pressure presents some difficulty. Blood pressure is a very reactive measure and varies a great deal (in both normotensive and hypertensive individuals) from one situation to another. Having a cup of coffee or a cigarette will elevate pressure—as will going to the doctor (and having your blood pressure taken). Small decreases in blood pressure are also easy to induce through suggestion, which makes the assessment of change over time difficult. It is useful to measure blood pressure repeatedly, at varying times and in varying places, in order to assess change.

Mechanism. Blood pressure is essentially a function of cardiac output and peripheral resistance. Cardiac output is the product of heart rate and stroke volume (how much blood is ejected in each contraction). Therefore, anything that affects heart rate, stroke volume, or peripheral resistance will ultimately affect blood pressure (Marcinek, 1980). Although cardiac output is increased in some hypertensives, the most common finding is of elevated peripheral resistance (Chobanian, 1983).

Although the cause of essential hypertension is (by definition) unknown, there are a number of possible etiologies. Most researchers agree that there are probably a number of interacting homeostatic mechanisms involved, rather than a single cause. Factors under consideration include:

(1) increased retention of salt and water by the kidneys, resulting in increased blood volume;
(2) increased peripheral resistance as a response to the increased blood volume;
(3) sympathetic nervous system hyperactivity (particularly as a result of stress), resulting in increased vessel resistance;
(4) inappropriate secretion of renin, a kidney enzyme, which may result in increased peripheral resistance;

(5) resetting of baroreceptors (sensory nerve endings which are stimulated by changes in pressure) to an inappropriate level, so that they respond to abnormally high pressure as if it were normal or low.

Hypertension is known to have a significant hereditary component, and is also more common in overweight individuals. A number of behavioral interventions are useful in moderating blood pressure. These include weight loss, dietary restriction of salt (sodium) intake, increased exercise, decrease in cigarette smoking and alcohol use, and alleviation of stress.

In a normal individual, exposure to stress results in increased heart rate and increased peripheral resistance, as part of the overall sympathetic arousal. Thus, stress can exacerbate symptoms in an individual who already experiences high blood pressure. In a previously unaffected individual, chronic recurrent stress may precipitate hypertension, particularly in the presence of other risk factors (such as age, cigarette smoking, positive family history, etc.). A review by McCaffrey and Blanchard (1982) suggests that a variety of stress management procedures have been found to be useful in dealing with hypertension; these include various relaxation and biofeedback techniques, self-monitoring, cognitive-behavioral approaches, and life-style management.

Migraine Headache.

Description. Migraine headaches occur in about 10 to 20% of individuals at some time in their lives, about one-third of whom require intervention.

Typically, migraines first occur in childhood, adolescence, or early adulthood, and diminish with age. They often abate during pregnancy. Women are affected three times as often as men.

Migraines are characterized by a throbbing unilateral pain, often in the forehead. "Classic" migraines, which are found in about one-third of migraine sufferers, are preceded by transient focal neurological symptoms such as visual, speech, and sensory disturbances. These symptoms may include seeing bright flashing lights, loss of vision in one side of the visual field, prickling or tingling sensations on one side of the body (usually in the hand), word-finding difficulties, and other sensory defects. These neurological symptoms rarely last more than 30 minutes, and generally abate before the headache begins.

The headache itself is frequently accompanied by nausea, vomiting, sensitivity to light and sound, and diarrhea. The pain usually lasts four to six hours, but may persist for days.

The syndrome of classic migraine has four parts:

(1) the prodromal phase (which occurs in a minority of patients) consists of mood alterations and/or increased hunger and thirst for 24 hours or more prior to the headache;

(2) the neurological symptom stage, as described above; these symptoms may also occur without the headache;

(3) the headache itself;

(4) the post-headache phase, characterized by exhaustion, tenderness of the scalp, and recurrence of headache on sudden movement.

Many patients with classic migraine also suffer from "common" migraine. Common migraine is similar to classic migraine, except that no prodromal or neurological symptoms occur.

Mechanism. The exact mechanism of migraine remains unclear. The symptoms of migraine are associated with changes in cerebral blood flow. The neurological symptoms are accompanied by arteriolar constriction and decreased cerebral blood flow. It is assumed that the headache phase is due to vascular dilation (although direct measurement of cerebral blood flow during the headache phase does not demonstrate this relationship).

There is a strong familial tendency toward migraine, with a positive family history evident in over 60% of cases. In addition, headaches are often precipitated by a number of factors, including food sensitivities (red wine, coffee, tea, chocolate, old cheeses), use of oral contraceptives, exposure to sunlight, changes in barometric pressure, stress and tension, menstrual status, and medications which induce vasodilation (Wyngaarden & Smith, 1985; Braunwald et al., 1987).

Although the actual mechanism whereby stress precipitates migraine headaches is not clear, it may be that the general sympathetic arousal and changes in blood flow that accompany the stress response trigger the vasomotor changes which initiate the migraine process. In addition, stress can increase the intensity and duration of migraines indirectly, through its effects on both blood flow and muscle tension. In those individuals who experience frequent and intractable migraines, secondary muscle tension appears to play a major role.

The most common behavioral approaches to migraine are thermal biofeedback training and relaxation approaches, although cognitive behavioral methods are also employed. Behavioral changes in life-style are also helpful.

Disorders of the Respiratory System

In a state of heightened physiological arousal, the individual relies heavily on increased consumption of oxygen to fuel and maintain the activity of all systems. This reliance can result in ongoing strain on the respiratory system, and therefore contribute to disorders such as bronchial asthma. Even in otherwise unimpaired individuals, hyperventilation is a common response to stress, as the organism strives to increase respiratory function.

Asthma.

Description. Bronchial asthma is a respiratory condition in which episodes of narrowing of the passages of the bronchi and bronchioles result in a characteristic triad of symptoms: wheezing, shortness of breath, and cough. Onset may be at any time in the life span, childhood or later. Some patients improve with age, others deteriorate.

During an attack, both inspiration and expiration are impaired; expiration in particular is prolonged and incomplete because air is trapped within the lung. The problem is complicated by the production of thick mucoid secretions which further obstruct breathing (Lachman, 1972).

Asthma is an episodic disease, with attacks interspersed with symptom-free periods of days, weeks, or months. Attacks are occasionally prolonged and resistant to therapy.

Asthma occurs in about 5% of adults and 7 to 10% of children (Braunwald et al., 1987).

Mechanism. Asthma is a complex disorder involving biochemical, neural, immunologic, infectious, endocrine, and psychological factors. The degree to which each of these factors is involved varies in different individuals (Cluss & Fireman, 1985).

The primary pathogenic event in asthma is the nonspecific hyperirritability of the tracheobronchial tree. Increased airway reactivity can be demonstrated in asthmatics even in an unaffected state, as well as in many disease-free relatives of asthmatics. The stimuli that increase airway responsiveness and incite acute episodes of asthma can be grouped into seven categories (Braunwald et al., 1987):

(1) *Allergenic.* Common allergens include pollens, dust, animal dander, feather, and mold.

(2) *Pharmacologic.* The drugs most commonly associated with acute asthmatic episodes are aspirin, coloring agents, and sulfiting agents (sanitizing and preserving agents in food).

(3) *Environmental.* Environmental causes are usually related to climatic conditions that promote the concentration of atmospheric pollutants. Heavily industrialized areas and urban centers are particularly problematic.

(4) *Occupational.* Bronchoconstriction can result from exposure to metal salts, wood and vegetable dusts, pharmaceutical agents, industrial chemicals and plastics, biological enzymes, and animal and insect residues.

(5) *Infections.* Respiratory viruses rather than bacteria are the major problems, particularly after the symptoms of a respiratory tract infection are present.

(6) *Exercise.* Asthma can be induced or made worse by physical exercise. The mechanism by which exercise provokes attacks seems to be related to thermal changes in the airways. Therefore, activities such as hockey and skiing are more problematic than would be swimming in a heated indoor pool.

(7) *Psychological.* Abundant data exist which demonstrate that psychological factors can interact with the asthmatic tendency to worsen or ameliorate the disease process.

Neural bronchoconstrictor activity is mediated through the autonomic nervous system, and hence is subject to the effects of stress. In spite of attempts to link asthma attacks to separation anxiety, overprotective mothers, suggestion, and conditioning, it appears most likely that the generally increased reactivity on the part of asthmatics can be in response to any highly emotional stressor. Since it is technically difficult and thus not normally feasible to work directly on respiratory function, stress management techniques are usually directed toward overall reactivity, rather than specifically toward airway activity.

Disorders of the Immune System

The immune system is responsible for providing the body's defense against invasion by foreign organisms. The effects of immune function are not localized in one organ, but function throughout the body. There is evidence that prolonged and excessive exposure to stress serves to disrupt the efficiency of the immune system (Asterita, 1985). The potential effects of such a disturbance are far-reaching. In some cases, the effect is simply to make the individual more susceptible to common infections such as colds, influenza, and other minor afflictions. At the other extreme, there is evidence that the course of cancer, which is itself a failure in immune function, can be altered depending upon the individual's level of stress and his or her associated cognitive response patterns.

Some disorders of the immune system have already been mentioned in the context of other systems; these include rheumatoid arthritis and the inflammatory bowel diseases. Thyroid disorders (both hypo- and hyperthyroid) are also immune disorders and thus may be subject to the effects of stress. Allergies represent an overresponse of the immune system. There is also some evidence that alteration in immune function plays a role in the development of some types of diabetes.

Other Systems

Eczema and Other Skin Disorders. Eczema, or dermatitis, is not a specific disease but an inflammatory reaction to a variety of stimuli, both internal and external. It may be chronic or acute. The skin may be red, swollen, and blistered, as in acute attacks, or scaly and thickened, as in chronic conditions. The chief symptom is intense itching.

There are a variety of types of eczema, and many causes. The latter include allergies, hay fever, asthma, exposure to irritants, and circulatory problems (Kiester, 1982).

The skin is an end-organ for the stress response in that the electrical conductivity of the skin surface changes and the temperature of the skin, which is a function of the vascular tone of small blood vessels, changes during stress. Thus psychophysiological arousal is thought to be one of the mediating factors in flare-ups of eczema and other skin disorders (including acne, psoriasis, and urticaria, Asterita, 1985).

Insomnia. Insomnia refers both to a lack of sleep and to inadequate quality of sleep. It may indicate difficulty falling asleep, or difficulty staying asleep. Insomnia is a common symptom of a variety of medical and psychiatric disorders. Numerous studies have suggested that 20 to 35% of the population have trouble sleeping at times; women tend to be more affected than men, and the frequency increases with age. Transient insomnia can occur in almost anyone in times of great stress or emotional upheaval. Chronic insomnia, however, can be a debilitating and frustrating affliction—one that frequently interferes with daily functioning (Kales & Kales, 1984).

Chronic insomnia can begin at any age, but in the majority of patients, persistent difficulty begins prior to age 40. Difficulty falling asleep is far more common than difficulty staying asleep or early morning wakening. Evaluation of sleep disturbances can be problematic, since sleep patterns and requirements vary from one individual to another, as well as within one individual over the life span. Thus, the diagnosis is often made based primarily on the subjective report of lack of sleep.

There are a number of types of insomnia; these are listed in Table 3–5. This list also identifies many of the various sources of insomnia, including various medical complaints, major psychiatric illness, alcohol use, and drug use. However, the most frequent cause of insomnia is stress. There is a significant body of research which indicates that the onset of insomnia is often associated with an increase in stressful life events. Kales & Kales (1984) suggest that stressful life events, when mediated by predisposing emotional factors and inadequate coping mechanisms, are closely related to the onset of long-term sleep difficulties. Once a major medical or psychiatric reason for insomnia has been ruled out, the current trend is to apply behavioral principles to dealing with insomnia. Attention to exercise, caffeine usage, diet, regularity in sleep habits, and relaxation is usually recommended for treating insomnia.

TABLE 3–5

Classification of Insomnia

A. Psychophysiologic
   1. transient
   2. persistent
B. Associated with Psychiatric Disorders
   1. personality disorders
   2. affective disorders
   3. other functional psychoses
C. Associated with Drugs and Alcohol
   1. tolerance to or withdrawal from CNS depressants
   2. sustained use of CNS stimulants
   3. sustained use or withdrawal from other drugs
   4. chronic alcoholism
D. Associated with sleep-induced respiratory impairment
E. Associated with sleep-related myoclonus and "restless legs"
F. Associated with other medical, toxic, or environmental conditions

Adapted with permission from E. Braunwald et al. (1987). *Harrison's principles of internal medicine*, p. 111. New York: McGraw-Hill.

Caution. It should be emphasized again that stress is generally only one of many factors which may contribute to the above disorders. In many cases, the primary treatment for these disorders is medical in nature. Certainly in all cases, a thorough medical evaluation should be completed before stress management is begun. In spite of the theorized mechanism by which stress may exert an effect on these disorders, it remains to be seen whether or not stress plays a role in the specific symptomatology of any affected individual. In individuals experiencing these disorders, the hypothesis that stress is a contributing factor should be entertained only if there is sufficient evidence to support such an approach. In any case, this hypothesis should be thoroughly tested before therapy is begun. In some disorders (e.g., tension headaches, anxiety), the hypothesis may frequently be supported. In others (e.g., migraine, thyroid disease) it often may not be relevant.

(This is not to suggest that behavioral interventions are not relevant if the disorder is not stress-related, but rather that they may better be applied in a context other than that of stress management. In the case of migraines, for example, biofeedback may be an effective technique, whether or not the headache is stress-related.)

CASE STUDIES

Cathy

Since Cathy had recently had a complete physical and had been found to be in good health, it appears that her intermittent insomnia is probably attributable to stress. She in fact identified the sleep problem as occurring primarily in response to stressful events. The most recent episodes of insomnia occurred during exam period. Cathy was slightly amused to discover that the others in her group who had had sleeping problems also found them to occur during the same period. In fact, many members of the group acknowledged experiencing various somatic complaints during exam periods. They spent some time in the group discussing not only the impact of exams on their physical health, but also the disruption in life-style (including eating habits, exercise, and regularity of hours) that happens at exam time.

Jean

Based on Jean's description of her headaches, and her obviously high ongoing stress level, the diagnosis of muscle tension headaches, made by her family physician, seems appropriate. There seems to be little doubt that stress is a major precipitating factor for her headaches. Working within this diagnosis, the therapist can elicit from Jean additional information about the frequency, location, duration, and intensity of the headaches. In addition, the therapist has explained to Jean, in conjunction with the general explanation of the stress response, the presumed physiology of tension headaches. A description of the muscles involved and the original importance of this aspect of the response is not only informative but also lends further legitimacy to Jean's discomfort. Increasing Jean's understanding of the physiology of her headaches also allows Jean to become more aware of the sensations of muscle tension as they develop into an actual headache. As she becomes increasingly aware of these sensations, she is in a better position to determine the relevant stressors, and to take some action before the headache reaches fulmination.

J. B.

In spite of his superficial awareness that his ulcers may be related to stress, J. B. had little idea of the mechanism involved. This was also true of his ideas about the relationship between his life-style, particularly eating habits, and ulcer flare-ups. J. B. had a simplistic notion that ulcers were attributable to too much stomach acid. His solution, therefore, was to take antacids frequently. Given a slightly more comprehensive view of the ulcer process, he was able to appreciate better the need for a more comprehensive approach to change. J. B. was also somewhat surprised to find that stress was not the primary cause of his ulcer. He reported having been told that he had a "typical ulcer personality," a statement which had made him somewhat defensive (a factor the therapist had already observed). J. B. did acknowledge a family history of ulcer, but had attributed it to his having similar personality characteristics as other affected family members. The therapist reviewed with him the interactive nature of personal physical predispositions and stress. J. B. eventually recognized that although he may have possessed a congenital tendency toward developing ulcers, his life-style and situational stressors have no doubt contributed to his current state, and may influence the frequency and severity of ulcer flare-ups.

4

Assessment of Stress:
Tools and Methods

By now, it should be obvious that there are three categories of variables which need to be assessed; these are (1) stressors, including major life events, hassles, and appraisals; (2) the stress reaction, including cognitive, behavioral, and physiological responses; and (3) personal characteristics of the client, including personal resources (strengths and weaknesses), behavior patterns, and coping styles. Measurement of these items is carried out for two reasons. First, problematic areas must be defined so that therapy can be planned appropriately. Secondly, the client's initial status must be clearly identified so that progress can be measured over the course of therapy.

MEASUREMENT APPROACHES

There are three approaches to measurement that can be utilized for each variable. First, the item in question may be examined in a general interview format. Second, the item may be assessed through use of rating scales, checklists, or other paper-and-pencil measures. Third, the item may be measured (or observed) directly. Each of these general approaches has its own strengths and weaknesses, and each has its own important role to play in the treatment of the individual client.

The Interview

It is difficult to conceive of a therapeutic relationship which does not begin with an in-depth interview between client and therapist. As was stated earlier, basic interviewing skills are as important in the management of stress as they are in any other type of therapy. It is not within the scope of this book to teach such interviewing skills. However, it is worth pointing out the strengths and limitations of the interview format.

The interview is the basic means of communication between therapist and client. In a semi-structured interview (i.e., an interview following a general format), the client has the opportunity to state his or her problems and interpretations of them, and to make his or her request for help. The therapist may request information about any aspect of the client's problem, and may pursue any line of thought or interest which arises. Thus, the interview is flexible, usually relatively pleasant, responsive to individual needs and personal styles, and as thorough or in-depth as the interviewer and client wish to make it. The interview is the foundation of any therapeutic relationship. No amount of testing, recording, and measuring will compensate for a poor or incomplete interview. It is generally from the initial interview that all other forms of assessment arise. However, the interview is an incomplete assessment tool. Depending upon the orientation of the interviewer and the comfort of the client, major areas of concern may be overlooked or minimized. The interview process also does not yield a measurable record of the client's status at any point in time. It is difficult to assess change by comparing one interview to another. Interviews are also quite time-consuming; it may take a great deal of time to elicit the amount of detail regarding symptoms and history that is necessary to begin therapy and monitor progress. Interviews are particularly susceptible to social desirability and expectancy biases. Thus, essential as it may be, the interview is not a sufficient measure for planning and evaluating therapy. Some of the limitations of the interview may be overcome by using a structured interview format, but at the same time, such a structure reduces the interview's flexibility, one of its major advantages.

The most satisfactory solution to this dilemma is to employ a semi-structured format (i.e., following a general outline), but to supplement the information from the interview with paper-and-pencil measures or direct observation of the variables involved.

Paper-and-Pencil Measures

Paper-and-pencil measures include standardized tests, rating scales, checklists, and questionnaires. Some of these measures yield a score, which can be compared to population norms and thus can categorize the individual client as high or low, normal or abnormal, in relation to the population at large. Others yield a score which may have no meaning outside of its relationship to the individual client. They may tell you whether the client is getting higher or lower, better or worse on a given dimension, but they will not tell you how that client compares to the population as a whole. Still other such measures are purely descriptive; they do not yield any type of score but do identify problem areas for the individual client.

Each of these types of paper-and-pencil measures has a useful place in measuring variables related to stress, but it is important that the therapist be aware of the strengths and limitations of each tool that he or she selects. Many rating scales and checklists are unstandardized or have been minimally applied to small populations, which may or may not be representative of the client's own population base. In order to employ an assessment tool properly, the therapist must be familiar with the psychometric properties (or lack thereof) for each measure. Paper-and-pencil measures are most appropriately used to confirm or deny specific hypotheses which arise from the general interview, and to monitor progress over time. The therapist may conclude from the interview that the client seems to be experiencing a certain type of stress response, or may be exposed to a certain type of stressor. A direct test of such a relationship can be carried out by examining these factors in the detail which can be found in a written measurement tool.

These measures have clear limitations as well. Although they are much closer to objective measurement than interviews typically are, they are self-report measures, and are subject to the biases inherent in this type of measure. They frequently rely on retrospection, which may be somewhat inaccurate. The tools themselves are also of variable quality, in terms of psychometric soundness, reliability, and validity. A measure which has not been demonstrated to have any reliability over time may be of limited utility in assessing change.

Finally, paper-and-pencil measures are only as useful as they are appropriate. It is up to the therapist to select the measure which addresses the problem at hand. No matter how good a rating scale of (for example) major life stresses is, it will not be helpful if the problem is actually one of hassles rather than major life events. Unless the therapist has conducted a comprehensive interview and accurately identified the problem areas, paper-and-pencil measures are not likely to be helpful. For this reason, it is desirable to select paper-and-pencil measures specifically for each individual client. Although each therapist will probably develop a repertoire of favorite measures, it is generally not as useful to administer a standard battery of measures as it is to give a few carefully selected tools, chosen specifically to address the needs of the individual client.

Direct Observation

Direct observation or monitoring of an identified variable has the potential to be one of the most useful forms of measurement. An accurate count of the number of times that a specified symptom or event occurs in a representative period of time provides the therapist with a clear description, a baseline against which to measure change, and a summary of factors which may impinge on the identified variable. The method of direct observation enables the therapist to avoid the errors and biases which accompany retrospection, and to focus on specific variables relevant to the individual client. The data collected by this method are easily quantifiable.

In its simplest form, direct observation entails the client keeping a count of how often a given event, symptom, or other variable occurs. How many times in a given period did the client sneeze? Smoke a cigarette? Have a headache? The observations may be made by the client, or by another person (a family member or the therapist). Sometimes the variable in question may be observed in a laboratory or other artificial setting, rather than in a natural setting. In order to assess the response to stress, for example, the therapist might artificially induce an environment of stress, then record the reactions of the client directly.

In order to measure a variable directly, the therapist must first decide what to measure, who will measure it, for how long, and with which units of measure. It is generally useful to measure antecedents and consequences of variables in question, as well as recording the variable itself.

There are several commonly used types of measurement which can directly assess behaviors and other observable variables:

(1) Frequency measures. This method entails a simple tallying of the number of times the identified variable occurs in a specified period of time (and is also referred to as the response rate; Kazdin, 1980). This measure is particularly useful for variables which are discrete and which usually last for the same period of time per occurrence.

(2) Discrete categorization. This method is used to classify behaviors into discrete categories such as correct-incorrect or normal-abnormal. If, for example, the hypothesis is proposed that each fight with the boss precipitates an ulcer attack, the client may be asked to record the presence or absence of an attack each time a fight with the boss occurs. In some ways, this measure is like a frequency count in that it is appropriate for discrete behaviors, but discrete categorization can also be applied to several behaviors simultaneously (e.g., of an ulcer attack, an argument

with one's spouse, and calling in sick to work, which occurred the day following the identified stressor?).

(3) Interval recording. For behaviors that may occur very frequently, a time-based method of recording such as interval recording may be effective. In this method, the identified behavior is observed for a predetermined block of time (e.g., one hour or one day) which is in turn subdivided into smaller intervals (10 minutes or one hour). For each identified block of time, the behavior in question is scored as simply present or absent. Time-sampling is a form of interval recording (Kazdin, 1980; Hersen & Bellak, 1981).

(4) Duration. Like interval recording, recording of duration is another time-based method of measurement. It is most appropriate for recording ongoing or continuous behaviors. It may be useful to record the amount of time in a given period that the variable in question occurs (for how many hours in the week does the client actually experience ulcer symptoms?) or to record the amount of time it takes the variable in question to occur (how long is the interval between the fight with the boss and the first ulcer symptoms?).

In spite of the apparent simplicity of direct observation approaches, there are many issues and difficulties associated with them. Specific variables need to be operationally defined—not always an easy task. Time intervals need to be determined. One hour a day of observation may be sufficient for a high frequency behavior, but several weeks or more may be necessary for an infrequent behavior. Furthermore, who is to do the recording? Introducing family members or "significant others" into therapy can have advantages, but may also have disadvantages.

Most commonly, the client is responsible for recording his or her own behavior, and the process becomes self-monitoring. The biggest problem associated with self-monitoring is compliance. Self-monitoring is only useful if the client actually does it! Often the client fails to carry out the assigned tasks, for a variety of reasons. At the surface level, the client may simply be too busy, not get around to it, may forget, or may find it inconvenient. At a less obvious level, a client's compliance is also a reflection of the client's general level of motivation, the perception of the severity of the consequences of complying or not complying with treatment, and the value or meaning of the specific outcome to that particular client. Self-monitoring puts the onus on the client to decide how much effort he or she is willing to put into changing. Self-monitoring may also force the client to address facts or issues that he or she would prefer to ignore or remain unaware of (such as how much he or she actually smokes or eats, or that it really is the dog that brings on the asthma attacks).

Exactly how much the client will be required to record on a regular basis will be a function of several factors: (1) what the therapist needs to know; (2) how motivated the client is; (3) how much trouble it is to do the recording. The last of these three items is the easiest to manipulate. It is useful to adjust the amount of recording required of the client in order to maximize the possibility that he or she will comply, while at the same time trying to focus on the most essential bits of information.

Although compliance is often a problem when self-monitoring is required, the degree of compliance with this task may also provide the therapist with useful information not only about the specific observed variables, but also about the general motivation of the client, and his or her likelihood of complying with future treatment-related assignments.

Of course, not all direct observation of behavior falls into the category of self-monitoring. As mentioned earlier, some observation is done directly by the therapist, particularly measurement of physiological responses. Although the possibility of noncompliance is effectively eliminated, the observation done directly by the therapist is likely to be very specific and limited to small samples of behavior. It may be difficult to generalize accurately from these small samples, as they may not be meaningful representations of the client's behavior in other situations.

As will become apparent in the rest of this chapter, each of the different types of description and measurement has its place in the management of stress. None of these approaches is intrinsically better or more useful than the others; each may be useful in its own context. Direct observation or self-monitoring may be unrealistically time-consuming if used to record major life events, which occur infrequently, and which can be listed in an interview or checked off from a list. Interviews are of limited utility for eliciting information about physiological symptoms, descriptions of which may be difficult to verbalize; checklists work well in that case. Cognitive content varies greatly from one client to another, so questionnaires identifying particular thought patterns may not contain items relevant to a specific individual; self-monitoring and recording are more useful in this instance.

The ability of the client to verbalize, describe, and follow through on assignments will also influence the choice of measurement strategies. Thus, there is no such thing as a standard protocol or a fixed assessment battery. The ideas presented below represent a potpourri of scales, lists, and ideas from which one can select, as appropriate, suitable methods, in the context of the individual client. This list is far from inclusive but does give a general indication of the types of instruments which are available. The instruments described here were selected primarily because they are relatively well known, or of particularly high quality, or easily available.

MEASUREMENT OF STRESSORS

Major Life Events

Major life events are fairly straightforward to measure. The therapist can usually simply ask the client what major events have occurred in the last six months or year. Although some kind of list, to which the therapist can refer and which can jog the client's memory, may be helpful, it is not essential. When this information is collected in an interview format, clients may have to be reminded to include positive as well as negative major life events in their lists, but generally anything significant enough to be considered a major life event can be elicited in an interview. This is not to say, of course, that clients will necessarily admit all major life events to the therapist in the early stages of therapy, but neither will they necessarily admit to them in writing.

In order to assure thoroughness, there are some paper-and-pencil measures which can be employed to assist in this process.

Social Readjustment Rating Scale (Holmes & Rahe, 1967). This most well-known of the life events scales lists over 40 major life events, each of which has been assigned a value of between 11 and 100 life change units. The total score has some predictive value in terms of anticipating disease or illness. This scale can probably be found in almost any book written about stress. There is a tremendous literature stemming from the development of this measure, particularly relating amount of life stress to the development of illness.

Interestingly, this scale is not particularly useful clinically. Most of the items are fairly obvious (e.g., the death of a spouse) and will emerge in the course of an interview notwithstanding. As noted in Chapter 3, the predictive power of the total score derived from this measure is significant but small, with other measures (i.e., hassles) being more closely related to illness. The scale may be useful in impressing clients with the need to manage stress; however, many clients have already made the decision to manage stress by the time that they are in therapy. Others may interpret reports back from the SRRS as "scare tactics." Finally, many women clients are annoyed by the scale, since it measures only discrete (not ongoing) stressors. The birth of a child would be included in the list, for example, but not the ongoing stress of parenting. Many of the items listed are of more relevance to men than to women, and most of women's major stresses are not included. There is no mention of items such as role conflict, physical or sexual abuse, or family responsibilities, such as caring for elderly relatives.

There are many other scales which represent variations on this general theme. Anderson (1972), for example, has developed a similar scale for college students. (For other examples, see Dohrenwend, Krasnoff, Askensay et al., 1978; Sarason, Johnson, & Siegal, 1978; Horowitz, Schaefer, Hiroto, et al., 1977.) Other authors (see Pilkonis's work below) have tried to amalgamate the major life events and appraisal approaches in a single instrument.

Life Events Questionnaire (Pilkonis, Imber, & Rubinsky, 1985; Marziali & Pilkonis, 1986). These two articles describe two very similar measures of major life events, which also incorporate questions about the individual's appraisal of any life event which has been experienced recently. Although the questionnaire described in the former article is somewhat more detailed than that described in the latter (98 potential events identified, versus 62), each consists of a list of potential major life stressors, with provision of space for the individual to add any others which are not listed. The client is then asked to answer a series of probing questions about his or her subjective response to the identified stressor. These questions concern such factors as the amount of adjustment required by the event, the perception of control over the event, desirability of the event, available social support, and general perception of stressfulness.

In both of the quoted studies, the primary intent of the developed questionnaire seems to have been to attempt to delineate the relative contributions of qualitative versus quantitative aspects of stress. Each article describes the relative contributions within its own subject group, and discusses the particular attributes of the scale which contribute significantly to the total variance. Although much of this is not particularly relevant when dealing with an individual client, either of these two questionnaires does provide a good structure or framework for taking a very detailed history of major life events, including the more subjective or qualitative aspects.

(It should be fairly obvious that self-monitoring and other direct observation methods are not very useful in measuring major life events. Major life events do not generally occur very often and are not expected to change systematically over time, so collecting a long baseline is quite inefficient.)

Hassles and Minor Life Events

Frequent and recurrent hassles are often identified by clients in an interview. Just as often, however, it is difficult for the client to figure out exactly what it is that is stressful or how often it is occurring. Keeping a daily log may be helpful; the client may be asked to record exactly what is happening when he or she feels stressed. There are also a number of scales which may help to clarify hassles.

The Hassles Scale (Kanner et al., 1981). The Hassles Scale (also discussed in Chapter 3) consists of a list of 117 irritants ranging from minor annoyances to fairly major problems. Subjects are to identify the hassles which have occurred in the past month, and rate each one as being somewhat severe, moderately severe, or extremely severe. The authors calculated three scores from these data. The frequency score is a simple count of how many items were checked. The cumulated severity score is the sum of the three-point severity ratings, and the intensity score is the cumulated severity divided by the frequency.

The original study by Kanner et al. presents a great deal of informative data about this scale, both in terms of psychometric properties and in relation to the theoretical role of hassles in the development of symptoms related to stress. There are analyses which address retest reliability, normative data, frequent items, predictive ability, and overlap with major life events. This particular study also addresses the role of uplifts, and their relation to hassles.

Clinically, the Hassles Scale provides an excellent complement to the major life events approach. The 117 listed items survey a broad range of subjects, many of which might be overlooked by a client who was simply trying to think up recent hassles in an interview setting. The noted study also addressed (to some extent) the issue of sex differences in the experience of stress—a matter overlooked in most scales and investigations. The extensive retest data quoted makes this tool useful for measuring change over time (although some questions about measurement over time are noted in the study), and the identification of both frequency and severity make the Hassles Scale useful in setting treatment goals.

Stressful Situations Questionnaire (Hodges & Felling, 1970). This 40-item instrument was originally developed to assess stress in anxious college students. The questionnaire consists of a list of 40 social situations which are believed to involve a loss of self-esteem, and which may occur frequently in young adults of college or university age (e.g., going on a blind date; asking a teacher to clarify an assignment in class; getting hurt in a fight; skiing out of control). The respondent is asked to state to what degree the identified situation is likely to cause him or her apprehension or concern. Factor analysis of the scale indicates that four dimensions may be present: (1) apprehension in physical danger; (2) apprehension in classroom and speech situations; (3) apprehension of social and academic failure; (4) apprehension in dating situations. No norms or reliability data are presented. Some validity is suggested through the moderate correlations between the latter three scales and trait anxiety measures.

In the context of stress management, this scale may be useful in formulating ideas about general categories of hassles which may be relevant for college students. The scale is quite obviously geared for this population, and the selection of items is probably not appropriate for other groups of individuals.

The Fear Survey Schedule (Wolpe & Lang, 1964). This 72-item checklist was developed to identify specific items which are related to maladaptive avoidance behavior, and which may be the target of desensitization procedures. It has a long history of use in behavioral psychology and is probably well known to many clinicians. Its primary use is not as a measure of stress, and the items listed are more typical of phobias than of stressors per se. However, for stressed clients who seem to experience a significant degree of trait anxiety, it may be worth spending the few minutes required to assess for minor phobias. In addition, ongoing avoidance of any of the items listed on the FSS would certainly render that item a hassle.

Once again, the FSS may aid in the identification of specific hassles for clients who are having difficulty verbalizing their hassles, or conceptualizing the idea of a hassle.

Appraisal

Appraisal of specific identified stressful situations might best be determined by asking the question, "What is it about that situation that makes it so stressful for you?" Careful discussion of specific situations in an interview setting, as well as systematic recording of stressful situations as they occur, can generate individual examples of the role of cognitive appraisal. Some of the scales identified for use in determining cognitive aspects of the stress response may also be useful in determining stressful appraisals.

In addition to specific appraisals, however, there is also the question of general tendencies and typical styles or approaches to appraisal that the client commonly exhibits. Pencil-and-paper measures are most useful in determining these general styles of appraisal.

Dysfunctional Attitude Scale (DAS) (Weissman, 1980). The DAS is a 40-item scale designed to identify cognitive distortions which may be related to depression. Each item is rated on a seven-point scale according to the extent to which the client agrees with the item. The items were selected to measure seven value systems (approval, love, achievement, perfectionism, entitlement, omnipotence, and autonomy). There are two parallel forms of the scale.

In addition to yielding a total score, the author does point out that clinically the scale can be used to examine areas in which the client is emotionally vulnerable; therefore, clinical work can be appropriately directed.

The DAS appears to have good retest reliability, and is internally consistent. No actual norms are reported, but an average value for nonclinical respondents is reported.

The DAS is a useful clinical aid in identifying tendencies toward nonadaptive thinking. The types of thoughts listed are fairly general and thus may be appropriate for a fairly wide range of subjects. Since automatic thoughts are sometimes difficult for clients to verbalize spontaneously, such a scale may be very useful in labeling cognitive distortions.

Irrational Values Scale (IVS) (MacDonald & Games, 1972). This is a brief nine-item scale designed to measure the extent to which the client supports nine irrational values derived from the work of Albert Ellis (see Chapter 8.) Each item is scored on a nine-point Likert scale, yielding a total score of from 9 to 81. Each of the nine items actually represents an entire arena of general but distorted beliefs, related to such notions as the necessity to be loved by all, or to be competent at all times. It is likely that one or more of these beliefs will underlie the appraisal of a situation as stressful in many subjects.

The initial investigation of this scale involved assessment of 11 items, but two were found to be inadequate psychometrically and were therefore dropped. There is evidence of concurrent validity, and internal reliability is adequate. No test-retest data are presented, but the format of this scale suggests that it could be used in such a context.

Rational Behavior Inventory (RBI) (Shorkey & Whiteman, 1977). The RBI is a 37-item scale designed to measure irrational and absolutist beliefs. Like the IVS, it is based on the work of Ellis. From the RBI, one obtains a total score as well as identification of 11 factors (such as guilt, perfectionism, need for approval, etc.). This instrument was specifically developed for use in assessing clients for cognitive therapies, and for evaluating the progress of such therapy. The RBI has been applied to both clinical and nonclinical populations and appears to possess reasonable psychometric properties. It demonstrates good internal reliability and homogeneity, split-half reliability and stability.

There are other general tendencies related to appraisal which might be considered; many of these are personality characteristics, which are mentioned later.

MEASURES OF THE STRESS REACTION

The Physiological Response

Direct Measurement. One way in which physiological response to stress can be assessed is by direct observation of end-organ responses, which are a result of sympathetic activation. This may be done in two ways: either by direct physiological recording of the systems in question, or by monitoring the occurrence of symptoms.

In the first instance, most of these responses require the use of specialized physiological monitoring equipment in order to be assessed properly. Fortunately, many clinics and hospitals do possess such equipment. Heart rate, blood pressure, muscle activity, and skin conductance are all measures which can be assessed directly by a therapist, given proper physiological monitoring equipment and appropriate knowledge and skills on the part of the therapist. These measures are not invasive, and do not require medical training in order to be utilized appropriately. (They do, however, require that the therapist have the necessary knowledge base in anatomy and physiology, as well as some basic acquaintance with electronics.) The equipment involved may be specialized biofeedback equipment, a multichannel polygraph, or computer-assisted recording equipment.

The decision to monitor physiological response will be determined largely by the availability of equipment and therapist expertise. In addition, such monitoring is indicated in instances in which the client has identified physiological response symptoms as a primary or significant aspect of his or her complaint. Routine assessment of physiological response is time-consuming and may be misleading; therefore, it is generally not recommended to develop a standard assessment procedure for all clients.

If the client does indicate specific physiological symptoms, there are several reasons why physiological monitoring may be useful:

(1) to determine whether or not a specific physiological response does occur in times of stress;

(2) to create a baseline against which to measure change;

(3) to aid in selecting appropriate treatment techniques.

In order to address these concerns, the monitoring process may include the following observations:

(1) Is the general resting level of the particular response high? For example, is the resting heart rate fast? Is there a generally increased level of muscle tension? It should be borne in mind that there are tremendous variations between individuals (and between various types of equipment) in resting levels for the various physiological responses. An elevated resting level may mean any number of different things. However, the resting level can provide a general indication of which systems may be responsive to stress, and which treatment techniques may be helpful. For example, employing muscle biofeedback techniques with a client who exhibits very low levels of resting muscle tension may not be very useful, even if the client experiences tension headaches.

(2) Regardless of the resting level of the response, does the response seem reactive to stress? Using the above example, even if the level of resting muscle tension is low, are there pronounced increases in muscle tension in the presence of stressful stimuli? The therapist can induce stress through use of mental stressors (e.g., subtracting serial 7s or performing mental arithmetic), or by having the client imagine particular stressful situations which have been identified as being relevant to that client. This procedure allows the therapist to see if the particular response system does indeed react to stress. In cases in which several responses are monitored simultaneously, the therapist can determine which response system is most affected.

(3) If the response is exaggerated or pronounced, does it return to the baseline level when the stressor is removed, or does it remain elevated? Even if the initial resting level and immediate response to stress appear normal, it may be that the client has a slow recovery from stress. Stoyva

(1979) suggests that a period of 14 minutes of relaxation followed by a six-minute period of stress and a six-minute recovery period should be sufficient to generate a physiological stress profile of the individual.

The direct monitoring of physiological symptoms also allows the therapist to demonstrate to the client the connection between stressors and stress response. Some clients, particularly those who are chronically stressed, may find it difficult to identify or describe specific physiological changes that accompany stress. Use of physiological monitoring can provide a graphic representation of exactly what is happening in the body, under what conditions. If several systems are monitored simultaneously, their interrelations can be examined, and suitable systems for intervention identified. Particularly for clients who may be offered some type of relaxation therapy, direct monitoring can lead to a more informed and more accurate choice of methods.

(Many research protocols measure the presence of circulating stress hormones as indicators of adrenal medullary and cortical activity. Blood and urinary levels of the catecholamines and corticosteroids can be measured, but for obvious reasons this is generally not done in the context of ongoing therapy.)

The second type of direct observation of physiological symptoms is self-monitoring or recording of specific symptoms. Particularly for individuals with diagnosed medical problems or clearly delineated problem symptoms, a record of the frequency, duration, and intensity of symptoms is essential in order to monitor the effects of therapy. One of the more common formats for obtaining this information is presented in Figure 4–1. The client is given an index card sized form, which has a week (or other time interval) broken down into time blocks of one hour (or another convenient interval). For each interval on the card, the client notes the status of his symptom, rating it on a scale from "not present" to "the worst it has ever been." This system is portable, easy to complete, requires little time, and yields a great deal of information. It can reveal the frequency, duration, and intensity of symptoms, as well as information about patterns over time, and sudden changes in any of the parameters noted. Depending upon the expected frequency and duration of symptoms, the row and column headings may be adjusted. Similarly, intensity ratings are usually constructed taking into account the individual client's own range of experience. The therapist may also request that additional information be obtained concurrently, either by recording additional data on the card itself (e.g., "put an asterisk beside the rating if the symptom occurred at work") or by having the client keep separate notes relating additional items of concern. In the latter case, the

Time	Sun	Mon	Tues	Day Wed	Thurs	Fri	Sat
7 am	1	1	1	4	2	1	1
9 am	1	1	1	4	2	1	1
11 am	1	1	1	4	2	1	1
1 pm	1	2	1	4	2	1	1
3 pm	1	3	1	4	2	1	1
5 pm	1	4	3	4	2	1	1
7 pm	1	4	4	5	2	1	1
9 pm	1	4	4	5	2	1	1
11 pm	1	4	4	5	2	1	1

Intensity Rating:
  1= no symptom
  2= mild symptom
  3= moderate symptom
  4= severe symptom
  5= extreme symptom

Figure 4–1. A simple recording system for symptoms.

therapist must again consider the relative weights of the need for information, the motivation of the client, and the likelihood of compliance with additional recording requirements.

This system is most useful for symptoms which occur fairly often, and at discrete intervals (that is, not continuously). It is less useful with diseases or symptoms which flare up only occasionally but for prolonged periods of time (e.g., peptic ulcer, colitis). These symptoms might better be monitored in a diary fashion, with the client simply noting when attacks occur, and how long they last. For extremely infrequent symptoms, retrospective observation is most useful. In spite of the bias which may occur with retrospective observations, it is simply impractical to try to carry out a baseline on symptoms which may occur only a few times a year.

Finally, any self-monitoring is only useful for symptoms which are readily detectable by the client. Recording episodes of high blood pressure, for example, may be difficult since most people can not accurately tell when their blood pressure is elevated, unless aided by the use of a blood pressure cuff or other measuring device.

Paper-and-Pencil Measures. There are several paper-and-pencil self-report measures which may be used to monitor physiological reactivity, either in conjunction with direct observation, or in its absence when direct physiological measurement is not possible.

Cues for Tension and Anxiety Survey Schedule (CTASS) (Hersen & Bellack, 1976). The CTASS is a 20-item list of sensations or behaviors which may accompany tension or anxiety. There are items related to autonomic responses, voluntary motor responses, and symptoms of panic attacks. The CTASS also asks clients to describe what they do to alleviate feelings of tension or anxiety. This scale is almost more of a structured interview than it is a measurement scale. It does not yield any type of numerical score or quantifiable data. It does not compare the individual client to any reference group nor can it be used to assess change over time. However, it is a useful intake instrument in that it touches upon a wide variety of symptoms which enable the therapist to select appropriate intervention techniques, particularly in the area of relaxation. The experienced clinician may well find that he or she has elicited all the information contained in the CTASS in the course of the intake interviews, but a less experienced interviewer may find this scale useful to ensure that a broad range of symptoms are considered in the assessment stage of therapy.

The Self Rating Anxiety Scale (SAS) (Zung, 1971). The SAS is also a 20-item measure which includes 15 somatic and five affective symptoms of stress. The frequency of each symptom is rated by the client on a four-point scale and a total score is obtained. Unfortunately, the total score represents the sum of five cognitive, as well as the 15 physiological, symptoms. While this total score is useful if one is attempting to formulate a DSM diagnosis or to compare a client's overall level of anxiety with either him or herself or with a reference group, the apples-and-oranges nature of the total score does limit its utility.

Like the CTASS, the SAS is composed of fairly obvious items which may all be covered in the initial interview. It does provide somewhat more information than the CTASS, in that clients can rate individual items on a scale of one to four, rather than responding in a simple yes-no format. There has also been some attempt to establish the reliability and validity of the scale, as well as to establish general norms. In addition, since it does yield a general composite score, it may be useful to assess global change over time.

Allen and Hyde Symptom Checklist (1980). A more specific checklist of symptoms has been developed by Allen and Hyde (1980). This scale is comprised of seven groups of symptoms (cardiovascular, respiratory, gastrointestinal, muscular, skin, immunity, and metabolic), each of which is rated on a frequency scale of 0 (never) to 5 (daily). An overall symptomatic score is derived, and categories for interpretation are offered (i.e., low, moderate, or excessive stress symptoms). This particular list is more detailed and thorough than those listed above.

The Cognitive Response

Of all the aspects of the stress response, the cognitive components are probably the most difficult to define and measure. Part of this difficulty arises from the confounding described earlier among cognitions as stressors, cognitions as part of the stress response, and cognitions as part of the coping process. Schwartz (1982) has pointed out that the word "cognition" is used to mean any of (1) a response class composed of private events; (2) mediators of behavior; and (3) complex structures which organize and generate behavior, but which also function independently of the laws of behavior. Clearly, the word "cognition" can be used in a variety of ways, in a variety of contexts. In this chapter, a somewhat arbitrary decision has been made to limit the role of cognitions as stressors to those cognitions involved in the process of appraisal—that is, cognitive interpretations of events which are labeled "stressful." Cognitions which follow a stressful event are assumed to be part of the stress response; cognitions which reinterpret the experience are part of the coping process.

If this seems about as clear as mud to the reader, it should be kept in mind that to a large extent, in the practical sense, it does not really matter which role faulty cognitions are playing at any point in time; the measurement and treatment of faulty cognitions will be the same no matter which hat the cognitions are wearing. Furthermore, in spite of the theoretical vagaries, it is generally quite clear to the therapist which role the cognitions are playing. Consider the following example: Mary works extremely hard to earn a promotion at work. She thinks, "If I don't get this promotion, I'll die!" She does not get the promotion. She thinks, "This is the end of my career—I'll never be good enough to get ahead." She goes home and thinks, "It's probably just because I'm a woman that I didn't get the promotion." Here, it seems relatively apparent which thought is a stressor, which is part of the stress response, and which is part of the coping process.

Much of the work of identifying cognitions is begun in the initial interview. By asking repeatedly such questions as, "What did you think about that?", "How did that make you feel?", "What were you thinking while that was going on?", and "Why is that so important to you?", the therapist can begin to get an idea of the sequence of thoughts, images, and behaviors that the client is experiencing. The goal of the cognitive focus in the interview is to enable the client to entertain the notion that part of his or her problem is what he or she says to him- or herself. (Some examples of cognitive distortions are supplied in Table 4-1.) Once this first step has been accomplished, the therapist may proceed to employ more structured analyses of cognitions, including self-monitoring and use of rating scales.

TABLE 4-1
Cognitive Distortions

1.	*All or Nothing Thinking:* The tendency to see things as either black or white, without acknowledging intermediate ground.
2.	*Overgeneralization:* Interpreting a single incident as being indicative of a never-ending pattern.
3.	*Mental Filter:* Picking out a negative detail from an event and focusing on it, to the exclusion of any positive aspects.
4.	*Jumping to Conclusions:* Making a negative interpretation of an event, even when there are no negative facts to support the conclusion.
5.	*Disqualifying the Positive:* Rejecting positive aspects of a situation, so that you can hold on to negative interpretation, even in the face of little evidence.
6.	*Magnification/Minimization:* Either exaggerating (usually negative aspects of yourself) or shrinking (positive aspects) so that you appear worthless in comparison to others.
7.	*Emotional Reasoning:* Assuming that negative feelings are valid, even when there is no other evidence to support such a belief: "I feel worthless; therefore I am worthless."
8.	*Should Statements:* Motivating oneself through the use of "shoulds" and "shouldn'ts," usually resulting in guilt feelings.
9.	*Labeling/Mislabeling:* An extreme form of overgeneralization in which labels are applied in an emotional and negative manner: "I'm a real loser."
10.	*Personalization:* Attributing to yourself blame or responsibility for some event outside of your control.

Adapted with permission from D. Burns (1980), *Feeling good*, pp. 40–41. New York: William Morrow & Co.

There is a danger in relying too heavily on information derived retrospectively in interviews: the cognitive interpretations described by the client in the interview represent the client's thoughts at the time of the interview, but may not actually represent the client's thoughts at the actual time of the incident in question. It is difficult to determine whether or not the cognitive analyses done in the interview do actually represent the client's original thoughts, or whether they represent the later attempt of the client to make sense of the original incident.

Another difficulty with the interview format is that some clients, particularly those who are less skilled verbally, may have problems trying to identify and articulate cognitions. Use of checklists or artificial situations (see "Direct Observation," immediately following) are particularly helpful with these clients.

Direct Observation. One of the most direct ways of establishing the role of negative or faulty cognitions is to have the client attempt to listen to and record his or her own cognitions over a period of time. Usually this is done in conjunction with the recording of specific stressful events identified earlier. For example, the client may be asked to note (in writing) each time he or she felt stressed, what was happening, and what he or she was saying to him or herself at this time. A typical recording format is presented in Figure 4–2. The focus of the monitoring can be

Who, what, when, where, etc.	Event	Cognitions
Monday, 2:00 p.m. at work	Boss asks me to stay late again.	Why is he after me again? If I don't stay this time, I'll really be in trouble.
Tuesday, 5:00 p.m. driving home	Stuck in traffic.	I knew I should have gone the other way—why don't I ever get it right? I'm so dumb.
Wednesday morning	Getting up—forgot to get stuff for kids' lunches.	How could I forget again? I bet I'm the only mother who does this. I'm so hopeless, I'll never get organized.

Figure 4–2. A recording format for cognitions related to stress.

adjusted to suit the needs of the individual client. For example, if the client's presenting problem is work stress, he or she may record only items related to work situations. Additional information about the severity of the stressor, other people involved, the duration of the reaction, and so forth may also be included if it is relevant. Meichenbaum (1976) cautions that the therapist must also be concerned about what the client says to him or herself about the assessment process. Meichenbaum's tendency is to keep recording requirements to a minimum, to avoid the exercise itself becoming a stressor which would then engender its own negative thoughts about not measuring up to the therapist's expectations. (On the other hand, such a situation may provide ideal material for therapy.) Meichenbaum also suggests that the exact nature of the self-monitoring assignments should emerge naturally from the interview, and represent a collaborative effort between therapist and client. This is especially important in the context of stress management therapy, given its foundation in the compensatory model (i.e., putting responsibility on the client for the solution to the problem).

An alternate way of observing and recording cognitions directly is to create an artificial but relevant situation to be carried out in the therapeutic context. One possibility is to employ pictures of situations related to the client's own identified stressors. The client is then asked to describe what is happening in the picture, what the people in the picture are feeling and thinking, what the expected outcome is, and how the situation might be handled. Similarly, the client and therapist can role-play specific situations, then analyze the client's resultant feelings and thoughts. (Or as mentioned above, the therapist and client can discuss the cognitive reactions to failure to comply with homework assignments, if such noncompliance has in fact occurred.) Such approaches are one step removed from the client's actual day-to-day behavior, but should be able to provide useful information about the ways in which the client typically responds to stressful situations.

Once a sufficient body of descriptive information about cognitive responses is generated, it may be useful to categorize the client's typical manner of responding, using a classification system such as that described by Burns (1980) and presented in Table 4–1. Although these particular categories are derived intuitively rather than psychometrically, they provide a convenient language for describing the errors and biases that a client might demonstrate in his or her thinking.

Paper-and-Pencil Measures. Because of the highly individual nature of cognitions, it is difficult to create a specific measure which has general applicability to all clients. However, there are several measures which are useful with some clients. First, some clients do have a hard time grasping the notion of self-statements at all, or identifying their own cognitions. Checklist-type instruments can help these clients understand the task and provide a concrete starting point for them to generate their own lists. Second, it is quite difficult to assess changes in cognitions over time. Quantifiable data do not usually emerge from self-monitoring of cognitions, as happens in self-monitoring physiological symptoms. Thus, a scale which yields some kind of numerical score would be useful. However, such scales are easily subject to bias, especially in the form of expectancy, and so should be interpreted cautiously. It may be useful in some cases to administer one of the following scales with instructions to respond only in the context of an identified stressful circumstance (i.e., ask the client to identify only those cognitions that occur when he or she is late for work).

Thought-Stopping Survey Schedule (TSSS) (Cautela & Upper, 1976). The TSSS consists of 51 items which involve thoughts, images, or feelings which accompany anxiety and depression. These items are fairly general and broad ("I feel lonely," "People don't like me," "I am not worthwhile"), and are rated by the client as occurring from "not at all" to "very much." As the title suggests, the scale is intended to be particularly useful in the implementation of treatment programs using the technique of thought stopping (see Chapter 8). The questionnaire also provides space for the client to list other problematic thoughts that occur frequently.

This scale is purely descriptive, does not yield a score, and has not been assessed psychometrically. It is also (as noted) fairly broad and general. However, as an intake instrument it covers a wide range of areas and does provide a general rating of frequency. For clients who are otherwise having difficulty identifying problematic cognitions, it is a place to start.

Automatic Thoughts Questionnaire (ATQ) (Hollon & Kendall, 1980). The ATQ is superficially somewhat similar to the TSSS. It is a 30-item instrument that measures the frequency of automatic negative statements about the self. The ATQ taps four aspects of automatic thoughts: (1) personal maladjustment and desire for change ("I wish I were a better person"); (2) negative self-concepts and negative expectations ("I'm no good"); (3) low self-esteem ("I hate myself"); and (4) helplessness ("I can't finish anything").

The primary intent of the ATQ was to differentiate depressed from nondepressed subjects, and to measure changes in cognitions attributable to clinical interventions. The latter attribute makes it particularly appealing.

The fact that these 30 items were selected from a pool of 100 with the intent of differentiating depressed subjects may mean that other items related to the experience of stress (but not necessarily depression) are not included. Nevertheless, if the items seem relevant to the individual client, the scale is relatively sound. There has been some effort to assess internal reliability and to establish norms. Interestingly, although the scale is specifically intended to assess change, no data for test-retest reliability are presented. The provision of subscales within the ATQ may provide some additional conceptual information about the individual client.

The Cognitive-Somatic Anxiety Questionnaire (CSAQ) (Schwartz, Davidson, & Goleman, 1978). The CSAQ is a brief 14-item scale which assesses both cognitive and somatic aspects of anxiety. Since it focuses only on symptoms, it is equally appropriate for the measurement of the stress response. Cognitive items emphasize persistent thoughts, imagining terrifying scenes, worry, and concentration. Somatic items include references to gastrointestinal complaints, increased heart rate, pacing, and general jitteriness. The lists are of course not comprehensive, given the brevity of the questionnaire. However, this questionnaire was designed with the intent of helping the therapist select intervention tools more precisely, and preliminary data suggest that it may in fact differentiate those with predominantly cognitive symptoms from those with predominantly somatic symptoms.

The data collected by the authors in the original article are not sufficient for the development of true norms, but this questionnaire may be useful in that it is short and focused in its efforts.

The Impact of Event Scale (Horowitz, Wilner, & Alvarez, 1979). This 15-item scale is designed to assess the stress associated with a particular traumatic event. The scale itself does not specify the event (which is to be identified by the client and therapist jointly). The 15 items include two categories of experience: intrusive events, such as ideas, feelings, and bad dreams ("I had bad dreams about it," "Pictures of it popped into my mind") and avoidance of certain ideas, feelings, and situations ("I tried to remove it from my memory," "I tried not to talk about it"). The client is to identify to what extent each item was true for him or her in the past seven days. Normative data were obtained from two small adult samples, and some evidence of validity is offered. The authors also maintain that the scores are sensitive to change over the course of therapy.

This scale provides a structured framework for assessing a variety of aspects of the client's cognitive response to an identified stressor. The scale leaves identification of the particular stressor to the individual situation, rather than asking for anticipated responses to situations which may or may not be relevant to the individual client. This scale is particularly useful in dealing with reactions to major traumatic events. For the client who experiences many minor stresses, and who may experience each of them differently, this scale would not provide the breadth of information required to deal with all the various cognitive responses.

Social Anxiety Thoughts Questionnaire (SAT) (Hartman, 1984). The SAT is a 21-item scale which is intended to measure the cognitive aspects of social anxiety. It lists what are essentially self-defeating and negative thoughts related to general discomfort, concern about others' awareness of distress, fear of negative evaluations, and perceptions of performance anxiety. This is a short and easy-to-complete questionnaire which may serve as a starting point for the discussion of cognitive distortions or self-defeating statements for clients whose stress is associated with social situations. Since the instructions refer to thoughts that have occurred only in the past one week, it may also be useful to assess change over time.

There are a number of other possible scales which may be used to assess cognitive functioning, depending upon the presenting complaints of the client. A number of these are summarized by Hollon and Bemis (1981) in their general discussion of cognitive assessment.

Note: One additional multipurpose scale should be mentioned here. Although it is not specifically a measure of any one component of the stress response, it is a widely used and very helpful measure.

The Hopkins Symptom Checklist (HSCL) (Derogatis, Lipman, Rickels, Uhlenhuth, & Covi, 1974). The HSCL has a long and healthy history of use as a criterion measure in many studies of stress, as well as in a variety of other contexts. The original scale is a 58-item list of symptoms which can be subdivided into five dimensions (somatization, obsessive-compulsive, interpersonal sensitivity, depression, anxiety). Each symptom is rated by the client on a four-point scale. There are a number of variations of this scale in use as well. These include the Behavior Symptom Index (Derogatis, 1983) and the SCL-90 (Derogatis & Cleary, 1977a, 1977b). Although the focus of these questionnaires varies slightly from one to another, all are psychometrically sound multidimensional measures which document a number of factors that may be very relevant to the individual client. They are useful as general indicators of problem areas, and as measures across time. For the clinician who may want to collect some systematic data across all clients for clinical research purposes, these are very useful instruments.

The Behavioral Response

Direct Observation. It is probably fairly obvious that the best way to assess behavior is through behavioral assessment—that is, the direct observation and recording of the behaviors in question. Some of the mechanics of this approach were described earlier. Essentially, there tend to be three ways in which one can record specific behaviors.

The first method consists of keeping a structured diary. The usual form is for the client to record a specified behavior, along with the antecedents and consequences of the behavior. Thus, if being late for work is the behavior in question, the client simply records when he or she is late for work, what led to the lateness, and what the consequences of being late were.

The second method is the frequency count. For the individual who would like to stop smoking, for example, a frequency count of the number of cigarettes smoked per day might be a logical place to start.

Finally, the client may keep a daily log, an approach described quite well by MacDonald (1977). The daily log combines aspects of the frequency count, a daily diary, and a rating scale. It is particularly useful for recording information about emotional responses to a specified behavior along with information about the behavior itself. For example, if the client feels that he or she smokes when feeling frustrated, then degree of frustration may be rated on a scale of 1 to 10 along the Y axis, while time is plotted along the X axis. The client plots a point on the graph each time the designated behavior (smoking) occurs. Such an approach is described in Figure 4–3.

Although these methods are particularly appropriate for recording specific behaviors, interviews and paper-and-pencil approaches have a clear role in the measurement of behavior as well. Morganstern (1976) and Morganstern and Tevlin (1981) describe a behavioral approach to interviewing, which stresses not only the importance of eliciting information related to the antecedents and consequences of behavior, but also carefully considers the issue of determination of objectives—an area in which the behavioral approach differs significantly from some traditional and dynamically oriented therapeutic approaches.

Further discussion of the finer points of behavioral interviewing is outside the scope of the present discussion. However, it is worth noting that information from the interview will determine which behaviors are to be measured and subsequently modified. Therefore, competent behavioral interviewing skills are a prerequisite for employing this type of approach.

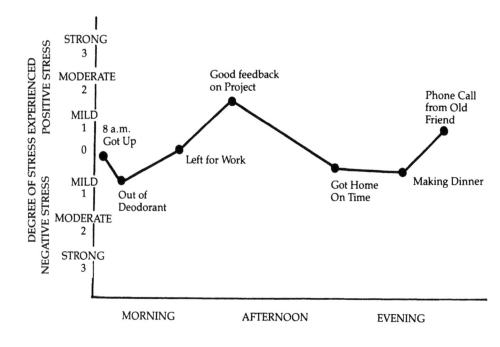

Figure 4–3. A daily stress log. Adapted with permission from D. L. Watson and R. G. Tharp, *Self-Directed Behaviour: Self-Modification for Personal Adjustment* (3rd Ed.), Monterey, California: Brooks/Cole, p. 64.

Paper-and-Pencil Measures. **Paper-and-pencil measures become particularly important once a specific behavior has been defined as a concern. The specific measures which may be employed will of course depend upon the behavior in question. One general scale which may be useful is the *Behavioral Self-Rating Checklist* (Cautela & Upper, 1976), a list of 73 adaptive behaviors which the client may feel the need to master. In the present context, the client may be asked to identify those behaviors which he or she may want to master in order to better tolerate or moderate stress.**

There are also innumerable scales which assess such behaviors as alcohol usage, sexual behavior, smoking, eating habits, social skills, and assertiveness. Many of these are described in Hersen & Bellack (1976,

1981) and in Corcoran & Fischer (1987). Because assertiveness is often an issue of importance in stress management, a few of the available scales which measure assertiveness are described below:

The Rathus Assertiveness Schedule (Rathus, 1973). This 30-item scale is one of the standard instruments in the field; it has been around since 1973 and is fairly well known. There is also a simplified version (McCormick, 1984) for individuals with low reading ability.

The schedule consists of a series of 30 statements about assertive behavior; the client is asked to rate each one on a scale from +3 (very characteristic of me) to −3 (very uncharacteristic of me). The items include a broad range of everyday situations, nonspecific enough to be applicable to a wide range of people.

Internal reliability and test-retest reliability were demonstrated in the initial studies of this questionnaire. Since it has been used so widely for so many years, both clinical and in research, there is a great deal of data from a variety of populations available.

Assertion Inventory (AI) (Gambrill & Richey, 1975). This 40-item scale is designed to measure three aspects of assertion: discomfort with assertion, probability of engaging in assertive behavior, and identification of problem situations. In order to assess all three dimensions, each of the 40 items must be answered three times. However, as a diagnostic instrument, the AI clearly provides more information than most assertiveness scales. It can be used to classify individuals as "assertive," "unassertive," "anxious performer," or "doesn't care."

The AI has also been used successfully to measure change during therapy. Its stability over time is good. Given the additional information which may be generated from this scale, it may be a good choice if time permits.

The Assertive Behavior Survey Schedule (ABSS) (Hersen & Bellak, 1976). In contrast to the above scales, the ABSS is not primarily a measurement scale per se, but rather a descriptive scale. It might almost be considered as a structured interview technique. The survey consists of four sections. First, the client is asked to anticipate his or her reaction in six situations requiring assertive behavior. The second and third sections ask questions about the anticipated consequences of acting assertively with a variety of people (e.g., parents, friends). Finally, the client is asked to identify his or her general behavioral tendency in a situation of inequality with other important persons in his or her life.

This scale does not yield any scores, nor would it be particularly helpful to assess change over time. However, it does provide useful descriptive information.

There are many other assertiveness inventories available. Of additional interest in some cases is the information which can be obtained from inventories which accompany role-play protocols (see Hersen & Bellack, 1976).

PERSONALITY, PERSONAL STYLE, AND PERSONAL RESOURCES

There are a number of personal characteristics of the client which should be considered in the assessment process. None of these is specific to the conduct of stress management in particular, but all are important in carrying on any type of therapy. These will be mentioned only briefly, since a complete discussion of these general factors is outside the scope of this book.

There are many sides to the arguments about personality assessment, its reliability, and its predictive validity. Given the generally cognitive behavioral approach advocated in this book, formal personality assessment is not considered to be a matter of prime importance. However, it may sometimes prove to be of interest in helping to sort out the nature of stressors in an individual's life. In those cases in which stressors seem to be more a function of the individual than of the situations, it may help to examine the individual's personality structure. In addition, there is some belief that personality variables may provide information about the prognosis of the individual (particularly for problems such as chronic pain syndrome).

Somewhat more useful are measures of specific aspects of personality, such as locus of control. Both general locus of control scales and health-related locus of control scales (see Lefcourt, 1981) may provide insight into the client's perception of the responsibility for his or her ailment, as well as the responsibility for the treatment. There is some evidence that internally oriented and externally oriented individuals may respond best to different approaches to treatment. Particularly externally oriented individuals may have some difficulty with the compensatory approach in general, and with a cognitive behavioral approach in particular. Such clients may be less inclined to assume responsibility for their problems, and more likely to attribute them to matters outside of their own control. In such cases, therefore, therapy may be more effectively directed toward altering external circumstances rather than altering internal responses.

A related personality characteristic of interest is "hardiness" (Kobasa, 1979). Hardiness is described as a strong commitment to self, an attitude of vigorousness toward the environment, a sense of meaningfulness, and an internal locus of control.

Hardiness is proposed to be a source of resistance, a resource that can neutralize the potentially harmful effects of stress (Antonovsky, 1982). Hardiness is a construct composed of three dimensions: commitment, control, and challenge. Commitment is expressed as a tendency to be involved rather than alienated; committed persons have a sense of purpose that allows them to find meaning in themselves and in their work. Control is expressed as a tendency to feel and act as if one is influential. Challenge is expressed as the belief that change is normal and desirable. The combination of these dispositions seems to keep persons healthy despite encounters with stressful life events. Kobasa (1979) and Kobasa, Maddi, and Kahn (1982) have demonstrated an interactive relationship between hardiness and the effects of stressful life events (as well as demonstrating a significant main effect for each) in predicting illness symptoms. Individuals who displayed the commitment, control, and challenge typical of the hardy personality were less likely to experience illness than were less hardy individuals who had experienced the same level of stressful life events.

There is no single measurement tool which addresses the total concept of hardiness, but Kobasa (1979) and Kobasa, Maddi, and Kahn (1982) propose a series of scales which may be useful if formal assessment of hardiness is indicated.

Finally, it may be worth looking at particular coping styles. As mentioned previously, coping styles tend to vary across situations and across time within an individual. Taking this into account, Folkman and Lazarus (1980, 1985) have developed the situation-specific *Ways of Coping Checklist (Revised)*, a 66-item questionnaire containing a variety of cognitions and behaviors that people may employ to deal with stressful encounters. The 66 items yield eight scales, each of which represents a way of coping, including such strategies as problem-focused coping, wishful thinking, and self-blame.

The authors caution against using the checklist as a means of classifying individuals according to general coping style, since it is not clear that such a tendency exists. The scale is more appropriately used to assess changes in coping style relative to a specific situation. The authors also do not claim that any one coping style is necessarily better than another, but maintain that appropriateness depends upon the individual and the situation.

The *Ways of Coping Scale* is a useful clinical tool in spite of these cautions. It does allow the therapist to determine which behaviors are in the client's repertoire, and which he or she might use in a given situation. It is also a good measure of change over time.

Another major individual factor of some importance is simply the level of intelligence and educational attainment of the client. Several references have already been made to the considerations which must be made for clients who are less verbally skilled than others. In most cases, an alert therapist who has taken a good history can readily estimate the level of intelligence of the client and adjust the therapy accordingly. In some cases, an educated guess is not sufficient and formal assessment of intelligence is recommended. Many therapies have been criticized as being suitable only for reasonably bright, middle-class, and well-educated clients. Because of the wide range of treatment modalities which can be employed within the stress management perspective, this problem can be avoided to a great extent, but only if the therapist is aware of the strengths and limitations of the individual client. Clients who have less skill in the verbal area may well benefit more from behavioral approaches, whereas particularly intelligent individuals may be offended by purely behavioral approaches and may prefer more cognitive content.

An additional consideration is the individual's social context. Social suport is known to be a moderator of stress, but the exact nature of the role is complex. Social contacts may contribute to stress as well as help to ameliorate it.

CASE STUDIES

In each of these cases, the assessment procedure consisted of three sections. First, of course, each client was interviewed in some detail. Second, each was asked to complete a variety of rating scales, all of which could be done at home. Finally, each was asked to keep some kind of a diary or record over time, to examine specific issues in greater detail.

Cathy

At the end of the first group session, each participant was given a packet of scales to complete before the next group session. Also, as mentioned earlier, each subject was asked to keep a diary of stressors and responses to stress. Had Cathy been participating in individual therapy, the instructions for the diary would probably have been significantly more detailed, and she may have been asked to keep records of her sleep (due to her complaints about insomnia). However, in the group context, the purpose of the diary was primarily to provide general information for discussion in subsequent groups, so the same degree of rigor was not necessary. Similarly, the rating scales were selected because of their general appropriateness to the group, rather than because of any specific applicability to Cathy. Included were the following:

1. The Anderson (1972) adaptation of the *Social Readjustment Rating Scale*.
2. The *Stressful Situations Questionnaire*.
3. The *Cognitive-Somatic Anxiety Questionnaire*.
4. The *Irrational Values Scale*.

Jean

At the conclusion of the second session, Jean was given some homework assignments to complete before the next session. Knowing that one of Jean's major problems was her sense of time pressure, the therapist gave Jean a minimum of homework—only enough to elicit the bare minimum of information necessary to complete the next session of planning. She was asked to do the following:

(1) To complete the Allen and Hyde Symptom Checklist. Although it appears that headaches and insomnia are Jean's major complaints, it is also apparent that she has a variety of vague symptoms, all of which may not have come up in the initial interview. In order to ensure that significant symptoms have not been overlooked, she was asked to complete this checklist.
(2) To focus more specifically on the headaches by keeping a daily log of them, essentially like that in Figure 4–1.
(3) To complete the Hassles Scale, in order to begin to recognize the validity of her many minor daily difficulties as stressors.
(4) To complete the *Dysfunctional Attitude Scale*, to assist in pinpointing the cognitive aspects of her stress. It will clearly be necessary to ask Jean to record specific thoughts and reactions in the future, but this was not started at present, in order to avoid overloading her.

Finally, Jean was asked to give some thought to her own personal goals and priorities, as a worker, as a mother, and as an individual. The therapist suggested that she might want to jot down some of these thoughts before the next session.

J. B.

This client is still not convinced of the relationship between his behavior and his symptoms. However, he seems to be a perfectionistic worker and is willing to continue to pursue all options. Thus, he was given a rather substantial amount of work to accomplish before the next session. (Notably, since J. B. is on the road a great deal, the next session would not take place for three weeks).

His assignments included:

(1) Completion of the Multidimensional Health Locus of Control Scale, to further illuminate J. B.'s notions of responsibility for his illness.

(2) Completion of the Hopkins Symptom Checklist. J. B. seems to edit his reports to the therapist somewhat, so a relatively thorough review of symptoms seemed warranted in order to ensure that significant items were not overlooked.

(3) Completion of the Hassles Scale, in order both to collect data about hassles, and to educate J. B. as to the broad range of hassles that may affect him.

(4) Keeping of a structured diary (see "The Behavioral Response," this chapter). He was asked to keep track of the behavior of his ulcer by noting the following each time his ulcer began to act up ("acting up" was defined by the sensation that J. B. noted which led him to take an antacid):
   a. the time, place and date
   b. what he was doing
   c. what he was thinking about
   d. when and what he had last eaten
   e. what action he took

Like Jean, J. B. was also asked to think about his goals and priorities in life. Unlike Jean, J. B. was not specifically asked to address his various roles, since the therapist wanted to see which roles that he would address voluntarily.

5

Planning Interventions

The first four chapters of this book are concerned primarily with the definition, description, identification, and measurement of stress. The last four chapters are concerned with specific physiological, cognitive, and behavioral treatment techniques for managing stress. The purpose of this chapter is to provide a transition from assessment to treatment, from formulation to application.

In stress management, there is not necessarily a one-to-one connection between identified stressors and proposed solutions. The individual who is experiencing four types of stressors will not necessarily need four types of treatment; more or fewer may be appropriate. As was mentioned earlier, it is fairly common to employ a variety of techniques within a treatment program with stressed clients. As a result, treatment can easily become disjointed and scattered, jumping from a bit of relaxation to a little assertiveness training. It can also appear to be an endless series of vaguely related treatment techniques. In order to avoid either of these possibilities, systematic planning is essential.

The approach to stress management advocated in this book is a cognitive-behavioral approach. As such, it relies on a self-management or self-control perspective. This approach is described in more detail in Chapter 9. An essential part of such an approach is the reliance on developing coping skills which can be employed by the client when necessary. Treatment focuses on developing a range of coping skills which can be employed to address a range of stressors, rather than simply working to eliminate the particular stressors which are currently an issue for the client. Thus, one coping skill may address several stressors; conversely, one stressor may require several coping strategies.

PLANNING

The Planning Grid

A convenient mechanism for determining a plan of intervention is presented in Figure 5–1. This planning grid can be utilized at two levels. First, stressors can be categorized according to the interventions required. Second, specific treatment strategies can be proposed to address the most significant areas of need.

The first step in this process is to list the relevant stressors for the individual client. For each stressor, two questions are asked. First, can the stressor be changed or must it be tolerated? Stressors which can be changed require problem-focused interventions; stressors which must be tolerated require emotion-focused strategies.

Secondly, regardless of whether change or tolerance is indicated, would the most effective intervention be in the cognitive, behavioral, or physiological sphere? Answering these two questions allows the therapist to insert each stressor into one (or more) of the six blocks of the planning grid. The distribution of entries in the planning grid at this stage provides a clear indication of what direction therapy should take. What remains is simply to translate the results of this analysis into a concrete plan.

Figures 5–2 and 5–3 demonstrate the completion of the planning grids for Jean, the second of the case studies. In Figure 5–2, the stressors which have been identified include time pressures, family expectations, role conflict, mild chronic health problems, lack of personal discretion-

	Physiological	Cognitive	Behavioral
Problem-focused			
Emotion-focused			

Figure 5–1. The basic planning grid.

	Physiological	Cognitive	Behavioral
Problem-Focused		Role Conflict	Time Pressures Family Expectations
Emotion-Focused	Time Pressures Health Problems	Time Pressures Family Expectations	Discretionary Time

Figure 5–2. The basic planning grid: categorizing Jean's stressors.

ary time, and unrealistic personal expectations. Solutions to these problems can be found in five of the six areas of the planning grid. Dealing with time pressures, for example, might involve several steps: trying to reduce the time pressures by changing behaviors, or dealing with the effects of time pressures through physiological or cognitive means. Similarly, Jean might change the expectations that her family has of her by changing her behavior, or she may learn to live with the expectations by changing her cognitions. In Figure 5-3, the specific strategies which might be used to address these problems are identified.

The completion of the planning grid is the essence of the "integration" in integrated stress management. The specification of the overall goal, and later, the prioritizing of the steps involved in reaching this goal, provide the general order and structure that therapy will follow. Within this structure, the individual techniques become part of a coherent whole.

Some common examples of each of the six types of interventions specified in the grid are described below.

	Physiological	Cognitive	Behavioral
Problem-Focused		Changing Beliefs and Cognitions	Time Management
Emotion-Focused	Relaxation		

Figure 5–3. The basic planning grid: identifying strategies for Jean.

1. Problem-Focused Physiological Strategies. These are physiological strategies which may impinge on the stressor itself, and thus alter the problem. These strategies are most often used when the stressor itself is physiological in nature. If, for example, the stressor is that the client suffers from a chronic disease, a problem-focused physiological strategy might involve alteration of life-style habits that may affect the course of the disease.

2. Problem-Focused Cognitive Strategies. In this case, cognitive strategies are employed to alter the perception of stress, the appraisal process. Thought stopping of ruminative or obsessive thoughts, cognitive hypothesis testing, and problem-solving techniques might fall into this category.

3. Problem-Focused Behavioral Strategies. These are behavioral strategies which serve to alter the nature of the stressor. Such techniques include assertiveness, time management, and acquisition of new skills.

4. Emotion-Focused Physiological Strategies. These are techniques which enable the client to deal more effectively with the physiological arousal which accompanies stress. Such strategies include the relaxation therapies, and some life-style interventions. These techniques do not alter the stressor or stressful situation, but do allow the client to moderate the physiological response.

5. Emotion-Focused Cognitive Strategies. These are cognitive strategies which alter the client's emotional, affective, or cognitive response to stress. Cognitive hypothesis testing, challenging negative thoughts, and cognitive reinterpretation are examples of strategies which allow the client to deal with the cognitive sequelae of stress.

6. Emotion-Focused Behavioral Strategies. Like the two categories above, this category consists of strategies which address the response to stress, in this case the behavioral response. These strategies may include learning new behaviors to counter maladaptive responses, and utilizing recreation and leisure time to offset the effects of stress.

Many of the specific techniques which may be entered into the grid are described in the following chapters. The planning grid format enables the therapist to present his or her ideas for therapy to the client, to introduce the client to the various approaches which may be pertinent, to relate them to the conceptualization of stress which has already been discussed, and to propose a plan of action. The client has the opportunity to verify that the therapist has accurately assessed his or her needs, and to become aware of the long-term plans.

Depending upon the client, all or only a few of the boxes may be filled. Each box may contain no strategies, one strategy, or more than one strategy. Some strategies may appear in more than one box. Whatever the case, when the therapist and client have inserted the appropriate strategies into the appropriate boxes, a plan begins to emerge—a plan which is able to accommodate a number of different interventions in a coherent and organized structure.

Once the strategies have been identified and discussed, the next step in the process is the determination of order and priority. It is difficult, of course, to embark on several different types of therapy simultaneously. Some order of priority must be established. The most obvious determinant of what goes first is the potential pay-off to the client. Typically one expects to deal with the most important problems first, the problems which are the source of greatest distress to the client. The assessment of importance is largely determined by the client, with consultation by the therapist. (As experienced therapists will recognize, there is enormous variation among individuals in terms of their tolerance of different problems.) Unfortunately, the question of what goes first is not as simple as this. There are a number of considerations to be made, many of them practical.

Client Considerations

Practical concerns aside, there are a number of aspects of the individual client which will determine the course of therapy, regardless of the specific nature of the stress problem.

Motivation. Most experienced therapists have encountered the client who wants to be "fixed" in the course of a single session. In some cases, this is merely an indication of ignorance on the part of the client as to the nature of therapy. However, there is always a balance to be struck between the level of distress that the client is experiencing and the amount of work that changing entails. The relative balance between these two factors may determine the overall motivation of the client. A client in a great deal of distress is likely to put out more effort toward change; the less distressed individual may decide to opt for a simpler, if less effective, approach. In some cases (particularly those individuals displaying a Type

A behavior pattern), there is clear ambivalence toward change. The same behaviors that are the source of stress may also be quite rewarding to the client. The Type A person may believe that it is his or her overcommitment of time which is in fact responsible for his or her success. J. B., for example, clearly feels that his long hours and many responsibilities are essential to success in his job. They are also activities that he enjoys, in spite of their potential risks to his health. These conflicting demands and time pressures may also contribute to feelings of importance and self-worth. In such a case, priorities can be determined only after some investigation of the real meaning of the various behaviors to the client. Motivation may also be related to time-limited factors. If the stressor in question is the month-long visit of one's father-in-law, then strategies which require several months to learn are not particularly helpful.

Motivation can be difficult to assess initially, since most clients come to therapy with intentions to persevere. Assessing the balance between distress and required output may shed some light on the likelihood of continuing motivation and compliance. Observing compliance with any homework requested during the assessment process may also be helpful. The client who is unable to keep baseline recordings may also have difficulty with ongoing assignments.

(It is important to note that motivation is not totally the preserve of the client. It is also up to the therapist to ensure motivation and to promote and facilitate compliance as part of the therapeutic process.)

Capability and Limitations. Each client who comes to therapy does so with an inherent set of strengths and weaknesses, which must be taken into account in selecting intervention strategies. A healthy, intelligent, and insightful client will surely respond differently to most techniques than will a dull individual who suffers memory loss secondary to alcohol abuse. Each client can in fact be accommodated within the stress management framework, but the selection and application of techniques will reflect the particular idiosyncrasies of the individual client.

Unfortunately, the literature on psychotherapy and behavior change is of little use to the therapist in tailoring strategies for individual clients. Researchers tend to persist in the belief that clients are randomly assigned to types of treatments. Clinicians rarely select treatments randomly, or assign clients to treatments without consideration of the clients' individual characteristics. In addition, many clients come to therapy with preconceived notions of what will help. If one considers the client as an informed consumer (who of course may need further information), then the expectations of the client will also affect the choice of specific techniques.

Client characteristics which may be significant include:

- level of education and intelligence
- memory function
- age
- general mental health
- sense of time urgency
- problem-solving style
- physical health status
- personality style
- sense of commitment

Life-style. Depending upon the daily habits and life-style of the client, the suggestions for specific techniques may vary. The time constraints and flexibility possessed by the client will vary tremendously, depending upon whether the client is a retired bachelor or a single mother of three preschoolers. In addition, some individuals will find that their life-style is dictated by others (e.g., military personnel), whereas others have a great deal of control over their life-style (e.g., university students). These considerations may be significant in selecting techniques which require specific predetermined periods of time to master (e.g., meditation), or techniques which focus on behavioral aspects of life-style (alcohol use, exercise).

Personal Agenda. Although it is rewarding to think that all clients approach therapy with the goal of personal enlightenment and control over one's future, it is worth remembering that this is often not the case. A reasonable understanding of the specific agenda of the client will generally result in the most effective plan for that client—even if it is not the plan that the therapist would have devised. Some clients enter into therapy with a specific goal in mind, or at the request of a third party. The client's agenda may in fact be to appease the third party (employer, family doctor, spouse), rather than to overhaul his or her life. The determination of the therapeutic agenda must be a collaborative effort between therapist and patient. Therefore, the therapist must recognize and work with the agenda of the client. This is not to suggest that the therapist must support fraudulent motivations or unhealthy agendas. Rather, each party has an obligation to respond to and address the concerns of the other in goal-setting. (In cases in which a major discrepancy cannot be ameliorated, it may be best for the client to see another therapist.)

Previous Attempts. The client who has never before sought help with a stress problem allows the therapist the privilege of selecting from a wide range of hitherto untouched techniques. Many clients, however, come to therapy with a past history of treatment, or having made some attempts to change on their own. The relative success or failure of the past interventions will have an effect on the current selection of techniques. (As mentioned earlier, previous unsuccessful attempts at a technique may sabotage further efforts in the same direction.) This often occurs in the context of relaxation therapies. Some degree of judgment on the part of the therapist will be necessary in order to assess how much of the previous failure is attributable to the technique itself, and how much stems from other extraneous factors. In the latter case, it is also up to the therapist to judge whether or not he or she can convince the client that another try might be effective, without suggesting that the previous therapist was a quack!

It would be ideal if one could suggest that a specific combination of motivation, intelligence, life-style, and history yields a favorable prognosis for a particular type of therapy. Alas, it is largely not so. However, the therapist who proceeds to select techniques without considering all the above aspects of the client's situation may well find that he or she is not as successful as was hoped.

Practical Considerations

Among the obvious practical considerations are those related to time and money. How much time does the client have to devote to therapy? How much time does the therapist have? How often will the two meet? And at what cost to whom? It may appear that relaxation training is the most important aspect of therapy, but if the client is out of town more often than not, or if the therapist's idea of intensive psychotherapy means monthly meetings, this may not be a feasible plan. Time limitations often arise in institutional settings. In such a case, it may be more effective to select a quicker technique aimed at another area of concern, one which can be accomplished within the available time frame. (Often, in an inpatient setting, the role of the therapist may simply be to identify the problems and make recommendations, rather than actually carrying out the therapy. In this case, the "treatment" may be considered to be a problem-focused cognitive approach; the problem is defined and specific directions identified, so that the client can pursue help outside the setting in an informed and organized manner.)

As a general rule, it is probably best to embark on therapy with a task which has a reasonable probability of completion, even if the task may not appear to be the single most important issue. Experience suggests that poorly or incompletely taught techniques tend not to be particularly effective. Not only is this discouraging to the client at the time, but it may also discourage him or her from trying that technique again in the future, even under optimal circumstances. ("I tried that before but it didn't work.") Similarly, some techniques require relatively intensive work, with sessions occurring at least once a week, whereas others can be spread out further over time.

In addition, one is often bound by the constraints of money. If the client is paying for the service out of pocket, it clearly behooves the therapist to select the most efficient means of treatment. In some cases, third party payments are limited in terms of total dollars or number of sessions. These financial considerations are less obvious in the case of salaried workers in hospitals and clinics, but remain somewhat salient nevertheless. In situations in which two treatments have an equal likelihood of success, it is prudent to employ the most cost-effective strategy.

Finally, one must also consider the limitations inherent in the therapist him- or herself. Regardless of how effective a technique may appear to be according to the literature, if the therapist has no experience with that technique, and if supervision or consultation is not available, it may be preferable to substitute another technique. In other cases, a referral elsewhere may be necessary, either in addition to or instead of treatment with the original therapist. Given the variable nature of stress management techniques, it seems unlikely that any one therapist would be able to address all aspects of all stress problems. Obviously, knowing one's limitations is essential in this area of practice.

ESTABLISHING A CONTRACT

Once the planning grid has been completed, and the order of priorities established, the next step is to establish a contract of treatment between therapist and client. If the planning process has been carried out with appropriate thoroughness so far, the contract will be largely self-evident.

Essentially, a therapeutic contract will specify the following:

- the responsibilities of the client
- the responsibilities of the therapist
- the initial target of change (and subsequent targets if appropriate)
- how change is to be assessed
- the length of time the contract is to be in effect

Therapeutic contracts in this context are not necessarily written out formally and signed, although this may be useful in some cases. It is essential, though, that the contract be clearly stated, and referred to periodically. An initial contract might be simply that "You (the client) and I (the therapist) will meet weekly for five weeks to begin learning a relaxation technique for your headaches. At that time, we will review your headache diary to see how the headaches are doing. If progress is satisfactory, we will discuss the next step, which is assertiveness training."

Some contracts may be more involved and formal, and may specify to a greater extent exactly what is to be done in therapy. The contract may need to be more comprehensive in cases in which the client is expected to be difficult, insincere, or unreliable. (From the client's standpoint, a more specific contract might be employed when the therapist is expected to be incompetent, insincere, or unreliable!) Contracts might also be more specific in cases in which the therapist and client have not reached total agreement as to the goals and methods of therapy. In this case, the duration of the contract might also be quite brief. ("Let's get together for one session of relaxation training so you can get an idea of what I am talking about. If the idea still does not appeal to you, we'll revise the plan.") Although contracts are usually thought of as binding, in therapy they actually serve the purpose of allowing both client and therapist greater freedom. Both parties participate in the formulation of the contract, and both parties are able to revise and alter the contract at regular intervals. Thus, if techniques do not perform as they should, or if the client's life situation changes, there is a prearranged time for change or revision. Neither party is locked into an endless and perhaps unsatisfactory relationship.

Nevertheless, there are often times when the plan is clearly not working, and when the contract needs to be violated. Good clinical judgment will generally dictate the need for deviating from the plan. Good reasons to deviate from the plan include:

- The failure of one party or the other to keep to the contract (e.g., the client fails to come to appointments or fails to complete homework; the therapist cancels appointments, or goes off on tangents unrelated to the contract);
- Sudden and significant changes in the client's life alter the circumstances which led the client into the contract (e.g., the difficult father-in-law cancels his plans to visit; the problem boss dies);
- The techniques being learned seem to be making things worse rather than better;

- The client makes a late disclosure in therapy, which significantly alters some of the previous assumptions and plans (e.g., a woman may reveal that she is being abused at home);
- The practical concerns relating to therapy are altered in such a way that the plan is no longer viable (e.g., the client is called out of town for a prolonged period; the therapist becomes pregnant and decides to work for only a few more weeks).

Some of these factors will result in a temporary suspension of the contract; others require that it be scrapped altogether. At no time, however, should deviation from the plan occur from neglect, lack of perseverance, or inertia. A brief review of the state of the contract should be made frequently (in many cases, at each meeting). A simple reminder such as, "We are now in the fourth week of our five-week series on relaxation. It looks like the headaches are letting up, but it is important that you keep up your headache diary so we can review our plans next week," provides an opening for either party to propose a deviation from the plan if it is indicated. Deviations should only occur with the consent of both parties, and should be labeled as temporary or permanent deviations. In some situations, the client may ask that one session be devoted to a specific and timely concern, whereafter the contract will be resumed. In other cases, the contract may be permanently abandoned. In either case, both parties must acknowledge the deviation from the plan, and the implications of such a deviation.

All this is not to suggest that the contract be taken lightly. Not all suggestions for deviation should be honored. Often, it is helpful to review briefly the total plan (as described in the planning grid) and the manner in which priorities were assigned to ensure that the deviation is justified. It is easy for both therapist and patient to lose sight of the long-term goals; loss of this vision will make breaking the contract dangerously easy.

WHEN ARE WE DONE?

One of the most difficult decisions in therapy can be determining when to end. The simplest answer to this is to end when all the items stipulated in the planning grid have been addressed. In an ideal case, a series of logical ordered contracts will include each of the techniques included in the grid in succession. The end will be clear.

However, it is often the case that there are diminishing returns from therapy as time goes on. If the most important and potentially most effective techniques are employed from the start, then the essential balance between level of distress and the work of change will be significantly altered. The level of distress will be reduced, and the work of changing will seem greater. Obviously, accurate continuous monitoring of whatever "symptoms" brought the client into therapy is essential. The overriding goal of therapy is of course to alleviate the symptoms which brought the client to therapy. Thus, regardless of the fact that the client is still unassertive and never exercises, if the presenting symptom was headaches and the headaches are under control, one should at least consider terminating. Of course, the client may want to address the other problems and therefore remain in therapy. Such a situation requires renegotiation of the contract, but is certainly not out of the question. Once again, the use of many short-term contracts will give both therapist and client the opportunity to broach the subject of termination whenever it may seem appropriate.

Regardless of the timing of the termination, the therapist should take care to allow the ending of therapy to occur in the same fashion in stress management that it does in any other type of therapy. The dynamics of the relationship between client and therapist are heightened, as are the feelings of both client and therapist about how well the therapy went, and whether either could have worked harder or done better. In addition to allowing time to carry out specific procedures and techniques in therapy, the client and therapist must also allow for time to separate and end. Shulman (1979) points out that termination of the client-therapist relationship is in itself a a real-life situation (or stressor), and thus may serve as a model experience through which the client can experiment with some of the strategies learned in therapy.

CASE STUDIES

Cathy

Since all of the members of Cathy's group were asked to complete the same homework tasks, the first part of the session was spent going over the homework assignments. Cathy made the following observations:

1. On the Life Stress Events Scale, her score was (as she had expected) quite low. She scored a total of only 121 points, for having changed her residence, changed her social activities (as she now has a steady boy-

friend), and taken a trip over the summer. Cathy was somewhat thankful, when she read the list of life stresses, that most of them did not apply to her!

2. Since the Stressful Situations Questionnaire does not have categorical norms, each group member was asked to look over the items to which they had given a score of "4" or "5," indicating an area of particular concern. Cathy observed that most of the items to which she had given such a score had to do with worry over academic performance. These included giving a speech in class, failing a test, doing poorly in class, and taking difficult tests.

3. On the Cognitive-Somatic Anxiety Questionnaire, Cathy's score indicated a great deal more concern over the cognitive aspects of anxiety (score=26) rather than the somatic aspects (score= 18).

4. On the Irrational Values Scale, Cathy's score of 42 was in the mid-range; on the scale of 1 to 7 she gave no responses over 6. Her highest response was to the statement, "It is a terrible catastrophe when things are not as one wants them to be."

The Plan and the Contract. In Cathy's case, the contract for treatment was largely in place before the group first met. Each prospective group member was presented with a list of group sessions and topics expected to be covered in the course of the group. By virtue of having enrolled in the group (and assuming that she continues to attend the group), Cathy has tacitly agreed to the contract as previously stated.

However, even given these limitations, Cathy is expected, as part of her participation in the group, to identify those particular items in the course which she expects to be of most use for her. Based on her knowledge thus far, she has stated that she is interested in learning some type of relaxation technique, preferably a cognitively based one, as well as obtaining some assistance with general life-style issues, including time management, since this seems to contribute to her difficulties around exam time. Cathy reiterated at this time, however, that her main goal was to become generally acquainted with the issues of stress management "for future consideration."

Jean

At this point, the first part of the session is spent going over the assigned homework. The following information is obtained:

1. Jean obtained a score of 53 on the Hyde and Allen Symptom Checklist, which is right in the middle of the average range. However, Jean's

symptoms are all clustered in two areas: cardiovascular symptoms, including heart pounding, cold, sweaty hands, and throbbing headaches; and muscular symptoms, including muscular headache, tremor, and muscular aches. She also complained of difficulty sleeping, frequent diarrhea, and feeling nervous. The information derived from this scale tends to support that which was obtained in the initial interview.

2. Jean was only able to keep the diary for four of the seven days since the last appointment. On two of the four days, Jean had a headache. In both cases it started in mid-afternoon, was particularly bad over dinnertime, and abated after about 8 P.M. (following consumption of pain medicine).

3. On the Hassles Scale, Jean reported an overall frequency of 39 hassles, with an intensity rating of 1.46. The frequency is quite high, indicating that Jean is exposed to many more minor stressors than is the average person. The severity of the stressors is generally not high, as is indicated by the intensity rating. Therefore, the problem does not seem to be any single or small group of particularly acute stressors, but rather the sheer number of them. Jean tended to identify hassles in the areas of time pressures, money, and family responsibilities in particular.

4. Jean's score of 142 on the Dysfunctional Attitude Scale is somewhat high, but the most notable feature of her responses was the high frequency of the "neutral" option as a choice. This might suggest that Jean is having some trouble identifying her beliefs, and is not sure where she stands in many of these areas. Her highest scores (most indicative of cognitive distortion) were in the areas of feeling obligation to others and the need to meet the expectations of others.

The Plan. Based on the results of the homework assignments, as well as the information obtained in the interview, the plan described in Figure 5–3 was developed with Jean. One of the goals of therapy that is being considered is to reduce her overall level of stress by working on her cognitions and beliefs about her various roles, and by teaching her time management techniques. In order to help her cope better with the existent stressors, Jean could be taught a relaxation technique, learn to moderate her cognitive reactions to stress, and develop some recreational interests of her own.

The Contract. Jean and the therapist agree that learning to decrease the demands on her time is a priority, but one which can be accomplished only by first reexamining her beliefs about her roles and self-expectations. They agree to begin by further identifying and correcting cognitive distortions that lead to perceptions of stress, and then restructuring time demands accordingly. When Jean feels that time permits, she will consider learning a relaxation technique. Initially, they agree to meet weekly for five weeks to work on these two areas conjointly (perceptions of stress and time management). At that time, if Jean can eliminate enough demands (real or perceived) on her time so that she feels comfortable taking time to work at relaxation at home, then she will agree to begin a course of relaxation training.

J. B.

The first part of the session was spent reviewing the homework assignments.

1. On the Health Locus of Control Scale, J. B. obtained an average score on the "internal" dimension (23), a slightly elevated score on the "powerful others" scale (25), and a very high score on the "chance" scale. These scores suggest that although J. B. does not deny that he has some influence over his health, he also attributes a great deal of influence to pure luck; his belief in the luck of the draw is much greater than that of most people. He is also somewhat more inclined than most people to think that physicians and other health care workers will exert significant control over his health. His tendency to attribute health status to chance may contribute to his failure to exercise much good judgment in areas such as life-style.

J. B. gave the highest scores to the items "my good health is largely a matter of good fortune," and "if it's meant to be, I will stay healthy."

2. On the Hopkins Symptom Checklist, J. B.'s scores were slightly elevated in the areas of somatization and interpersonal sensitivity. The latter finding is most interesting, in view of the client's reluctance to discuss or deal with matters related to apparent family conflicts. J. B. responded strongly to many items which reflect concern about the behavior of those close to him. Although J. B. has told the therapist that his family life is not an issue for therapy, his responses on this checklist clearly reflect problems in this area.

3. On the Hassles Scale, J. B. identified only 18 hassles which applied to him—an average frequency of hassles. Interestingly, his intensity score was 2.1, an above average score. Thus, although there are not a great many things bothering him, those that are of concern, are of great

concern. Many of the family-related items in this scale were also scored as 3s (extremely severe hassles).

4. J. B.'s diary revealed only one ulcer flare-up during the recording period. At the time he was on the road, and had eaten a very greasy dinner at a roadside take-out stand. He reported that he was thinking about not being home for his son's final baseball game of the season (the regional high school championship game). He also reported taking antacids to deal with the ulcer pain.

The Plan. J. B.'s plan is represented in Figure 5–4. He remained firm in his plan to learn some type of relaxation technique. However, based on the information which emerged from some of his homework, he also grudgingly acknowledged the need to address issues related to the family. The therapist proposed that life-style issues seemed to be relevant as well; J. B. conceded this point, but was not eager to address it immediately. He countered with an expressed interest in trying to learn to use his leisure time (or trying to create some leisure time) to offset some of the stress of his frantic life-style. J. B. expressed the hope that his eating and drinking habits might "take care of themselves" if he were more relaxed and doing things he enjoyed. The therapist also suggested that J. B. might want to take a look at his expectations and self-induced demands in general, to see if altering these might reduce his level of stress. Again, J. B. was willing to acknowledge the point, but did not seem inclined to pursue it at present.

The tentative plan which emerged from this session represented a combination of the ideas proposed by both J. B. and the therapist. They agreed to give priority to relaxation training and family work, and to readdress the other concerns at a later date.

	Physiological	Cognitive	Behavioral
Problem-Focused	Life-style		Changing Family Behavior
Emotion-Focused	Relaxation Training		Leisure Education

Figure 5–4. The basic planning grid: identifying strategies for J. B.

The Contract. J. B. and the therapist agreed to meet twice weekly for three weeks to begin work on a relaxation technique. (This schedule seemed ideal, since J. B. was expecting to be on the road very little during the next month.) During this time, J. B. would also discuss the possibility of family therapy with his wife and son. A decision about that would be made at the conclusion of the three weeks.

6

Physiological Approaches to Managing Stress Part I: The Relaxation Therapies

The relaxation therapies are without doubt the cornerstone of any stress management program. It is difficult, in fact, to imagine any client who would not readily benefit from some form of relaxation therapy. The terms "relaxation therapy" and "relaxation training" are commonly used to refer to any one of several techniques whose major purpose is to offset or diffuse the normal but negative physiological symptoms which the human body displays under stress. The goal of teaching an individual to relax is to enable that individual to produce voluntarily an alternate physiological response, a state in which the individual deliberately eliminates the undesirable physiological effects of stress. Thus, just as the stress reaction results in increases in muscle tension, blood pressure, heart rate, and gastric activity (as well as other changes described earlier), the voluntarily induced state of relaxation reverses these actions. Keable (1985a) describes relaxation as "the combined and integrated actions of the autonomic nervous system, the endocrine system and the brain cortex and subcortex . . . in a generalized trophotropic or relaxation response" (p. 99). The effects of relaxation include:

(1) decreased oxygen intake and carbon dioxide excretion;
(2) decreased respiration rate;
(3) decreased blood flow to skeletal muscles and decreased sweat output;
(4) decreased blood cholesterol and lactate;
(5) decreased heart rate;
(6) decreased blood pressure and volume;
(7) decreased muscle action potential;

(8) increased galvanic skin response;
(9) increased alpha and theta brain waves;
(10) increased saliva output;
(11) stabilization of gastric motility;
(12) relaxation of sphincters to allow emptying of rectum and bladder;
(13) dilation of blood vessels to salivary glands and external genitalia.

Although there are a variety of different methods of inducing relaxation, they share the common goal of countering the physiological aspects of the stress reaction by producing the physiological effects listed above. The specific goal of relaxation therapy will, of course, vary somewhat from one client to another. If the client tends to stiffen his or her shoulders under stress, which then causes a headache, then the goal of relaxation training would be to teach the client to relax the involved muscles, to avoid developing headaches. If the client tends to suffer from headaches which are more migrainous in nature, then the goal of relaxation training is to teach the client to alter the pattern of vasoconstriction/vasodilation which typically occurs. Although the specifics may vary, the goal of relaxation training is the same in these two (and, indeed, in all) instances. That goal is to offset whatever adverse physiological effects the client is experiencing.

Although the idea of utilizing relaxation strategies as agents to counteract the effects of stress seems obvious and natural, such strategies are learned responses, which must be developed over time. Contrary to the beliefs and expectations of some clients (and some therapists), the effects of relaxation are not the same as the effects of sleep, or "rest" in its generic sense. In contrast to a sleeping or resting state, the client in a clinically meaningful relaxed state is not simply drowsy, or sedated. Rather, the client is able to attain a lowered state of physiological arousal, while maintaining the cognitive alertness usually associated with higher levels of arousal. As Figure 6–1 indicates, most individuals think and problem solve most effectively under some degree of stress. Under "normal" conditions, the level of problem-solving ability and cognitive acuity increases as physiological arousal increases—to a certain point. However, beyond that point (the top of the curve), cognitive ability begins to fall off in the presence of increasing physiological arousal. Many individuals (particularly Type A behavior pattern individuals) are subjectively aware of the relationship evident in the first part of the curve; these individuals may be reluctant to relax physiologically, because of their perception of the con-

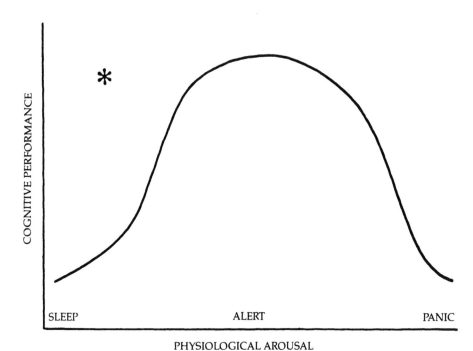

Figure 6–1. The "normal" relationship between physiological arousal, cognitive performance, and the clinically relaxed state (denoted by *).

comitant decline in cognitive performance. Contrary to their expectations, however, application of a relaxation technique will allow them to achieve a lower level of physiological arousal without suffering this loss of cognitive acuity. Being able to induce a "trained" state of relaxation enables the client to retain the cognitive "edge" without enduring the damaging physiological side effects.

There are a number of well-established relaxation techniques from which to choose. Despite the variety, there is an unfortunate tendency among clinicians to acquire skill in utilizing one particular technique and to apply this technique indiscriminantly to all clients in need of relaxation therapy. If all techniques produced identical results, if all clients experienced the stress reaction in identical ways, and if all symptoms responded equally to all techniques, then mastery of one type of technique would indeed suffice. Benson (1975), in fact, has argued that all relaxation techniques do indeed produce a single uniform "relaxation response." However, the literature tends to support the position of Schwartz, Davidson, and Goleman (1978), who suggest that although a general relaxation response (such as Benson describes) does seem to be induced by a variety of relaxation techniques, also evident are specific effects, attributable to the individual techniques.

Some of the common aspects of the various relaxation methods have been mentioned. They all have the effect, to a lesser or greater extent, of lowering physiological arousal, as well as altering the subjective experience of anxiety. Individuals who are adept at relaxing tend to fatigue less easily, and have less need to rely on maladaptive "relaxation" tools such as smoking, alcohol, and other drugs.

Aside from the similarities in results, there are also a number of similarities in the mechanisms of teaching and learning the various relaxation techniques. First, all relaxation strategies are self-control strategies which depend upon active client participation. Although proper instruction is necessary, the end result will depend primarily on the amount of effort expended by the client outside of the therapy sessions. Second, learning to relax is like learning any other skill; most people are not very good at it initially, but gradually improve with practice. Third, no relaxation method is intended as a form of treatment in and of itself. Relaxation therapy is part of an overall treatment plan. It is often an appropriate first step in the plan, in that it has good face validity to clients, is clearly definable, usually creates rapport between client and therapist, and frequently leads to measureable and concrete results. It is also a technique with which clients are often familiar; therefore, it is often requested specifically. However, the client and therapist must both be clear that it is only one aspect of a comprehensive treatment plan.

Fourth, all relaxation strategies require some amount of concentration—often difficult to sustain in an anxious client. Finally, all relaxation techniques may create some unusual and initially frightening feelings in clients who are unused to relaxing. Complaints of dizziness, ringing in the ears, lightness (or conversely heaviness), feelings of tingling, loss of control, sudden muscle contractions, and disorientation may occur. It is worth remembering that for the chronically tense person, being relaxed is a foreign state.

Once the decision has been made that the client will indeed benefit from relaxation training, the question becomes, "Which relaxation strategy should this client learn?" The question is not which technique is better, but rather which technique is most effective for what disorder in whom? In order to answer this question, it is important first to have a general understanding of the various types of approaches and their conceptual as well as practical differences. These differences are best appreciated through a historical perspective.

HISTORICAL DEVELOPMENT

There are two separate trends in the historical development of relaxation techniques. By far the older type of technique is the meditation approach. More recent but also more familiar to Western therapists is the coping-skill approach, which derives from the medical model (see Figure 6–2).

Meditative practices that induce a profound state of relaxation have been an important part of Eastern culture, in particular, for thousands of

Date	*Preventive*		*Curative*	
3000 B.C.	Early Eastern Religions			
	Yoga			
	Zen Buddhism			
		Hypnosis		
			Modern Medical Model	
1900		Autogenic Training		
1938			Jacobson's Progressive Relaxation Training	
1958	Transcendental Meditation		Wolpe's Systematic Desensitization	
1969				EMG BIOFEEDBACK
1973			Abbreviated PRT (Bernstein & Borkovec)	
1974	Clinically Standardized Meditation			
1975	Relaxation Response			
1976			PRT as a Coping Skill (Goldfried & Trier)	
				COMBINED EMG/PRT

Figure 6–2. Historical evolution of relaxation strategies.

years. Yoga, which includes meditative components, appears to have been practiced at least as early as 3000 b.c. (Johnston, 1970). The practice of yoga meditation allows the individual to strive for the achievement of his or her utmost potential (Patel, 1984). It is a personal self-help system, whose focus is preventive rather than curative. Zen Buddhism employs similar practices. In fact, in the East, these types of meditative practices have been systematically developed, to the extent that they are considered integral parts of everyday life. Although similar practices are evident in the writing of Western Christian figures such as St. Augustine and Martin Luther, these so-called "contemplative exercises" were not in general practice and tended to be limited to those in religious life (Benson, Kotch, Crassweller, & Greenwood, 1977). Of all the various forms of meditation which have been introduced in the West, transcendental meditation (TM) is the most widely practiced and investigated. TM has remained largely outside the sphere of the formal mental health system, as it is usually taught by members of a private organization rather than by mental health practitioners. Nonetheless, the essential elements of TM have been extracted and developed in the "noncultic" methods of "clinically standardized meditation" (Carrington, 1978) and "the relaxation response" (Benson, 1975).

What all the meditative techniques have in common is their focus on the development of prevention through self-help. These techniques require the individual to carry out periods of meditation on a regular basis, usually twice daily. Thus, at regular intervals, the stress-producing effects of daily life are offset or reversed. The periodic forays into a state of profound rest are thought to mitigate the potentially harmful cumulative effects of stress, and to enable the body to revitalize itself. These techniques may therefore help to prevent the development or recurrence of stress-related somatic problems.

In contrast to the preventive nature of the meditation approaches, the more familiar Western relaxation methods evolved from the medical model. As technological medicine began its advance in the late 1800s, two relevant influences came into play. First, the idea of treatments specific to ailments gradually began to replace the notion of general nonspecific cures (e.g., meditation). Second, the need for demonstrating the scientific validity of treatments was more pronounced. Both of these influences are evident in Jacobson's (1938) pioneering work on progressive relaxation training. Rather than advocating "rest" as an integral part of a healthy life-style (as was the case in Eastern cultures), Jacobson identified it as a remedy, albeit a versatile one, for those suffering from specific disorders. His immediate goal was to "seek by scientific means the most effective form of rest" (Jacobson, 1938, p. 2). Jacobson's original formulation of progressive relaxation training required that the patient undergo a long and arduous course of therapy, involving three to four weekly sessions of one half hour to one hour, over a course of months. In addition, the individual would practice by him- or herself for an hour or two more each day!

Although there seemed to be little doubt that such a regimen was effective, due to the extensive training required, little attention was afforded this technique for many years. However, a considerably condensed version of progressive relaxation training emerged when Wolpe (1958) proposed the notion of reciprocal inhibition as a method of fear reduction. Wolpe suggested that an undesirable emotional response could be suppressed or eliminated by the conditioning of a stronger but incompatible response. He selected relaxation, as described by Jacobson, as the competing response. The emergent treatment package became known as systematic desensitization. Bernstein and Borkovec (1973) further popularized a shortened version of progressive relaxation training through the publication of a training manual.

Wolpe's application of progressive relaxation training evoked a purely behavioral explanation of effect, and attributed the technique's effectiveness to counterconditioning. However, as the predominant behavioral trend in psychology began to fade and clinicians and researchers began to acknowledge (again) the role of cognitions in behavior, the mechanism by which progressive relaxation training was effective came into question. Goldfried and Trier (1974) suggested that desensitized individuals were in fact voluntarily choosing to utilize their relaxation skills. A model of relaxation as a coping skill emerged. This is currently the predominant model.

In spite of the evolution of progressive relaxation training, the essential features of the medical model are retained. It is curative rather than preventive; it relies on formal instruction by a trainer; it is a technique which is to be invoked in particular problematic situations.

There are other relaxation methods currently in use, some of which follow the same general approach of progressive relaxation training. Biofeedback is another example of this type. Autogenic training also encompasses some aspects of the curative approach but in combination with some aspects of the preventive approach.

The fundamental difference in techniques remains the distinction between preventive and curative approaches, a distinction of both historical and clinical significance. This conceptual difference plays a major role in the selection of an appropriate technique for a given individual. In the simplest terms, meditative or preventive approaches may be most effective for individuals experiencing chronic ongoing stress, related to life-style and occurring across a wide variety of situations. Coping skill or curative approaches may be most effective for individuals confronted with specific problematic situations.

MEDITATIVE OR PREVENTIVE APPROACHES

Regardless of the form that meditation takes, there are four essential components of the practice. These are:

(1) a quiet place, free from external distractions and the urgencies of daily living;
(2) a comfortable position, one which can be maintained without distress for 20 minutes;
(3) an object, sound, feeling, or thought to dwell upon;
(4) a passive attitude, reflecting a lack of critical appraisal of performance (Benson, 1975; Davis, Eshelman, & McKay, 1982).

The most frequently encountered meditative approaches to relaxation training are yoga, transcendental meditation, and Benson's relaxation response. In the first two types, the role of the mental health practitioner will not actually be to instruct the client in the meditation approach, but rather, to steer the client toward the appropriate technique and to facilitate his or her finding instruction elsewhere. Because most meditation approaches grew out of religious and life-style practices rather than from mental health research, they tend to be espoused by groups that are outside the mental health system. Thus, the therapist must be sufficiently familiar with these techniques to make properly informed referrals and suggestions, but not necessarily be adept at the techniques themselves.

Yoga

Yoga, in its most general sense, is not a specific set of exercises or a procedure, but a way of life, a "science by which the individual approaches truth" (Vishnudevananda, 1960, p. 6). According to yogic philosophy, the goal of life is to achieve a state free from death, pain, sorrow, and disease. Vishnudevananda (1960) maintains that "yoga philosophy holds not only the answer to all man's problems but also offers a scientific way to transcend his problems and suffering" (p. 11). If, indeed, yoga promotes a healthy state and allows one to transcend one's problems, then its utility as a stress management technique is obvious!

There are various forms of yoga practice. Hatha yoga, most familiar to Westerners, focuses on the physical body and progresses in stages. First is the training of the physical body itself, through purification and postures. The second stage focuses on the spirit and involves controlled breathing, stilling the mind, and mental control. Third is meditation itself. Finally, one attempts to merge one's own ego with the Supreme Ego or God.

When the yoga philosophy is adhered to in full, its discipline is reflected in all areas of an individual's life, including diet, physical care of the body, exercise, thought patterns, breathing, and personal beliefs. However, since yoga is more of a religion or philosophy than a measurable technique, there is little empirical evidence of its effectiveness.

But yoga philosophy is an Eastern philosophy, and a complete yogic life-style is unlikely to appeal to many members of Western culture. For most it would entail a fundamental and complete alteration of personal philosophy and life-style. Although one may encounter the occasional client, perhaps undergoing an existential crisis, to whom such a fundamental change appeals, these clients will be in the minority.

There are, however, elements of yoga which can be extracted and integrated into a Western philosophy of stress management. These elements are the "postures" and meditation. They are physiologically oriented and meant to serve the function of diffusing the effects of stress and increasing the resistance of the body to future stress.

The postures are, in effect, physical exercises which emphasize slow continual stretching movements. The most basic difference between yogic exercises and ordinary physical exercises is that the latter emphasize violent and strenuous movements of the muscles, whereas yogic exercises focus on gradual development of elasticity, improved circulation, and mobilization of the joints. The exercises are isotonic, so that contraction of one group of muscles is accompanied by the relaxation or stretching of the counterposed muscles (Patel, 1984). A typical yoga exercise session involves a series of well-defined postures which focus on different parts of the body in sequence so that a balanced and comprehensive state of fitness is achieved. A session would conclude with a period of directed physical relaxation which lasts approximately 10 minutes. Such a relaxation exercise ("the sponge") is described in Table 6–1.

Yogic meditation follows the above steps of exercise and relaxation. Once the physical musculature has been relaxed, breathing becomes the target of regulation. The individual then begins a stage of sensory with

TABLE 6–1
A Yoga Relaxation Exercise

THE SPONGE: teaches one to relax the whole body and free it from anxiety, nervous tension; is an energy recharger.

Technique:

(1) Lie on the floor, legs slightly apart, arms limply by your side.

(2) Point your toes away from you and hold for 5 seconds. Relax.

(3) Pull the toes up toward the body, bending at the ankle.

(4) Pull your heels up two inches off the floor and then straighten the legs, pushing the back of the knees firmly against the floor. Hold. Relax.

(5) Point the toes toward each other and pull the heels under and up, keeping the legs straight. Hold. Relax.

(6) Pinch your buttocks together. Hold. Relax.

(7) Pull your abdomen in and up as far as possible. Hold. Relax.

(8) Arch the spine back, pushing the chest out. Hold. Relax.

(9) With arms straight by your side, palms down, bend the fingers up and back toward the arm, bending at the wrist. Hold. Relax.

(10) Bend the elbows and repeat step 9, bending the hands back toward the shoulders. Hold. Relax.

(11) Make a tight fist of your hands, bring the arms out to the sides and move the arms up perpendicular to the floor. Move very slowly, resisting the movement all the while to make the pectoral muscles of the bust stand out.

(12) Pull the shoulder blades of the back together. Hold. Relax.

(13) Pull the shoulders up beside the ears. Hold. Relax.

(14) Pull down the corners of the mouth. Hold. Relax.

(15) Bring the tongue to the back of the roof of the mouth. Hold. Relax.

(16) Purse your lips, wrinkle the nose and squeeze the eyes tightly shut. Hold. Relax.

(17) Smile with the lips closed and stretch the face. Hold. Relax.

(18) Yawn very slowly, resisting the movement.

(19) Press the back of the head against the floor. Hold. Relax.

(20) Frown, moving the scalp forward. Hold. Relax.

(21) Squeeze the eyes closed. Hold. Relax.

(22) Pull your head under and against the shoulder without moving anything else.

(23) Relax, melting into the floor, for up to 10 minutes.

Reprinted with permission from K. Zebroff (1975), *Beauty through Yoga.* Vancouver: Fforber.

drawal and gradually begins to narrow down the focus of attention. The eventual object of focus or contemplation is a matter of personal discretion—a sound (mantra), a flower, a candleflame, a sense. The final stage of yogic meditation arises from this narrowing of awareness. The mind is said to "transcend an ordinary plane of awareness" (Patel, 1984, p. 84). The beginner will not attain this last stage; however, achievement of the earlier state of contemplation is purported to be sufficient to restore health and energy in the ordinary individual.

Comments. It is unlikely that the therapist will have sufficient expertise in yoga to teach it unless he or she is a practitioner of the yoga philosophy in his or her own life. However, a familiarity with the basic tenets of the practice as outlined here will enable the therapist to make properly informed recommendations to clients. For those clients experiencing stress-related musculoskeletal problems which benefit from exercise regimes (e.g., low back pain, some forms of arthritis), yoga is a logical choice. It may also be of benefit to clients who would prefer to deal with their problems outside the mental health system, since yoga classes are frequently offered at local fitness centers, clubs, schools, community centers, and the like. There are also televised yoga instruction programs, as well as instructional books. Thus yoga can be performed at home or outside the home, in groups or individually. Yoga would seem to be well suited to the normal healthy individual who is conscientious about keeping his or her body strong and resistant to stress. Also, the client with multiple needs in therapy can enroll in a yoga program independent of the ongoing therapy, so that cognitive and behavioral interventions can be begun simultaneously.

The disadvantages of yoga are fourfold. First, given its philosophic and religious overtones, it simply does not appeal to some clients. Second, because it does tend to occur outside of the primary therapist/client relationship, it can be difficult to integrate into the therapeutic package. There is always the possibility of some conflict between what the yoga instructor advises and what the therapist is advocating. Third, it may not be readily available in all geographical areas at all times. Fourth, for the particularly severely affected client, the practice of yoga through classes or other group instruction may not be sufficiently intensive or individualized to address the therapeutic needs.

Transcendental Meditation

Of those forms of meditation which have been popularized in Western culture, transcendental meditation is the most well known and most widely practiced. Neither a religion nor a philosophy, transcendental meditation (TM) is described as a natural technique for reducing stress and expanding awareness (Bloomfield, Cain, & Jaffe, 1976). Although TM retains some of the features of the Hindu culture from which it derives, it is less cultic than other Eastern meditations (i.e., Buddhism, Taoism, Sufi), and does not require any prior acceptance of dogma or concepts. Thus, it may be viewed as a transitional technique, between the more traditional cultic meditations and the more "modern" techniques such as Benson's (1975) Relaxation Response, discussed below, or Carrington's (1978) clinically standardized meditation.

TM has been popularized in North America by Maharishi Mahesh Yogi, who claimed that any individual with a reasonably intact mind could learn to meditate readily. With this claim, he differed greatly from most teachers of meditation, who have argued that many years of practice are necessary in order to meditate properly (Campbell, 1975). Maharishi also claims that TM is, specifically, a method of removing stress, a method for the cyclical rhythmic release from the negative physiological effects of stress. He defines stress as a failure of the brain to achieve balance, and TM as a technique for facilitating the regaining of this balance.

TM is a structured form of meditation in that it carefully and precisely defines the inner activity toward which the practitioner is striving. It is a "mantra" meditation in that the object upon which the practitioner dwells is typically a word, syllable, or name. According to TM philosophy, each person has an individual mantra (sound), selected for him or her in consultation with the TM instructor. Maharishi maintains that selection of the proper mantra for a given individual is a vital factor in TM (Goleman, 1977). The mantras come from standard Sanskrit sources used by many Hindus. TM instructors believe that particular sounds bestow certain feelings, and are therefore appropriate to certain types of individuals.

Bloomfield et al. (1976) point out that the danger of using a mantra of unknown effect is demonstrated by the many anecdotal reports of individuals who have failed to meditate successfully when using nonsense syllables or when "borrowing" another's mantra. For these reasons, instructors admonish novice meditators to refrain from revealing their mantras to others. (This silence also avoids the inevitable chagrin experienced by some meditators who discover that other meditators of the same general gestalt—age, sex, education, and so on—have the same mantra.)

Procedure. The mechanics of TM are relatively straightforward. The four basic components of meditation outlined above (a quiet place, a comfortable position, an object to dwell upon, a passive attitude) are applied in conjunction with the individual's personal mantra. The meditator is to learn to avoid effortful concentration and is to center his or her thoughts on the mantra, gently bringing his mind back to the mantra as his or her thoughts wander. The goal is to achieve a focal narrowing of attention on the meditation object (the mantra) and to transcend the object, turning the mind inward.

The process of TM is typically learned by enrolling in an introductory course offered by the Students' International Meditation Society or one of its affiliated organizations (the International Meditation Society; the American Foundation for the Science of Creative Intelligence; the Spiritual Regeneration Movement; the Maharishi International University). The basic course begins with one or two public lectures outlining the nature of TM, the benefits of regular practice, and the mechanics of the technique. After the lectures, individual appointments with instructors are arranged. Follow-up meetings are also arranged. There is a fee for the introductory course. More advanced training, involvement in activities at training centers, and ongoing "checking" to ensure proper practice are also available. The goal is for the practitioners to meditate twice a day, every day, for about 20 minutes per session.

Empirical Support. Interestingly, in spite of TM's status outside the mainstream of the health system and mental health practice, it has been subject to a significant amount of empirical evaluation, much of which has in fact supported its claims of effectiveness in countering the physiological effects of stress. Much of this work has been carried out by Benson and his colleagues (Wallace, 1970; Wallace, Benson, & Wilson, 1971; Wallace & Benson, 1972; Benson & Wallace, 1972). In fact, it was this research which led Benson to derive his own meditation approach, the relaxation response (described below).

Comments. TM shares many of the advantages and disadvantges of yoga and other meditations. It is taught by individuals outside the therapy situation, which both frees up time and allows for contradiction. It is simple and straightforward to learn, but may be insufficient for particularly distressed clients. It requires faithful practice, twice daily, in order to be effective. It is not primarily a coping skill, but is an effective preventive measure.

There are several factors specific to TM that should be considered. First is the issue of availability. Although the practice of TM was at one time quite widespread on college campuses, TM instruction does not seem quite so widely available as it was in the 1960s. If it is not available in the client's town, then it will not be very useful. Second, there is a significant cost involved. This may or may not be more than the cost of comparable training with a therapist. Third, like yoga, it simply does not appeal to some people. These individuals are not likely to comply with such an approach, regardless of the advantages it might offer. However, TM does benefit from having been assessed relatively well in clinical application, and is known to be an effective stress reduction technique, which gives it a decided edge over most other types of meditation.

Benson's Relaxation Response

Herbert Benson, a physiologist at Harvard University, was instrumental in bringing the practice of TM to the attention of the mental health community; he subsequently adopted some of the principles of TM and incorporated them into his own approach, known as the "relaxation response." Benson was involved in studies of the relationship between monkeys' behavior and blood pressure when he was approached by practitioners of TM who were interested in having their ability to control blood pressure assessed. As a result of Benson's studies of these practitioners of TM and his subsequent review of other relaxation methods (both meditations and others), he concluded that the various physiological changes that accompanied TM were part of a generalized and integrated response, opposite to the "fight or flight" response. Benson (1975) maintained that there were four essential components to the relaxation response (as outlined earlier) and that all relaxation methods shared these components. In extracting these four components, Benson sought to eliminate the religious and philosophic overtones of the meditations on the one hand, and to minimize the complicated and time-consuming instruction of progressive relaxation training methods on the other hand. The resultant set of standardized meditation instructions have come to be known as the "Relaxation Response" method.

Procedure. The technique is as follows:

(1) Sit quietly in a comfortable position.
(2) Close your eyes.
(3) Deeply relax all your muscles, beginning at your feet and progressing up to your face. Keep them relaxed.
(4) Breathe through your nose. Become aware of your breathing. As you breathe out, say the word "one" silently to yourself.
(5) Continue for 10 to 20 minutes.

Benson's method is presented as a self-help method in his book *The Relaxation Response* (1975).

Empirical Support. Investigations of the physiological changes accompanying practice of the relaxation response have generally been supportive (Hoffman et al., 1982; French et al., 1981) and indicate reduced sympathetic reactivity. However, there is some dispute over the extent to which the effects are attributable to positive expectancy (Goldberg, 1982) rather than any discrete therapeutic effect.

Comments. The major advantage of this approach is that it is simple to learn and cost-effective. Benson (1975) presents his technique as a form of bibliotherapy. For the therapist, it is largely a matter of handing over to the client a book or reference and building the technique into the existing treatment plan. As well as explaining the technique, Benson's book outlines much of the rationale for relaxation in general. (Actually, it is useful reading even for clients who are using other relaxation methods.)

One potential difficulty with this method is its reliance on cognitive control. For acutely stressed and anxious clients, it may be difficult to adopt the requirements of maintaining a passive attitude and concentrating on a single theme. Thus, its potential benefits for clients with substantial cognitive components to their stress reactions must be weighed against the potential difficulty these same individuals will have in producing the necessary cognitive attitude (Keable, 1985b).

A second and related problem lies in the simplicity of the approach. Although the bare-bones elegance of the instructions is appealing, it may be unrealistic to expect clients to simply be able to "relax all your muscles." For clinical applications, this approach might benefit from being combined with a more directive or structured method, such as progressive relaxation training.

These limitations notwithstanding, Benson has done an admirable job of extracting the essential components of meditation and presenting them in a straightforward and clinically useful fashion.

Although one potential drawback to these approaches is the necessity of twice daily practice, something which may be difficult for some clients, there is some evidence that clients do find meditation somewhat more appealing and are more likely to practice meditation techniques than they are progressive relaxation or autogenic approaches (Carrington et al., 1980; Lehrer et al., 1983; Zuroff & Schwartz, 1978).

CURATIVE TECHNIQUES

The two primary types of curative relaxation techniques are progressive relaxation training and biofeedback. In both instances, the therapist plays a major role as "coach" or instructor. Both techniques involve relatively long and exacting training which is dependent upon the therapist. But also in both types, proper training involves a gradual reduction in the time and effort required to relax, as well as decreasing dependency on the therapist. When these techniques are properly pursued, the client is able eventually to produce a state of relaxation quickly and on demand, thus demonstrating the acquisition of a coping skill.

Progressive Relaxation Training

As was mentioned above, progressive relaxation training (PRT) was originally developed by Jacobson (1938) and later abbreviated by others (Wolpe, 1958; Bernstein & Borkovec, 1973). There remains some controversy regarding the necessity of carrying out the full procedure which Jacobson initially prescribed (comprising 50 or more training sessions) or if indeed the shortened versions achieve the same result in a much shorter period of time (usually six to ten sessions). In spite of arguments to the contrary (Lehrer, 1982), the evidence in favor of the full unabbreviated version is weak (Bernstein & Borkovec, 1973; Bernstein & Given, 1984). There are a few studies which have attempted to compare the full-length version to the abbreviated version (Turner, 1978; Snow, 1977). Although these studies did suggest some degree of superiority for the original version, the results were marginal, the subjects were normal students rather than clinical cases, and the length of training was shorter than optimal for both conditions. Thus the question remains largely unanswered.

In addition, most therapists are not able to provide the time commitment necessary to carry out the full version. (The fact that there is very little literature comparing the two versions is probably attributable at least in part to this problem.) Nevertheless, it is worth keeping in mind that the question of the supriority of method has not been resolved. It is logically possible that for particularly difficult and intractable clients, the full-length version may have an edge.

Jacobson's Method. Jacobson's method (1964, 1976) involves focusing sequentially on 15 different muscle groups, one at a time. In a given session, the client and the therapist focus on one particular muscle group, concentrating on relaxing that muscle group differentially—that is, in isolation of other muscle groups. Each muscle group is the focus of from one to nine sessions of training (sessions are one hour long and are to be conducted daily). There are a total of 56 sessions of systematic training.

For example, the first muscle group of interest is usually the left arm. On the first day, the client is instructed to rest quietly for three to four minutes, or until such time as the eyes close voluntarily. Then he or she focuses on bending the left hand back (tensing) for several minutes. This is followed by several minutes of relaxation again. This sequence is repeated several times during the session until such time as an awareness of the produced tension is developed. The session concludes with one half hour of lying motionless, in a relaxed state.

On the second day, a similar procedure is repeated, with the client focusing on bending the hand forward. Over the course of seven sessions, the entire left arm is relaxed. The client is also encouraged to practice one to two hours daily.

These instructions are given in their entirety in Jacobson (1964) and in his self-help book *You Must Relax* (Jacobson, 1976).

Abbreviated PRT. There are actually many abbreviated versions of progressive relaxation training, a fact which makes the literature in this area very difficult to assess. This problem is compounded by the fact that since abbreviated PRT is much more common than the original Jacobsonian method, the abbreviated methods are also referred to as "Jacobsonian relaxation training." (Note: It is essential, when reading any literature in this area, to try to determine exactly what the experimenters did, and for how many sessions.)

For the sake of clarity and simplicity, the particular abbreviated method described here is that of Bernstein and Borkovec (1973), whose training manual presents a clear and systematic approach to the task.

In this approach, the client is initially presented with a rationale and explanation of the procedure. He or she is then asked to focus on a series of 16 muscle groups *in each session.* The basic procedure involves asking the client to tense the identified muscle for five to seven seconds, during which time the therapist aids in keeping attention focused by making statements which point out to the client what is happening. The client is then instructed to relax the muscle for 30–40 seconds while the therapist continues to discuss the developing feelings, and the contrast between tension and relaxation. (The continual narration by the therapist is usually referred to as the "patter.") Generally, this procedure is carried out twice on each muscle, so that the entire sequence may take up to 45 minutes.

Once the client has mastered the basic procedure, the number of muscle groups is reduced to seven or eight, then to four. At this point, the "tension" part of the sequence is eliminated and the client is directed to attend to any tension present in the body, and then to relax it away. Thus, the sessions become shorter and shorter until such time as the client is able to detect tension spontaneously and quickly relax it away.

A typical PRT protocol is described in Table 6–2.

Comments. Bernstein and Borkovec's abbreviated method of progressive relaxation training is comprehensive, thorough, and manageable clinically. PRT is an extremely useful structured relaxation procedure which has been shown to be effective in a variety of circumstances (see Woolfolk & Lehrer, 1984). It is also the most commonly practiced and frequently referred to type of relaxation training in psychological therapy. In spite of the apparent "cookbook" nature of the technique, it is actually very flexible and adaptable. These features, in combination with its convenience and demonstrated clinical utility, have earned PRT a solid position as an important component of any social learning approach to behavior change.

There are, of course, a few caveats to offer. First, there is an unfortunate tendency for therapists to cease training after the beginning stages (i.e., at a time when the client is able to lie down and carry out the prescribed exercises, but is not yet able to use the technique as a coping skill). This amounts to quitting halfway through. The goal of PRT is not to take to one's bed in times of stress! If a meditation-type approach is desired or if there is not sufficient time for a proper course of training, then another technique should be selected.

Second, some unknowing therapists have made the mistake of attempting to teach relaxation via audiotapes. This is a practice which should be avoided at all costs. Aside from the empirical evidence that it does not work (Lehrer, 1982), there are significant clinical risks associated with the practice. Without individual instruction and careful monitoring of the client's response to instruction, there is no way of ensuring that the technique is being carried out properly. The tapes may actually be reinforcing maladaptive behavior. Other therapists do conduct live training sessions, but hand out tapes to be used in homework assignments. The latter practice may be helpful for some clients who have difficulty remembering exactly what to practice in the early stages of

TABLE 6–2
Typical Progressive Relaxation Protocol

WEEK	SESSION	APPROX. LENGTH (MINUTES)	CONTENTS
1	1	60	Introduction and treatment rationale; training in 16 muscle groups; introduction to relaxing imagery; introduction in home practice.
	2	45	Check on home practice; training in 16 muscle groups; relaxing imagery; home practice audiotape offered.
2	3	35	Training on 16 muscle groups; relaxing imagery; introduce muscle discrimination training.
	4	35	Training on 16 muscle groups; relaxing imagery; muscle discrimination training.
3	5	30	Training on 8 muscle groups; relaxing imagery.
	6	35	Training on 8 muscle groups; introduce relaxation by recall.
4	7	30	Training on 4 muscle groups; relaxation by recall.
5	8	30	Training on 4 muscle groups; relaxation by recall; introduce cue-controlled relaxation.
6	9	30	Training on 4 muscle groups; relaxation by recall; cue-controlled relaxation.
7	—		
8	10	45	Review all procedures; diary check; schedule follow-up or additional treatment.

Reprinted with permission from E.B. Blanchard and F. Andrasik (1985) *Management of chronic headaches: A psychological approach.* New York: Pergamon Press.

training; however, there are also drawbacks to this procedure. It encourages the client to fixate at the early stage ("take to bed in times of stress") and shifts the locus of control away from the client to the tape. One does see clients panic or relapse when their tapes break or get lost.

If the client really appears to need an aid in order to practice independently, the therapist might consider assisting the client in making his or her own tape. Not only does the repetition of the instructions help the client to remember them, but also the tapes become a form of cognitive self-instructional training. In any event, the therapist should plan to repossess the tape after a couple of weeks so that dependence does not occur.

Finally, some therapists find it trying to keep up the "patter" of describing feelings, sensations and contrasts for an entire session. Only time and experience will lead to comfort in this procedure, but one can get ideas for developing a personal style from a number of sources. These include the aforementioned book by Bernstein and Borkovec, various commercial relaxation tapes, and the book by Blanchard and Andrasik (1985). There are also relaxation scripts in many of the biofeedback equipment manuals.

(This last source might lead one to inquire as to whether PRT and biofeedback are useful in combination. This issue is considered below, after the discussion of biofeedback.)

There remain many questions about the exact nature and mechanism of effectiveness and about critical procedural variables in PRT. These are discussed at some length by King (1980).

Biofeedback

The term "biofeedback" refers to "the technique of using equipment (usually electronic) to reveal to human beings some of their internal physiological events, normal and abnormal, in the form of visual and auditory signals, in order to teach them to manipulate these otherwise involuntary or unfelt events by manipulating the displayed signals" (Basmajian, 1979, p. 1). In the context of stress management in general and relaxation therapy in particular, biofeedback usually refers to electromyographic or EMG biofeedback (also referred to as myoelectric feedback). EMG biofeedback is a technique which enables the client to manipulate levels of muscle tension by means of electronic feedback. Other types of biofeedback which are sometimes used in stress management programs include galvanic skin response (GSR), alpha brain wave feedback, or electroencephalogram biofeedback (EEG), and skin temperature feedback.

EMG biofeedback. In 1969, the combination of a rapidly developing field of bioelectronics and a resurgent interest in relaxation therapies led to the publication of Budzynski and Stoyva's landmark article entitled "An Instrument for Producing Deep Muscle Relaxation by Means of Analog Information Feedback" (Budzynski & Stoyva, 1969). These authors contended that a central problem in other relaxation techniques was that of determining whether the client was actually relaxed, or if the demand characteristics of the situation merely encouraged him or her to think so. By using an objective measure of tension/relaxation (i.e., muscle tension), the therapist could verify the state of tension in the client. By feeding back this information to the client by means of auditory or visual signals, the therapist could encourage the client to alter his or her performance in such a way as to ensure success. The essential strategy of biofeedback is therefore purely operant. A signal is presented to the client and he or she is instructed to alter it. Through trial and error, the client will eventually develop an effective means of manipulating the signal in the desired direction and thus will produce the appropriate physiological response (i.e., muscular relaxation).

Procedure. The procedure, again in its purest form, consists of attaching a set of biopotential surface electrodes to the muscle in question, establishing a baseline, and then instructing the client to make the tone/light vary in the appropriate direction. Several trials of a few minutes each, or one longer continuous period of effort may comprise an individual training session. In the research literature, instructions to relax are often omitted in order to avoid confounding the effect of the instructions to relax with the effect of the biofeedback itself.

However, biofeedback in its purest form, as described above, is virtually never practiced by the clinician, who is generally most interested in assisting the client in obtaining the desired result, regardless of exactly which aspect of the treatment brings about the change.

Clinically, EMG biofeedback is generally carried out in conjunction with another relaxation technique. A reasonable and comprehensive course of training in EMG biofeedback is described by Stoyva (1979) and is summarized in Table 6–3 (Stoyva, 1979, p. 100). The preparation phase involves acquainting the client with the technique as well as assessing the client for appropriateness for this particular technique. Since the goal of EMG biofeedback is to reduce muscle tension, it is logical to determine first if the client does indeed exhibit excess muscle tension, either at rest or when stressed. (It is well documented in the literature [viz. Schwartz et al., 1978] that the various physiological indicators of anxiety

TABLE 6–3

Typical Biofeedback Training Protocol

Preparation Phase

---

1. *Explain Biofeedback* training and why it could be helpful in:
   a. Reducing localized muscle tension, or
   b. Counteracting the effects of psychological stress. Make certain your patient understands the reason for biofeedback training in his case.
2. Make sure the *physical setting* is a good one for relaxation training.
3. Make sure your *apparatus* is in working order and ready for use before the patient arrives.
4. *Obtain baseline data.*
5. *Obtain a stress profile.*
   This consists of three phases: *Relaxation, stress and recovery.* A useful stressor is the subtraction of serial sevens. In what system does the patient respond too powerfully?—for example, in EMG, peripheral temperature or in GSR activity?

Training Phase

1. Make sure the patient knows what the feedback signal is telling him.
2. *Step 1: Cultivating the muscle sense.* Do the *tense-relaxation* exercises in order to develop an awareness of muscle tension. These can be started at the end of the baseline session(s).
3. *Step 2: Forearm EMG Training.* Give the patient a couple of minutes to experiment with the feedback. "What makes it go up; what makes it go down?" For a 20-minute period, (±5 minutes), the patient practices letting the tone go to low levels (or on reducing the click rate). Afterwards, *discuss the session* with the patient. Train the patient on forearm EMG until he reaches an average level of 2.0 μV. Encourage patient to develop awareness of internal cues such as heaviness and warmth. Encourage home practice—twice a day for 15 to 20 minutes each time.
4. *Step 3: Frontal EMG Training.* Train the patient on frontal EMG till he reaches an average level of 3.5 μV. Encourage awareness of internal cues. Emphasize continuing importance of *home practice.*
   Is the patient mastering a thorough relaxation response? Is he having any difficulties? Work on correcting them.
5. *Step 4: Autonomic responses.* With patients who are strong autonomic responders under stress, hand temperature or GSR training can be useful. Note that the training's central focus is to promote a general relaxation response, so the therapist should be on the watch for remaining signs of high arousal. For example, is hand temperature low? If so, the patient should be taught the simultaneous mastery of peripheral temperature *and* profound muscle relaxation. Again, *encourage the patient to use the relaxation response frequently in everyday life.*

Reprinted with permission from J. Basmajian (1979), *Biofeedback—principles and practice for clinicians.* Baltimore: Williams and Wilkins Co.

do not tend to covary. Thus, one cannot readily assume that clients with predominant symptoms other than muscle tension will necessarily benefit from learning muscular relaxation.) Stoyva recommends assessing the client for autonomic reactivity and muscular reactivity at the same time, so that an alternate form of biofeedback training can be implemented if it seems more appropriate. If excess muscle tension is evident, the client will begin the training phase, which focuses on cultivating muscle sense.

In a training session, a criterion level of muscle tension is identified, and the client attempts to manipulate the feedback in such a manner as to reach the criterion. Generally, some form of instruction to relax or to produce particular sensations is offered to the client. Over the course of the training sessions, the criterion is gradually lowered, and the amount of time required to reach the criterion is shortened. In addition, the feedback itself is eventually eliminated, so that the client is finally in possession of a voluntary response which can be invoked as a coping skill.

In general, the literature suggests that the effect of EMG biofeedback is approximately equivalent to that of other relaxation strategies, and may have some differential effect in the case of predominantly musculoskeletal disorders such as tension headaches (Surwit & Keefe, 1978).

Other Biofeedback Approaches.

Thermal biofeedback. Probably the second most common form of biofeedback, thermal feedback centers on teaching the client to alter hand temperature. Like EMG biofeedback, it is purely operant when applied in isolation. A thermistor is attached to one finger, usually on the dominant hand, and the client is instructed to increase or decrease hand temperature. This method is believed to be particularly effective in treating Raynaud's phenomena (Surwit, 1982) and migraine headaches (Blanchard et al., 1982).

Electroencephalogram (EEG) biofeedback. EEG feedback evolved from observations in the mid-1960s that individuals skilled in meditation showed high levels of alpha wave activity during the practice of meditation. However, subsequent research failed to support the utility of specific alpha training and it is not currently a major treatment technique. As Basmajian (1979) points out, " 'alpha feedback' is still a mystery but it is not an acceptable treatment method" (p. 1). (There is at present some interesting experimental work being carried out, on altering EEG patterns in epileptics; (viz. Mostofsky & Balaschak, 1977.)

Galvanic skin response (GSR). GSR reflects sweat gland activity and changes in sympathetic nervous system activity, as well as some changes in peripheral nervous system activity (Fuller, 1977). Although it has a long and prominent history as an indicator of anxiety and stress, the exact nature of GSR and related responses remains unclear. Almost any type of emotional arousal appears to produce changes in GSR. For that reason, it is both a good general indicator of change, and a difficult measure to interpret. In general, GSR and related measures (electrodermal response, skin resistance, skin potential, etc.) tend to be used more often to identify patterns of response in clients than as agents of change. There is some evidence, however, that GSR training may be helpful in the treatment of hypertension (Patel, 1973) and for exploration in the course of psychotherapy (Toomin, 1974).

Biofeedback Combinations. If one accepts Schwartz et al.'s (1978) contention that all the various relaxation techniques evoke a global relaxation response but that each technique adds a specific individual effect as well, then the notion of combining techniques has good face validity. As Lehrer and Woolfolk (1984) point out in their general review of stress reduction techniques, the literature does generally favor use of combinations of techniques over the use of individual techniques. One particular combination which stands out in the literature is that of abbreviated PRT and EMG biofeedback. For exactly the reasons given originally by Budzynski and Stoyva (1969), EMG biofeedback can be used conjointly with PRT to ensure that the client is in fact relaxed—and tensed—at the appropriate times. The two techniques share the same philosophical orientation, as well as the same physiological focus.

Ideally, PRT and EMG biofeedback are taught concurrently—not sequentially. That is, the client is actually attached to and is receiving feedback from the EMG equipment while the PRT session is in progress, and the therapist uses the feedback as verification of the client's progress. Thus, reference to the feedback is actually integrated into the PRT patter. (Note that in many studies assessing the "combination" of EMG biofeedback and PRT, the two types of training are actually carried out separately, with the therapist alternating between the two techniques (i.e., Staples, 1978; Nigl & Jackson, 1979), so that the subjects were in essence participating in two different types of training within the same time frame.)

A second combination of approaches which may be useful is that of autogenic training (see below, "Other Approaches") and thermal biofeedback. In fact, in some thermal biofeedback equipment manuals, one finds what are essentially autogenic instructions. Both approaches focus on the development of relaxation through induction of feelings of warmth, so it may be that combining these approaches potentiates the individual results. Norris and Fahrion (1984) describe a technique called autogenic biofeedback, which is in effect a combination of the two techniques.

Comments. The period of the late 1970s saw the dramatic introduction and popularization of biofeedback techniques, to the extent that biofeedback began to be regarded as a panacea (viz. Surwit & Keefe, 1978). However, as time passed and more rigorous and controlled studies emerged, biofeedback fell from grace in the 1980s. First viewed as a treatment revolution, it became merely another reasonably effective relaxation technique, indistinguishable from the rest. Some would have it completely dismissed from the armamentarium of the clinician (Roberts, 1985). In a stimulating bit of editorializing, Roberts points out that "there is little relationship between research findings in the area of biofeedback and the clinical practice of biofeedback" (p. 938). He attributes this failing to the inability of graduate training programs to produce students who can think clearly and critically, and who are able to avoid the "pitfall of allowing fallible clinical judgments to supplant scientifically derived conclusions" (Roberts, 1985, p. 941).

The problem for the clinician, then, is whether to accept the literature which assesses the purely operant aspects of biofeedback, or whether to believe the collective wisdom of biofeedback practitioners who use the technique in a manner significantly different from that of researchers. Green and Shellenberger (1986) convincingly point out that "nothing whatsoever can be said about the efficacy of biofeedback training because the methodology prevents an accurate study of the procedure" (p. 1005). These authors, along with McGovern (1986), Smith (1986), White and Tursky (1986), and Norris (1986) point clearly to the need to employ biofeedback as part of a comprehensive and multimodal approach to treatment. In this context, biofeedback has been demonstrated to have meaningful impact, particularly in the treatment of tension or muscle contraction headaches (Blanchard et al., 1982) and other predominantly muscular conditions (Shellenberger & Green, 1986). The key to success is in adopting the proper rationale and in employing a comprehensive approach.

OTHER APPROACHES

There are a number of other approaches to relaxation training which combine some of the features of the two different models described above. The most significant of these is autogenic training.

Autogenic Training

The autogenic approach to relaxation does not fit neatly into either of the above categories of relaxation training, nor did it develop in conjunction with either of the two historical trends described earlier. Like the meditation techniques, autogenic training involves twice daily regular practice as a preventive measure. Like progressive relaxation training, it can be utilized in difficult or stressful situations to offset specific symptoms of distress. It did evolve from a medical intervention, but developed in Europe, separate from the North American evolution of PRT and biofeedback.

The term "autogenic" means self-regulation or self-generation. The essential thesis of autogenic training is that stress upsets the normal homeostatic balance in the body and that relaxation achieved through autogenic methods allows the body to regain the disrupted balance (Luthe & Schultz, 1969). Autogenic training techniques arose from the work of the German neuropathologist Vogt. In the course of his investigations of sleep and hypnosis, Vogt observed that some subjects were able to induce a trance-like state in themselves, outside of the experimental situation. He also observed that this state appeared to have a positive recuperative effect (Hastings, Fadiman, & Gordon, 1981). A Berlin psychiatrist, Schultz, went on to examine and develop the techniques further in hope of devising a technique which would produce the same beneficial effects as hypnosis, but which would eliminate the dependence upon the therapist. Schultz identified the sensations of warmth and heaviness as essential components of the practice, and developed these further into the standard exercises of autogenic training. Luthe, his colleague, is largely responsible for popularizing these techniques in North America (Luthe & Schultz, 1969; Luthe, 1977).

Procedure. The procedure is dominated by emphasis on the production of sensations of warmth and heaviness. Thoughts of warmth are believed to induce vasodilation, and thoughts of heaviness are believed to induce muscular relaxation. Concentration on these two sensations promotes a shift to the autogenic state which facilitates the process of self-normalization.

There are six standard autogenic exercises, described in Table 6–4. The subject begins by assuming a comfortable position and repeating the appropriate autogenic phrase to him- or herself, initially for intervals of a few minutes, several times a day. These periods of practice gradually evolve into two periods of 30 minutes twice daily. Thus, in the first week

TABLE 6–4

Six Standard AT Exercises

Standard Exercise	Physiological State	Phrase
1	heaviness in the ex-tremities	"my arms and legs are heavy"
2	warmth in the ex-tremities	"my arms and legs are warm"
3	calm and regular function of the heart	"my heart is calm and regular"
4	calm and regular res-piration	"my breath is calm and regular" or "it breathes me"
5	solar plexus warm	"my solar plexus is warm"
6	forehead cool	"my forehead is cool"

Reprinted with permission from A. C. Hastings, J. Fadiman, & J. S. Gordon (1981), *Health for the whole person*. Boulder, CO: Westview Press.

of therapy, for example, the client may repeat to him- or herself "my right arm is heavy; my left arm is heavy; both of my arms are heavy" several times a day. Gradually, the legs are also included, until feelings of heaviness in the extremities can be induced at will. The client then progresses to the second standard exercise and a similar procedure is followed. Details of a typical course of autogenic training are outlined in Davis et al. (1982). In each of the six exercises, the content of the previous sessions is included and built upon. Thus, the client who has reached exercise four will quickly induce heaviness and warmth in the extremities and will regularize his or her heartbeat before working on his or her respiratory pattern.

Advocates of autogenic training view the technique as a potentially powerful medical tool which should be utilized cautiously in any individual in whom pathology is evident (International Committee on Autogenic Therapy, 1961). They recommend careful monitoring of any disease process in order to ascertain that there is no worsening of the symptoms over the course of therapy. (This is, of course, a commendable procedure in the application of any relaxation procedure.)

Comments. Until fairly recently, autogenic training was not well known in North America, but was more widely used in Europe. (In reading much of the professional literature in this area, one discovers that the phrase "relaxation training," used without qualification, generally refers to PRT in North American journals, but indicates autogenic training in most European journals.)

The actual mechanism by which autogenic training works is not well understood. It is thought to induce a trance much as hypnosis does—but alas, hypnosis is not well understood! Autogenic training highlights one of the major difficulties in assessing any relaxation technique, which is to identify the effects of nonspecific elements (such as suggestion) as opposed to technique-specific effects.

It may be that autogenic training's affiliation with hypnosis renders it suspect in the minds of some therapists and clients. Therapists may wonder if it represents a definitive placebo, whereas clients, particularly anxious ones, may fear the trance-like state and concomitant feeling of loss of control. Or, conversely, clients may find it excessively dull. Woolfolk and Lehrer (1984) report their own observation that clients were less apt to comply with autogenic training than with some other techniques. And consider the study by Glueck and Stroebel (1975) in which all the subjects in the autogenic treatment group dropped out of the study.

However, autogenic training also has some distinct therapeutic advantages. It does, as mentioned above, combine some of the advantages of each of the two major types of relaxation methods. It is physiologically oriented, but with a strong cognitive component. This combination can be useful in clients who find it difficult to attend to meditation techniques. It may be more effective in dealing with problems involving autonomic functioning than are more muscularly oriented techniques, such as PRT and biofeedback (Lehrer, Atthowe, & Weber, 1980). Consistent with this, however, are findings by Staples, Coursey, and Smith (1976) which suggest that autogenic training has less effect on muscular tension than do PRT and biofeedback.

As mentioned earlier, autogenic training has also been gaining popularity as part of an "autogenic biofeedback" technique (Norris & Fahrion, 1984), which combines autogenic phrases with biofeedback. The logic for doing so is particularly compelling in the case of thermal biofeedback for disorders such as Raynaud's Disease or migraine headaches, since these disorders seem to represent malfunctions which may respond directly to the effects of vasodilation in particular.

Other "Other Approaches"

There are many other relaxation techniques which will not be discussed here. These include "simple" relaxation (i.e., the general instruction to relax); scanning; somatic focusing; guided imagery; controlled breathing; hypnosis; and others. Many of these have been subjected to little empirical research and are therefore not as well established in clinical practice. Davis et al. (1982) and Smith (1985) provide much useful information about alternate forms of relaxation.

CHOOSING A TECHNIQUE

Much of the research that has been carried out in the past two decades concerning relaxation techniques has posed the simple question, "Which technique works best?" Alas, it has become clear that there is no simple answer to that apparently simple question. A second generation of research has addressed a somewhat more complex question: "For this particular disorder, what technique works best?" There is some evidence, albeit equivocal, that some techniques do have differential effects, depending upon the specific disorder. There remain, however, two other aspects of treatment selection which have not been addressed to any great extent in the literature. These are: (1) characteristics of the therapist and therapeutic situation; and (2) characteristics of the client (other than diagnosis). To some extent, the therapist will have to rely on his or her own clinical judgment to address these concerns.

The first step in selecting a relaxation technique is, simply, to ask the proper question. "Given this therapist treating that client with those symptoms, which technique is most likely to be effective?"

Characteristics of the Therapist and Therapeutic Setting

Fortunately, these are questions which only need to be asked and answered once—and they are questions which can be addressed directly. First, with which techniques is the therapist familiar and comfortable? Regardless of the "official" status of any technique, it is not likely to be effective if the therapist is not convinced of its efficacy, comfortable with its philosophy, and adept at its administration. No therapist should shy away from experimenting with new and different treatment strategies— but proper preparation and supervision are essential. As important as skill in application is belief in efficacy. If the therapist feels that TM is hype, biofeedback is annoying, and autogenic training is boring, these messages will not escape the client!

Similarly, the philosophy of the approach should be consistent with the general treatment philosophy of the therapist. The eclectic therapist may not face any difficulties, but a nondirective Rogerian therapist may be uncomfortable with a technique as directive as PRT, just as a strict behaviorist may find a cognitive meditational technique foreign to him or her. Selection of a philosophically incongruous technique will not only strain the therapist, but may also create a lack of cohesion in the treatment package as a whole.

Once the therapist has identified the specific techniques which he or she might offer, the question of time commitment arises. Is the therapist able to see the client daily? Weekly? Monthly? Once only? What portion of the therapist's time is to be devoted to training in relaxation? Some relaxation techniques are very time-intensive (i.e., PRT, biofeedback), whereas others can be taught fairly quickly (Benson's approach) or by someone outside of the therapy situation (yoga).

There are also equipment considerations. In order to carry out biofeedback training, one must have biofeedback equipment! Most techniques require at least a quiet and private place with a comfortable chair—modest expectations, perhaps, but ones which might not be met in some institutional settings. Other considerations notwithstanding, it may be preferable to refer the psychiatric inpatient housed in a crowded dormitory to the Recreation Department for yoga, rather than embarking on the hopeless task of having him or her search for two 20-minute periods of solitude a day.

In the case of a therapist who provides services on a fee-for-service basis, ethical practice would dictate that the most cost-effective procedure should be selected. Regardless of the therapist's personal fascination with biofeedback, such a time-consuming and expensive procedure should be selected cautiously, and used only in cases in which a shorter form of treatment would clearly not suffice.

Finally, what other options are open to the therapist? It can be advantageous to have other sources of input into a comprehensive stress management program. If yoga and TM programs are available locally, if a biofeedback technician is employed by the agency, if the therapist in the next office conducts weekly group relaxation sessions, then the available options are increased.

The therapist who intends to include relaxation as one of his or her therapeutic tools needs to assess all these factors and to determine his or her own options independent of specific clients. Once these factors have been addressed, then the needs of a specific client can be addressed.

Client Characteristics

There are a number of considerations specific to the client which should be taken into account in selecting an appropriate treatment modality. The most obvious, of course, is the client's particular symptomatology. Although for most disorders there is no clear evidence of the superiority of one type of technique over another, some techniques have greater face validity or intuitive appeal for individuals with a given problem. Suggestions for dealing with six of the most frequently presented somatic problems are given below.

Headaches. Given the theoretical mechanism of tension headaches, one might logically predict that EMG biofeedback and progressive relaxation training would be the preferred choices for clients with tension headaches. Silver and Blanchard (1979) have reviewed the literature in this area and have concluded that both of these techniques are effective but that neither has a significant advantage over the other. Pinkerton, Hughes, and Wenrich (1982) suggest that a combination of the two might be more effective than either treatment alone.

Similarly, autogenic training with or without biofeedback is often considered to be the most effective treatment for migraine and other vascular headaches. However, the reviews by Pinkerton et al. (1982) and Beatty (1982) indicate that no differences have been consistently found among the different types of relaxation therapy when applied to migraines.

Blanchard and Andrasik (1985) suggest a hierarchical scheme of treatment for chronic headache sufferers. Regardless of the type of headache (tension or migraine) they propose beginning with a thorough (ten-session) course of abbreviated PRT. Those clients who do not show satisfactory improvement from this course of action then progress to the second level strategy, which is biofeedback. As recommended by the Biofeedback Society of America, EMG biofeedback is used in the case of tension headaches; thermal biofeedback in the case of vascular headaches. These authors recommend use of autogenic phrases in conjunction with thermal biofeedback. Suggested procedures for dealing with headache clients are given in detail in Blanchard and Andrasik (1985).

General Anxiety. A thorough review of all studies assessing the effect of the various relaxation strategies on anxiety would fill this entire volume—and would probably not shed a great deal of light on appropriate clinical procedures. There are three major points which can be drawn from the literature, however, and which should be kept in mind when treating anxious clients:

(1) All established methods do indeed produce significant changes in both clinical manifestations and self-reports of anxiety (viz. Mathews, 1982).

(2) The contemporary wisdom in selecting techniques is to try to match clients to treatments on the basis of the individual client's specific symptomatology, and the apparent focus of the techniques, as described earlier. Although this approach has good face validity (Schwartz et al., 1978), there is little empirical research to support it. Unfortunately, researchers tend to randomly assign subjects to treatments; therapists rarely do this.

(3) No relaxation treatment alone is very successful in dealing with severe anxiety problems. Raskin, Johnson, and Rondesvedt (1973) and LeBoeuf and Lodge (1980) have demonstrated that EMG biofeedback and PRT have minimal effect on anxiety neurosis. Other studies have noted a high dropout rate for severely anxious clients (Glueck & Stroebel, 1975; Lavallee et al., 1977). The therapist should be aware that the vast majority of studies investigating relaxation effects on anxiety have dealt with "normal" anxious subjects. Clinical populations do not fare as well as normal subjects when exposed to relaxation training. Multimodal approaches are generally the most effective for severely affected clients.

Gastrointestinal Problems. Much of the work that has been done in treating gastrointestinal disorders has involved direct biofeedback training of the affected area (i.e., teaching control of gastric acid production for ulcer patients; teaching anal sphincter control for fecal incontinence). While the results in this area are quite encouraging (Whitehead & Bosmajian, 1982), the methods and mechanics are often outside the capabilities of the average clinician.

There is also evidence that stress management packages, including relaxation components, may be effective. Schwartz, Blanchard, and Neff (1986), for example, found a combination of PRT and thermal biofeedback to be effective in treating clients with irritable bowel syndrome. Brooks and Richardson (1980) also found PRT to be part of an effective treatment package for duodenal ulcer.

Generally, the literature in this area is not sufficiently comprehensive to warrant any specific comments about the superiority of one technique over another. However, there is evidence to support the application of relaxation training procedures to clients with gastrointestinal disorders.

Insomnia. In a literature review of studies investigating various types of relaxation training applied to insomnia, Knapp, Downs, and Alperson (1976) concluded that "Almost any variant of relaxation training produces statistically significant reductions in latency to sleep onset and a reduction in the number of awakenings" (p. 623). This finding may actually be an oversimplification, since it appears that some treatments work better for some types of insomnia (Borkovec, 1979). Hauri (1981), for example, found that appropriate matching of subjects to specific biofeedback treatments increased treatment effectiveness substantially. Thus, combinations of treatments (logically) seem to offer the greatest chance of success. Lehrer and Woolfolk (1984) indicate that psychologically produced insomnia is probably the result of a number of factors, including somatic and cortical arousal, worry, conditioned anxiety, and operant reinforcement. If this is the case, it may be preferable to select treatment strategies on the basis of a thorough analysis of situational determinants, as well as by symptom identification.

Hypertension. McCaffrey and Blanchard (1985), in their review of stress management approaches to the treatment of hypertension, conclude that all relaxation methods seem to have a significant beneficial effect on hypertension, but that no one approach appears to be clearly superior to the others. Many studies have used combinations of treatments (consider Patel's 1984 study which found a combination of GSR biofeedback plus PRT plus meditation to be effective). McCaffrey and Blanchard also cite preliminary evidence that a combination of thermal biofeedback and autogenic training may be more effective than PRT, but this is not well established.

Interestingly, although it was through studies of hypertension that meditation entered the mainstream of psychological therapies, Pinkerton et al. (1982) point out that studies of the effects of meditation on hypertension have had less consistently positive results than studies of PRT.

Chronic Pain. Fordyce (1976) has described a comprehensive approach to the operant management of pain, which includes relaxation training. EMG biofeedback and PRT have been employed widely in this context; there are dozens of reports and studies of these techniques, which have been reviewed by Turner and Chapman (1982). These authors have expressed some concern that the popularization of EMG biofeedback in particular is not warranted, and that use of such methods may merely exacerbate the chronic pain patient's preoccupation with physiology and tendency to somatise his or her problems. However, Turk et al. (1979) conclude that biofeedback training is warranted and effective in some individuals, but that the mechanism remains elusive. (Here keep in mind the aforementioned limitations of most biofeedback studies.)

Because of the assumption that muscle tension is implicated in chronic pain, PRT has usually been selected as the relaxation method in chronic pain studies. Brownell (1984) points out that autogenic training and meditation may have a similar effect, but this is not well established in the literature. It should be noted that all comprehensive pain management programs also include a physical exercise component, geared at increasing flexibility and strength (Follick et al., 1985). For this reason, yoga may also be an appropriate choice.

Other Client Considerations. Clearly, even a specific diagnosis leaves the way open for a variety of interventions. There are a number of other factors which the therapist might take into account in making a choice.

Some are simple pragmatic concerns. How much time and money does the client have (particularly if cost is a factor)? Does he or she lose time from work (and thus money) to attend appointments? Is distance from the therapist a concern? Poor clients who live far away might best be given Benson's book and a few training sessions, which are generally sufficient for this technique, rather than having them embark on what is likely to turn out to be an inadequate trial of a more complicated method.

Conversely, one might try to avoid suggesting meditation-type techniques to women with small children or people who work rotating shifts. Meditation requires not only a strong commitment to keeping a daily schedule of practice, but also some assurance that the client will be left undisturbed for the required interval of time.

There may also be relevant personality dimensions to consider. Although this area is not well investigated, there is some suggestion that subjects high in internal locus of control may show better compliance in general with relaxation training (Lewis, Biglan, & Steinbock, 1978), but that relatively external subjects may benefit more from biofeedback training (Prager-Decker, 1979).

Related to personality is simply personal preference. The idea of TM or yoga just does not appeal to some clients, while others find this type of approach preferable to being caught up in the mental health system, with all its accompanying implications.

Intelligence and memory function should be assessed in any client who may be below the average range of functioning, such as individuals with neurological or neuropsychiatric disabilities. Success in PRT relies on the ability of the client to remember a fairly complex series of instructions and to perceive the accompanying physiological sensations. Although this has not been formally assessed, it seems likely that individuals of limited intellect or impaired memory function might have difficulty learning and remembering such a procedure.

Finally, it bears repeating that relaxation techniques do have a potentially significant physiological impact. Thus all prospective candidates for training should be carefully screened for any health problems which may be affected by these procedures. (There have been some anecdotal reports, for example, of diabetics who have become unstable after courses of relaxation training.) It may be wise to have all potential candidates screened by a physician.

CONCLUSIONS

It is usually not difficult to convince a stressed client that he or she needs to learn to relax. Many clients approach therapy for the express purpose of learning to relax. However, the apparent simplicity of the request should not mislead either the client or the therapist into thinking of relaxation as a simple technical procedure which can be carried out mechanically. In many ways, teaching relaxation is a more complex procedure for the therapist than it is for the client. The therapist must elicit from the client a detailed description of the client's own experience of the stress response, then attempt to obtain the proper "fit" among the client's symptoms, the therapist's capabilities, and the attributes of the various techniques. The therapist who merely masters one particular relaxation technique and applies it indiscriminantly will be at a disadvantage in serving a varied clientele.

Fortunately, there are a number of different relaxation approaches available to the therapist. Many of these are relatively well researched and have been demonstrated to be clinically effective. The question of differences among approaches is less clearly documented. It may be that future research will suggest that all approaches yield a common response, as Benson (1975) suggests. Conversely, it may be that the common element is supplemented by a distinctive approach-specific component, unique to each variant of relaxation training, as Schwartz et al. (1978) maintain. In either case, it is likely that the elements of style in each technique will have important implications for the outcome of therapy with an individual client. Regardless of the presence or absence of a unique effect for each technique, the approaches vary in the manner in which they approach the problem, the appeal they have for various types of clients, the length of time they take, and a host of other nonspecific therapy effects. These factors may be deemed to be "placebo" effects by some, but there is no doubt that they contribute significantly to the overall efficacy of therapy.

Complex as the task of matching techniques to clients may seem, it can be justified by the knowledge that most relaxation techniques are effective, and that learning to relax is a fundamental part of most stress management programs.

Below, the selection and application of specific techniques are discussed in the context of the three ongoing case studies.

CASE STUDIES

Cathy

Cathy returned to her group the following week, having completed the daily diary of stressful events as well as the Cues of Tension and Anxiety Questionnaire. As has been noted, Cathy did not consider herself to be under severe stress at any point during the recording interval. She had noted two moderately stressful events. First, she had to present a brief seminar in one of her advanced level courses; second, she had had an argument with her boyfriend. Cathy found it somewhat difficult to define the specific symptoms that she experienced in conjunction with these events. She had checked off a number of somatic symptoms on the Symptom Checklist, but felt that the list seemed to exaggerate her actual discomfort. She did clearly identify insomnia as a problem, since it had taken her several hours to get to sleep on the evenings prior to both of the identified events.

Finally, Cathy did note that although her subjective impression was that her own level of stress was not particularly high, she did tend to feel increasingly harassed and pressured over the course of the day, so that by evening she was usually feeling tense and somewhat uptight.

Although Cathy described a number of symptoms and problems which might benefit from her learning to relax, she did not appear to be in particular distress. Thus, she may have been reluctant to embark upon a course of treatment as complex as PRT or biofeedback, even though an approach such as either of these would certainly have helped her with some of the situation-specific stresses that she experienced. The possibility of seeking such treatments is also made somewhat less likely by the fact that she was attending a group program and thus would have to seek out an individual therapist to pursue such a course.

However, Cathy is reasonably well motivated, fairly bright, and relatively "internal" in terms of locus of control. Given these factors and her expressed concern over the general "downhill" course of her day, a meditation approach such as Benson's seemed most appropriate.

Fortunately for Cathy, this approach also seemed appropriate for several other members of her group, so the group leader went over the technique with the group, then handed out some printed material for them to review.

Over the next week, Cathy was able to practice the technique at least once daily, but found it difficult to push the irrelevant thoughts from her mind while meditating. At the next group meeting, she brought up this concern. The group spent some time discussing the necessity of achieving a passive attitude. As Cathy thought over the week, she concluded that she had been trying too hard and had been focused more toward striving than passivity. In addition, when the group practiced as a whole during that meeting, the group leader pointed out that Cathy tended to keep her fist clenched throughout the practice session.

Over the course of the following week, Cathy incorporated this new knowledge into her practice and found the technique to be more effective.

Jean

Since Jean's presenting complaint was headaches, it seemed appropriate to consider a technique which focused on muscular tension. However, from the intake information, it was also clear that most of Jean's distress did not come from her headaches, but from her frenetic life-style and her concerns about being a single parent. Thus, although Jean would probably benefit from a combination of PRT and biofeedback, it did not seem appropriate to devote the therapy time that would be required to teach this method when Jean had a greater need for time management and cognitive interventions.

It was suggested to Jean that she consider taking up yoga, both as a relaxation method and as a way of increasing her level of fitness in general. Although she agreed in principle, Jean was concerned about finding the time to participate in such a program, as well as about spending more time away from her children. She was amused when the therapist pointed out that these two concerns (time management and cognitive interpretations) were exactly the two items that they had identified as priorities. Although Jean appreciated the logic of the argument, she remained hesitant about committing herself to a course of action.

Jean and her therapist reached a compromise by deciding to begin working on time management and cognitive strategies, but to use the goal of enrolling in a yoga program as a medium for therapy. Jean agreed that once she could make available the necessary time and not feel overwhelmingly guilty about going out without her children, she would begin taking yoga. She also agreed to discuss this possibility with her family doctor on her next visit.

J. B.

J. B.'s meticulous and detailed diary revealed him to be a man who experienced sudden and dramatic mood shifts, many of which were quite predictable. The sources of friction over the recording period were threefold: arguments with his 16-year-old son; surprise visits from the out-of-town supervisor, and computer system breakdowns at work. His reaction to any of these situations was the same: he would experience generalized muscular tension, get red in the face, and "blow my top." Whenever two or more of these episodes occurred close together, he could be virtually assured that his ulcer would flare up. Although J. B. had been aware of this connection for some time, he regarded it as unalterable, since the problematic situations were (mostly) not under his control (he thought).

J. B. was extremely motivated to learn any type of physiological technique which would give him control over his own body. He had, in the past, attempted to learn TM, but found the slow pace and lack of immediate and concrete results frustrating. In contrast, he had read a little about biofeedback and had expressly asked about its appropriateness in his case. EMG biofeedback combined with PRT was suggested to him and was well received. Because of the flexibility he had in his own job, he was able to complete the first four sessions of training in a two-week period so that treatment got underway quickly. J. B. was extremely surprised to see the reaction of the biofeedback machine during the stress induction phase of the assessment. He was also somewhat frustrated by his inability to relax as quickly as he had expected. However, careful coaching permitted him to adopt a less aggressive attitude toward the training so that after the initial two weeks he was beginning to experience some positive changes.

Since he was now able to relax to some extent after only a few minutes, he was asked to begin utilizing the skill in troublesome situations. The first occasion arose when he had to confront his son about violating

166 Stress Management: An Integrated Approach to Therapy

an agreement that the two of them had made. J. B. was surprised and somewhat puzzled to discover that when he relaxed, much of the anger and hostility that he felt toward his son also abated. Unfortunately, J. B. felt that his anger and aggressive manner were necessary in order to keep his son "in line," and thus he questioned the wisdom of using the technique. This situation provided a good opportunity to begin working with J. B. on other skills related to interpersonal behavior.

7

Physiological Approaches to Managing Stress
Part II: Life-style Management

It should be obvious from Chapters 2 and 3 that the stress reaction places enormous demands on the physiological system of the individual. It makes sense to assume that the better the physiological condition of the individual, the better he or she will be able to withstand the adverse effects of stress (and thus remain healthy). For this reason, the notion of promoting a healthy life-style is an integral part of the practice of stress management.

The practice of health promotion is based on a number of assumptions, one of which is that certain behaviors increase the risk of certain diseases (Kaplin, 1984). This assumption is sufficiently well supported by available evidence to lead the Institute of Medicine of the National Academy of Sciences (1982) to implicate several individual behaviors in the cause and maintenance of disease states. Some of these disease states are among those listed in Chapter 3; in others, such as cancer, stress may play a less significant but nevertheless meaningful role in the etiology and progression of the disease.

For many diseases, direct links between faulty health life-style practices and the disease have been established. Diseases of the heart are related to smoking (Report of the Inter-Society Commission for Heart Disease Resources, 1972), inadequate physical activity (Paffenberger, Hale, Brand, & Hyde, 1977), and excessive caloric intake (Dawber, 1975). Cancers have been linked to smoking (Armstrong & Doll, 1974) and diet (Burkitt, Walker, & Painter, 1974). Cerebrovascular diseases are also related to smoking (Freis, 1976) and sodium intake (Kannel, 1971). Dietary factors are obviously related to diabetes and (again obviously) smoking is linked to respiratory disease.

In fact, evidence in favor of changing health life-style behaviors has been significant enough to have found its way into both the surgeon general's report on health promotion in the United States (Richmond, 1979) and *A New Perspective on the Health of Canadians* (Lalonde, 1974). These studies and actuarial data suggest that diet, exercise, cigarette smoking, and alcohol use are all related to excess mortality.

In the case of an individual who is also being adversely affected by stress, the potential consequences of faulty life-style are magnified. As will be discussed throughout this chapter, the individual who is experiencing the physiological effects of stress is already at somewhat of a health disadvantage. If he or she is also practicing health habits which are compromising the body's ability to endure and resist stress, the effect of stress may well be potentiated. Clearly, the stressed client would be well advised to participate in healthy life-style behaviors.

Management of life-style is most often an emotion-focused physiological coping strategy. As a rule, eating properly or exercising regularly will not change or eliminate the stressors in an individual's life (unless, of course, the stressor is a chronic disease which may be affected by life-style). Healthy life-style behavior may, however, reduce the intensity of the physiological aspects of the stress reaction, as well as moderating the effects of the reaction. In this chapter, the role of eating habits, exercise, cigarette smoking, and alcohol use in augmenting or reducing the effects of stress will be discussed. In each area of life-style, two questions will be addressed:

(1) What is the relationship between this behavior and stress?
(2) Which means are most effective for altering this behavior?

Before these questions are addressed, however, it is worth mentioning briefly the notion of health life-style in general.

HEALTH LIFE-STYLE: A UNITARY CONCEPT?

It is appealing to think that the above-noted behaviors comprise a single dimension or factor which might be called "life-style." Such an assumption implies that some individuals tend to live a healthy life-style, characterized by good eating habits, moderate alcohol intake, no smoking, and regular exercise. Other individuals, the "comprehensive slobs," would therefore be expected to display systematically poorer health behaviors, including poor eating habits, excess comsumption of alcohol and cigarettes, and no exercise. Although there are undoubtedly some individuals who fall into each of these camps, the tendency to be consistent across life-style behaviors is by no means universal. Langlie (1979), for example, has attempted to delineate two different types of individuals—"consistents," for whom preventive health behaviors are unidimensional or multidimensional, and "inconsistents," for whom behaviors are independent.

Research on the issue of consistency across health behaviors has yielded conflicting results. A variety of authors have addressed the question of the interrelationships among the health behaviors of interest here; the general conclusion must be that one cannot assume any consistency within individuals across behaviors (Cotton, 1986; Williams & Wechsler, 1972; Harris & Guten, 1979; Kannas, 1981; Tapp & Goldenthal, 1982; Norman, 1985).

What do these findings mean for the stress therapist? Primarily, they suggest that health life-style behaviors must be assumed to be independent, and therefore must be assessed independently. It would be unwise to assume that a smoker, for example, is generally negligent about his or her health and therefore must also eat poorly and drink to excess. Similarly, it would not necessarily be wise to assume that a militant and vocal anti-smoker is equally virtuous in other life-style areas. For the purposes of assessment and treatment, each behavior of interest is best dealt with separately.

Having offered these caveats, however, there are two relationships which are fairly well established—relationships of which the therapist should be aware.

The first of these is the positive relationship between alcohol use and cigarette smoking. It is well known (and demonstrated in the above-noted studies) that individuals who drink also tend to smoke. Not only do these two behaviors often occur in the same individuals, but they also tend to occur in close proximity in time. The therapist attempting to address either of these behaviors may want to consider it in relation to the other.

The second relationship to note is that of eating habits and weight. Contrary to popular wisdom (and the relentless dictum of the popular media) these two are *not* related (Cotton, 1986; Williams, Martin, & Foreyt, 1976). Studies have consistently failed to link weight to amount eaten or any of the topographical variables accompanying eating. The therapist who assumes that his or her overweight clients have poor eating habits and that normal weight clients have good eating habits is making an unwarranted (and often invalid) assumption.

The task of the therapist is therefore to assume, by and large, that each health life-style behavior occurs independently, but to remain alert to the possibility of interactions between behaviors in some clients.

EXERCISE AND STRESS

It is probably not entirely coincidental that the rise in frequency of stress problems in the twentieth century has occurred simultaneously with a fall in the level of physical activity. The relatively low level of physical activity of most members of contemporary society may also account for the dramatic increase in the amount of obesity in the population, despite an overall decrease in caloric consumption (Brownell, 1982c).

Although it is difficult to provide definitive cause-and-effect support for claims of a relationship between exercise and reduced risk of problems such as heart disease, it certainly appears that exercise is associated with decreased risk. The most prominent effects of exercise have been found to be on blood pressure, coronary efficiency levels, plasma insulin levels, and plasma lipid and lipoprotein levels (Brownell, 1982b). At least the first two of these have clear implications in the area of stress management. It may be that exercise can moderate or offset the potentially deleterious effects of stress on cardiac function and blood pressure. Targan, Britvan, and Dorey (1981) have also suggested that physical exercise can affect some immunological functions, functions which may in turn be adversely affected by stress (Rogers, Dubey, & Reich, 1979).

Fitness and Response to Stress

The relationship between life stresses and pathology is well documented, but may be moderated by a number of variables. One of the potential moderator variables is physical exercise. Some studies have indicated that aerobic exercise engenders more adaptive physiological responses to specific laboratory stresses. Sinyor et al. (1983), for example, found that individuals who trained in aerobic activities tended to recover more quickly, both in terms of heart rate and in ratings of anxiety, than did untrained subjects, when exposed to a series of psychosocial stress situations in the laboratory.

Roth and Holmes (1985) took this relationship one step further, to determine whether or not physical fitness affected the relationship between stressful life events and subsequent illness. Their results confirmed that physical fitness did act as a reliable moderator variable in the stress-illness relationship. Of those individuals in the study who had experienced high levels of stress, those individuals with relatively low levels of physical fitness developed more problems with both physical health and depression. Similarly, Kobasa, Maddi, and Puccetti (1982) found that male business executives who exercised regularly reported less illness in reaction to stressful life events than did executives who did not exercise.

This evidence suggests that aerobically fit individuals are more resistant to the physiological and psychological effects of stress, and that aerobically fit individuals may recover more quickly from stress.

It would be logical therefore to assume that increasing an individual's level of fitness would increase his or her stress tolerance. Evidence in this area remains equivocal. Sinyor et al. (1986) assigned subjects to aerobic, anaerobic, or waiting list control groups for 10 weeks, and did not find group differences on laboratory or self-report measures in response to stressors induced in the laboratory. On the other hand, Roth and Holmes (1987) compared the effects of aerobic exercise to those of relaxation training in a group of highly stressed individuals and found that exercise was useful for reducing depression, but did not alter physical symptoms. Holmes and McGilley (1987) found that aerobic exercise did result in reduced heart rate response to stressors in previously low-fit subjects, but fitness training did not influence the subjective response to stress. Hughes et al. (1986) also reported that in a group of sedentary males who displayed no initial psychopathology, exercise did not result in change in any of a number of psychological functions, including anger, tension, confusion, depression, fatigue, vigor, or total mood disturbance.

The results of these studies and others suggest that simply sending the stressed client off to the local "Y" may not be particularly effective. The initial evidence of reduced responsivity to stress may be related to some characteristic inherent in individuals who are fit, or who choose to become fit. Differences in the effects of training may also be attributable to differences in the type or length of training, or age or sex differences. Of the latter four studies mentioned, two employed men only (Sinyor et al., 1986 and Hughes et al., 1986); one employed only female subjects (Holmes & McGilley, 1987); and the fourth used half males and half females (Roth & Holmes, 1987).

It is worth noting that the supposed relationship between exercise and changes in mood is still not particularly well established empirically. Folkins and Sime (1981) have pointed out that while there are many studies which have associated fitness training with improvement in mood, the design of these studies is typically poor, rendering the conclusion tentative. Nevertheless, the consistent findings of reductions in anxiety and depression are impressive. McCann and Holmes (1984) did demonstrate the positive effects of aerobic exercise on depression in a well-controlled study of depressed women.

Clearly, the verdict is not yet in, as far as the effect of exercise in regard to stress is concerned. It appears that in some individuals, at some times, exercise does play a role in altering the response to stress. Studies with clinically depressed subjects tend to be more supportive of this relationship, which suggests that a ceiling effect may be operative. Finally, it is worth remembering that exercise is only one part of a comprehensive stress management program. As Roskies et al. (1986) observed, exercise alone is not as effective as a cognitive-behavioral stress management program.

Implementing Exercise Programs: The Problem of Adherence

On the surface, the steps toward implementing an exercise program for a client appear simple. A complete physical examination should indicate the level and type of exercise appropriate for the individual. A review of local facilities and programs will help determine what appeals to the client, is affordable, convenient, and available. The problem is not finding or starting an exercise program, but rather adhering to one. Brownell (1982b) estimates that attrition from exercise programs averages at least 50% after six months. Even among individuals who should be particularly well motivated to participate (e.g., cardiac patients), the rate of participation is not significantly better (Sanne, 1973; Wilhelmsen et al. 1975; Oldridge et al., 1978; Oldridge, 1979). The problem with exercising does not seem to be one of lack of conviction. Most people seem to believe that regular exercise will decrease their likelihood of disease (Cotton, 1986).

Martin and Dubbert (1982a) suggest that the most likely candidate for successful participation in an exercise program is "a white collar non-smoker with an active job and leisure pursuits, higher 'self-motivation' and an actively supportive spouse, who lives or works close to the place of exercise, where he exercises at a moderate intensity, with others" (p. 17). Conversely, a likely candidate for dropout from exercise is "an overweight blue-collar smoker with an inactive job and leisure pursuits, with low 'self-motivation,' and a spouse who is indifferent toward his exercise participation, who lives/works farther away from the exercise facility, and who exercises infrequently, alone, and at high intensity" (p. 17).

From retrospective data, smoking seems to be one of the most reliable predictors of exercise adherence; it is associated with both lower enrollment and higher dropout rates in exercise programs (Martin & Dubbert, 1982b).

A number of studies have attempted to manipulate and maximize adherence to exercise programs by behavioral means. These are summarized in Martin and Dubbert (1982b), Martin et al. (1984), and Brownell (1982b), and suggest the following strategies:

Reinforcement Control. This approach involves the manipulation of the consequences of exercising. In some studies, participants have deposited personal items to be earned back over time; participated in attendance lotteries; obtained the return of part of a monetary deposit; or received individual praise and feedback from instructors.

Stimulus Control. Posting reminders to exercise and having health clubs telephone participants tend to increase compliance. It is also useful to include the individual in the design and planning of his or her own exercise program, and to encourage input from the participant, thus creating the belief that individual preferences were taken into account.

Cognitive Self-Monitoring Approaches. Self-contracting and goal-setting, self-reward, and distraction/dissociation strategies have been effective.

Martin et al. (1984) suggest that instructor praise and feedback, flexible goal-setting (i.e., participants determining their own goals rather than following an arbitrary schedule of times and/or distances), and training in distraction/dissociation-based cognitive strategies have proven most efficient.

There are, of course, alternatives to participation in formal exercise programs. Physical activity can be introduced as a part of life-style. Although changing life-style activity patterns is not apt to provide as much benefit as a formal exercise program, it may be more practical and more likely to succeed. Charlesworth and Nathan (1984) suggest several ways of increasing life-style activity, including

- using stairs instead of elevators
- standing instead of sitting
- walking via a circuitous route
- parking the car farther from the destination and walking
- walking a pet farther or more often
- walking instead of taking a golf cart when golfing
- taking a walk during coffee break

To Exercise or Not to Exercise

Given the limited and contradictory evidence for the efficacy of exercise is ameliorating the effects of stress, and given the high probability of dropout from exercise programs, is it worth bothering to encourage exercise programs in stressed clients? There is no easy answer to this question, but it might be useful to respond with another series of questions that the therapist can ask about the individual client:

(1) Are there other physical or medical conditions that make exercise more (or less) desirable? The client with cardiac problems, hypertension, or asthma may well be advised to exercise regardless of his or her stress status. A physician should be able to advise such clients.

(2) Is the client motivated to exercise? Almost everyone pays lip service to the benefits of exercise, but the motivation actually to exercise is important.

(3) Is it practical and realistic for the client to exercise? Are there convenient and affordable facilities available? Is time a problem?

(4) Does the client possess any of the attributes of the "likely to adhere" person?

(5) How many other behaviors is the client trying to change, and how important is exercise in relation to the other behaviors?

(6) Is the behavior likely to be reinforced by social supports?

Only by weighing the responses to questions such as these can the therapist and client make an informed choice about the role exercise is to play in the client's life.

EATING HABITS

The relationship between stress and eating habits is a multifaceted one. First, proper nutrition is important in maintaining the body in optimal form, and in maximizing the body's resistance to stress. Second, stress may affect nutrient needs in specific ways which require alternation in diet. Third, when obesity is a problem, resistance to disease may be decreased and the potential for stress-related disease increased. Fourth, many people vary their eating habits when they are under stress; they may overeat, undereat, or simply alter their eating habits. Fifth, some eating disorders are stressors in themselves, such as anorexia nervosa and bulimia nervosa. Discussion of the fifth area is out-side the scope of stress management, but the other four areas are of direct concern to the stress therapist.

Nutrition and Stress

On a superficial level, it makes sense that a person who has sufficient intake of all basic nutrients will be in a better position to resist or tolerate the adverse effects of stress. This premise is supported by findings that indicate that under stress, a variety of changes in metabolism occur, including increased protein breakdown, decreases in insulin action, con-servation of sodium, and increased glucose synthesis (Berdanier, 1987). It follows that the body is best prepared to handle stress if there are adequate stores of all nutrients. Long-term undernutrition has been shown to affect the ability to handle stress. Barrett and Radke-Yarrow (1985) were able to demonstrate differences in how children reacted to moderately stressful situations as a function of nutritional supplementa-tion. McKinney and White (1985) also noted that those individuals who showed the greatest reaction to stress in terms of catecholamine levels tended to eat poorly, and were therefore not replenishing nutrient stores as needed.

Stress does appear to have some specific effects on nutritional status. The general increase in metabolism accompanying the stress response creates an additional need for B complex vitamins, especially thiamine and riboflavin. If protein use is increased, there is greater calcium use and increased need for pyroxidine. Water and sodium tend to be con-served, but potassium is lost (Edwards, 1987). Some literature also sug-gests that increases in phosphorus, zinc, vitamin A, vitamin C, and niacin may be indicated, although the extent of the need remains unclear (Berdanier, 1987).

Deficits of vitamins and other nutrients may also result in impaired immune response, which may already be compromised by the direct effects of stress. The combined effect results in poorer resistance to infection and disease (Edwards, 1987).

There are also indirect relationships between stress and nutrition. There are a number of studies which have documented the relationship between nutritional status and certain aspects of brain function and behavior. Some vitamins and minerals are required as cofactors for neurotransmitter function; these include iron, copper, zinc, thiamine, pyroxidine, and ascorbic acid. Behavioral changes in motor activity, ag-gression, and escape/avoidance behavior have been demonstrated in response to tyrosine supplementation. Other amino acids also seem to affect the response to stress and may affect symptoms such as insomnia and tension (Chapman & Greenwood, 1987). The individual who is under stress needs to think clearly and efficiently, and to be in control of his or her own behavior. Nutrient deficiencies which in themselves contribute to muddy thinking, aggressive or avoidant behavior, and related problems will only compound the stress problem.

Chapman and Greenwood (1987) also report that there are potentially both positive and negative effects from making nutritional adjustments. Drinking hot milk before bed can aid in sleeping; high-carbohydrate meals can bring about the decrements observed in reaction time tasks; nursing home patients have demonstrated improved functioning when they are given nutritional supplements.

Finally, some food substances can produce a stress-like effect in themselves. Items such as colas, coffee, tea, and chocolate, which contain caffeine, may mimic sympathetic nervous system activity; thus, they are called sympathomimetics (Greenberg, 1987). Sympathomimetics not only create a pseudostress response, but they also make the nervous system more reactive and thus more likely to react to stressors. Nicotine (found in tobacco) and theobromine and theophylline (found in tea) are also sympathomimetics.

Research on nutrition and stress is still in its early stages; most of the findings described above do not have clear implications for coping with stress through dietary manipulation. Nevertheless, the evidence does suggest that an adequate, balanced, and complete diet is essential for maximizing the performance and resistance to stress for any individual. It is even more important for the stressed client. As Edwards (1987) points out, "The prudent approach for the practicing health professional treating a stress-related disorder is to be aware that good nutritional status is a component of care" (p. 7).

Eating Under Stress

There is little doubt that significant changes in affect, particularly anxiety and depression, often lead to changes in eating habits. Certainly many weight control plans—both for the overweight and for anorexics—focus on the assessment of the relationship between emotional arousal and food intake. Leon and Roth (1977), for example, proposed that eating is an instrumental behavior which seems to reduce anxiety. Although there is dispute about the mechanism involved, the clinical literature certainly demonstrates an association between arousal and increased eating behavior. Similarly, a loss of appetite or decrease in eating behavior is often pathognomonic of depression.

Since anxiety and depression are often symptomatic of stress, it follows that stress is often associated with changes in eating habits.

Ruderman (1986) has examined the notion of dietary restraint, which suggests that some people—obese, normal weight, and underweight alike—consciously eat less than their physiological drives direct them to eat. These individuals, who are referred to as "restrained eaters," display eating habits which are influenced both by physiological factors prompting the desire for food and by their own efforts to resist that desire (Herman & Polivy, 1980). When the self-control of restrained eaters is interfered with for some reason, the physiological drive for food prevails and large quantities of food may be consumed. One type of interference that the restrained eater may face is the emotional disinhibitor, such as anxiety or depression.

Ruderman (1986) has reviewed the literature examining the relationship between emotional arousal and eating behavior. This relationship is complex: changes in eating habits vary depending upon whether the eater is restrained or unrestrained, whether the mood is positive or negative, and whether arousal is strong or weak. However, it is important to note that although the direction of the response varied in different studies, emotional arousal did bring about changes in eating habits.

There are also nutritional reasons why eating habits may change under stress. In the initial stages of stress, the increase in metabolic rate may require that caloric intake increase significantly; individuals experiencing severe stress may require increases up to 200% in caloric intake (Berdanier, 1987). Protein consumption may also increase. Immediately following periods of stress, cortisol serves to induce an increase in the production of enzymes important for fat synthesis. Thus, fat synthesis is enhanced and the individual becomes more efficient in his or her use of food eaten. If appetite remains good, the individual may actually be slightly fatter than before the stress began. Over a lifetime, the stressed individual may have a little less body protein and a little more body fat. One might argue that this is Mother Nature's way of ensuring that we have adequate energy stores to meet future stresses (Berdanier, 1987).

Obesity

It is difficult to devote a section to eating habits without addressing the issue of obesity. However, obesity may have little to do with eating habits. In addition, it is not clear whether or not obesity has an effect on stress tolerance or whether it contributes to disease at all.

At a grossly superficial level, one might make the same argument in regard to the relationship between obesity and stress that one makes for the relationships among exercise, eating habits in general, smoking, and stress; that is, the fitter and healthier the body, the more likely it is to resist the negative effects of the stress response. Unfortunately, in the case of obesity, the definition of "healthy" is not clear. A clinically "obese" individual may have good nutritional eating habits, and may be aerobically and muscularly fit. The notion of obesity unfortunately tends to convey more information about the distorted standards that our society advocates than about the health of the individual.

Obesity seems to be the function of a number of factors, including metabolism, heredity, eating habits, and exercise level. The implications of the latter two areas in regard to stress have already been discussed. Are there additional concerns related to size only (separate from eating habits and exercise) which relate to stress management? Of two individuals with comparable eating habits and exercise routines, is the heavier one at greater risk for stress-related disorders than the lighter one?

The answer to these questions is not clear. Andres (1980) has reviewed a number of epidemiological studies and has concluded that no relationship exists between obesity and mortality in individuals who are less than 30% overweight. Brownell (1982c) however points to evidence that obesity does greatly increase the likelihood of hypertension, hyperlipidemia, and diabetes, thereby creating an additional risk through this association. There are much clearer indications of risk for markedly overweight individuals, particularly those 50% or more overweight; these individuals seem to be at risk for heart disease and various cancers.

In the case of individuals who are 0 to 30% overweight, it is not clear that weight is associated with increased health problems. In fact, Brownell (1982c) cites evidence that lower weights may actually increase the risk of some diseases related to life-style.

An additional concern in relation to obesity is the difficulty and relative futility of dieting. In spite of the major strides made in the field of behavior therapy, weight loss programs are still difficult at best, and recidivism of 75% to 100% of initial weight loss is common (Jeffrey, 1987). These are sobering facts, and ones which must be considered seriously before embarking on a weight loss program.

One of the difficulties in ignoring the moderately overweight status of a stressed client is that concern about weight may be a stressor in itself. (It is listed on the Hassles Scale, for example.) However, cognitive therapy directed at the irrational weight expectations may be more effective in the long run than losing and regaining those few pounds one more time!

The most useful strategy for dealing with obesity in the context of stress management is to observe the following points:

(1) Weight loss per se should be considered primarily for those individuals who are significantly (more than 30%) overweight, or those who suffer from an illness related to their weight.
(2) In moderately overweight subjects, attention might better be directed to identifying
  • nutritional eating habits
  • exercise habits
  • beliefs about weight and body size.

Interventions may be directed at any of these areas if deficiencies are evident. In other cases, it may be most appropriate not to consider weight an issue.

Management of Eating Habits

Interestingly, there has been little attention paid to the issue of improving eating habits for nutritional purposes (as opposed to improving them for weight-control purposes). The most common method of addressing nutrition is through public health programs and general information dissemination.

Some interest in the development of nutritional eating habits comes from work in the area of diet compliance for individuals with medically indicated diets for diseases such as diabetes (Hamburg et al., 1979). In general, the following strategies may be useful:

Information. The practice of good eating habits presupposes a basic understanding of the elements of a good diet. Obvious as it may seem, many adults remain unaware of basic nutritional facts. Others may have difficulty translating this knowledge into functional behavior, particularly when eating away from home. Most dieticians and public health facilities can provide this information.

Self-monitoring. Almost any modification of eating habits requires that a record of what is eaten, when, where, with whom, and why be kept. Although self-monitoring procedures were initially developed as measurement tools, they are also very effective parts of any program to modify eating habits. In some cases, the act of recording is sufficient to alter the behavior in question.

Stimulus Control. Stimulus control techniques are those which attempt to isolate eating behavior from other activities or situations. Eating only at particular times and in particular places is helpful, as is stocking only healthy foods and keeping "junk" either out of the house or out of sight.

Social Support. It is hard to have a salad when your spouse is offering you chocolate cake. Familial reinforcement of proper eating habits is helpful.

Reinforcers. Built-in reinforcers will maximize the probability of adhering to any eating plan.

CIGARETTE SMOKING

Cigarette smoking is not good for you, and most of the population is now aware of this fact. Smoking prevalence is currently at its lowest point in 30 years, as is per capita consumption of cigarettes (Shopland & Brown, 1985). Even among those who smoke, the dangers inherent in the practice are generally recognized (Cotton, 1988). There is little doubt that smoking is related to heart disease, lung and other cancers, stroke, obstructive lung disease, low birthweight babies, and increased absenteeism from work and school. The potential links with stress are evident. The stress reaction places significant demands on the cardiovascular system, the immune system, and the respiratory system. The additional burden of impairment from cigarette smoking magnifies the risk of stress-related illness; in an individual already compromised by smoking, the stress reaction can more easily do harm.

There are also more specific relationships between smoking and stress. As mentioned earlier, nicotine is a sympathomimetic, and thus contributes to a general increase in arousal. In spite of the subjective impression of many smokers that a cigarette relaxes them, it may in fact have the opposite effect. Woodson et al. (1986) observed that in spite of the fact that their female subjects reported decreased levels of stress when they smoked, there were measurable increases in heart rate and vasoconstriction.

Many factors contribute to the initiation, maintenance, and cessation of smoking (Brownell, 1982c) and one of these is stress. Hadaway,

Beyerstein, and Kimball (1986) demonstrated that in spite of the negative health consequences it presents, smoking is often utilized as a functional behavior, an adaptive response to stressful situations. Factor analytic studies indicate that among other reasons, people smoke to reduce tension or anxiety, and to help themselves deal with social anxieties (Leventhal & Cleary, 1980). In addition, the act of stopping smoking can create a great deal of stress, by virtue of both the physiological withdrawal symptoms and the habit's strength. Clearly, in the short run, the least stressful option is to keep smoking! Unfortunately, in the long run, this is the least healthful option.

The stress therapist is in a difficult position in advising a client who smokes. Although the health implications for stopping are significant and obvious, the act of stopping is difficult in the short run and may increase stress temporarily. Many people who try to quit are unsuccessful, even with therapeutic intervention. (It is worth noting that about 95% of those who eventually stop smoking do so on their own, without aid of a formal cessation program (Lichtenstein, 1982). In general, the therapist might consider the following guidelines for advising clients who smoke:

(1) Ensure that the client is aware of the health hazards of smoking, and in particular is aware of the additional risk in conjunction with stress.

(2) Avoid trying to horrify the client into stopping by graphically depicting diseased lungs and other unpleasantries. In a smoker, such vivid information leads to cognitive dissonance and thus dismissal of the information at hand.

(3) Delay dealing with the smoking issue if the client is currently in a period of acute stress; the likelihood of success at such times is decreased.

(4) Modify only one aspect of life-style at a time. The client who decides to quit smoking, start exercising, and adjust his or her eating habits simultaneously is creating a greater risk of failure.

(5) If the timing is right and the client is motivated, encourage him or her to quit on his or her own, but provide constant reinforcement and support. (This is not necessarily the approach to be recommended in general for all people who want to quit smoking. However, in the case of stress management, it is assumed that there are a number of other changes and goals operative in therapy, which might preclude devoting a great deal of therapy time to smoking cessation strategies.)

(6) If the client fails, or has failed a number of times on his or her own in the past, consider implementing behavioral change strategies or referring to a specific smoking cessation program.

Behavioral Approaches to Smoking Cessation

Cigarette smoking is a problem particularly suitable for treatment from a behavioral perspective. Behavioral approaches to smoking cessation approach smoking as an overlearned habit which should be reactive to standard conditioning or contingency management procedures (Lichtenstein, 1982). In general, behaviorally oriented strategies are among the most successful strategies for smoking cessation. Below, some of the basic behavioral approaches are described.

Self-management Procedures. In self-management procedures, smokers are taught to identify the cues associated with smoking, and then to alter or avoid such cues, as well as to alter the reinforcers of smoking behavior. Specific strategies include self-monitoring (recording the time, place, and situation in which smoking occurs); contingency contracting; stimulus control; and relaxation training. Unfortunately, none of these strategies seems to be particularly successful individually. However, encouraging results emerge from multicomponent packages which include self-management methods (Kamarck & Lichtenstein, 1985).

Aversion Strategies. Three major types of aversive conditioning have been discussed in the literature: electric shock, imaginal stimuli, and cigarette smoke itself. The first two of these are now generally regarded as ineffective (Kamarck & Lichtenstein, 1985; Lichtenstein, 1982). The third method, developing an aversion to cigarette smoke itself, has shown some positive results. Two techniques have emerged from this line of research:

Satiation. This is a take-home procedure in which the client doubles or triples his or her baseline level of cigarette smoking. This technique appears promising, and is convenient to use. Unfortunately, it is difficult to monitor accurately, so results are inconclusive (Kamarack & Lichtenstein, 1985).

Rapid smoking. In this laboratory or clinic technique, the subject smokes continually, usually inhaling every six to eight seconds until tolerance is reached. Research on this method is generally but not overwhelmingly supportive. It appears to work best in conjunction with a multicomponent package.

A major concern with the rapid smoking techniques is the risk of cardiovascular complications. However, in spite of some observed irregularities in electrocardiogram recordings, no known serious consequences and few notable side effects have been reported. It is probably safe and beneficial in healthy individuals but should only be administered to clients with cardiovascular or respiratory disease under the guidance of a physician (Lichtenstein, 1982).

Additional Techniques for Smoking Cessation

Nicotine Fading. In this procedure, clients gradually switch to brands with less nicotine until they reduce their nicotine consumption by about 90%. Self-monitoring of tar and nicotine levels is usually part of the process. Nicotine fading can be used in cases in which clients are resistant to stopping altogether but would like to reduce the health hazard, or in clients who seem unable to stop by other means. Initial concerns that decreases in per-cigarette nicotine would result in a higher number of cigarettes being consumed have not been borne out (Brownell, 1982a).

Nicotine Chewing Gum. In contrast to nicotine fading, which reduces nicotine in the system, nicotine gum is intended to replace nicotine from cigarettes with nicotine in a less harmful and less addictive form. Once cessation of smoking behavior has occurred, withdrawal from the gum can be addressed. Again, this approach may be most effective as part of a combined gum and behavior-control program (Hall et al., 1985; Russell & Jarvis, 1985; Killen et al., 1984).

Social Support. Although little research in this area has been conducted, there is general agreement that social support is important, and should be a component of any multifaceted treatment program.

Programs Outside of the Therapeutic Relationship. There are a number of both commercial and nonprofit programs which are aimed at smokers. For the client whose therapeutic relationship revolves around the broader issue of stress management (or whose therapist knows nothing about smoking cessation) an outside intervention may be attractive. It is impossible to summarize these programs here. Some are costly; some free. Some are self-directed, self-help leaflets; others are programmed group activities. Some rely heavily on behavioral principles; others employ hypnosis, religion, or group pressure to achieve results. There are also increasing numbers of worksite programs available. Some physicians also participate in delivering interventions of this sort (past the level of giving advice not to smoke).

There is probably no "best" or "most effective" means of stopping smoking. However, given the number of currently available strategies and programs, a determined client should be able to find assistance that meets his or her needs.

ALCOHOL CONSUMPTION

Psychopharmacologically, alcohol is a nonselective general depressant. In structure and in its effect on the central nervous system, alcohol acts indistinguishably from other CNS depressants such as diazepam, chlordiazepoxide, and phenobarbitol (Estes & Heineman, 1986). For the stressed (and thus physiologically aroused) individual, this may be a desirable effect. Alcohol reduces anxiety—at least this is the subjective impression of those who drink. Drinkers typically report that tension reduction, a smoothing out of interpersonal irritants, and a distancing from problems are all benefits of alcohol ingestion (Cohen, 1983).

For the 90% of all drinkers who drink only socially and who are able to control their drinking, the subjective impression of anxiety reduction is not a problem. But for the remaining 10%, the relationship between drinking and anxiety reduction is indeed problematic. There are a number of reasons why drinkers become alcoholics; stress is one of them.

One of the most well-known lines of research into alcoholism has investigated the tension-reduction hypothesis. This hypothesis holds that alcoholics, when compared to normal drinkers, may have different baseline levels of anxiety, and that alcohol may have a differential effect in reducing tension for alcoholics (Estes & Heineman, 1986). Since 93% of all alcoholics can be classed as "escape drinkers"—that is, individuals who drink to escape unpleasant feelings or situations (Farber, Khavari, & Douglas, 1980)—there is clearly some support for the role of anxiety in alcohol comsumption.

Studies on alcohol intake following stress yield mixed findings. In Brownell's (1982a) review of studies in this area, it is apparent that some (but not all) drinkers increase their alcohol intake under some (but not all) situations of stress. The research on stress or level of arousal following intake is also not conclusive. Depending upon what aspect of the stress reaction is measured and whether it is measured objectively or subjectively, the results vary. Results also vary depending upon whether high or low dosages of alcohol are ingested. There is additional evidence that problem drinkers may have experienced an increased number of life stresses (Bell et al., 1976). Allan and Cooke (1985) have examined the evidence that life stresses play a particularly significant role in the etiology of alcoholism in women, but have concluded that such evidence is weak; that is, although it appears that stress creates increases in alcohol consumption in many people, it does not necessarily play more of a role in the case of women than men. (This popularly held belief seems to derive from the days in which alcohol consumption for women in general was much lower than at present.)

There is also general evidence that sociocultural factors that produce stress for members of a particular group will also result in increased alcohol consumption among members of that group. Zales (1985) cites evidence that both stressful conditions and stressful events did indeed result in increased rates of alcohol consumption in specific target groups.

In summary, many people experience a subjective decrease in the level of anxiety when they drink. Thus, people may drink more when they are under stress. For individuals who for other reasons are likely to become alcoholic, life stresses may precipitate the move from drinker to alcoholic. There is also evidence that some alcoholics may lack sufficient stress management skills to prevent their chronic abuse of alcohol.

Alcohol Consumption and Stress Management

To some extent, drinking is a satisfactory short-term solution to the problem of stress. It provides immediate relief, with few side effects or dangers. Unfortunately, in the longer run, use of alcohol as a mechanism for reducing stress often leads to increasing consumption, cognitive impairment, illness, family and job difficulties, and addiction. It also reduces the individual's level of self-control, leading to increased use of tobacco and other drugs, poorer eating habits, and less adaptive coping.

The role of the stress therapist is therefore to assure that drinkers do not progress to alcoholics, and to ensure that alcoholics receive treatment for alcoholism, not just for stress. It may be that stress plays a part in the alcoholic's problems, and that some stress management techniques may be of benefit to the alcoholic. Nevertheless, the primary problem of an alcoholic is drinking, not stress, and treatment should be directed accordingly.

Changing Drinking Habits

For the individual who would like to alter his or her drinking habits but who is not an alcoholic, any of the behavior change strategies discussed in Chapter 9 should be useful. For a nonaddicted person, alcohol consumption is much like any other behavior, and can be changed accordingly. For the true alcoholic, however, the situation is much more difficult and requires specialized assistance. It is beyond the scope of the present discussion to review the treatment literature on alcoholism. Should the stress therapist suspect that a bona fide alcohol problem exists, he or she would be well advised to refer to the client to an alcohol treatment facility (unless the therapist already has specialized expertise in that area).

FINAL COMMENTS ON LIFE-STYLE AND STRESS MANAGEMENT

A poor health life-style increases the body's vulnerability to stress; stress increases one's likelihood of engaging in unhealthful life-style behaviors. The relationship is obviously somewhat circular. One of the jobs of the stress therapist is to evaluate and clarify the relationship between stress and a given life-style behavior. In some cases, this task may amount to trying to solve a chicken-and-egg problem.

In conjunction with stress management, the therapist should of course attempt to encourage and facilitate healthful life-style behavior. However, the therapist should also remain aware of serious primary disturbances in life-style in a client who presents for stress management. Individuals who exhibit major problems in life-style, such as eating disorders or alcoholism, should have these problems assessed independently of the stress problem.

Finally, it is worth remembering that life-style behaviors are exceedingly difficult to change. In view of this difficulty, other areas related to stress may be easier to address initially. The potential gains of changing life-style behaviors must be weighed against the likelihood of success in each particular case. When and if life-style behaviors are addressed, only one major change at a time should be considered.

CASE STUDIES

Health life-style issues do not actually play a major role in any of the three cases being followed in this book. This is often the case when the client is experiencing acute stress-related problems. Since the effect of proper (or improper) life-style is often a long-term cumulative effect, direct intervention in life-style rarely has a significant immediate effect. The exception to this is, of course, those individuals who are experiencing disorders which are directly related to life-style behaviors (e.g., chronic bronchitis in a smoker).

Cathy

Life-style issues were dealt with only briefly in the sixth session of Cathy's program, along with other behavioral change issues. Cathy's life-style is generally not particularly unhealthful. She eats reasonably, does not smoke, and drinks moderately. She has expressed concern about her lack of regular physical activity, but is ambivalent about making a serious commitment to exercise regularly. She did state that she found the information about the mechanisms linking stress and life-style very helpful; although she had previously been aware that life-style was important, she had not known exactly why this was so.

Jean

None of the health life-style issues have emerged as being particularly important in Jean's life. She does not smoke, drinks moderately, and is reasonably conscientious about nutritional eating. Like Cathy, she does not participate in a regular exercise program. However, given the time constraints that Jean is currently experiencing, and the number of other areas of intervention which have been identified as priorities, the issue of exercise does not seem particularly important at present, and is not included in the current plan.

J. B.

J. B. is one for whom life-style issues seem much more salient. The initial recordings in his personal diary suggest that eating habits are certainly a significant factor in his ulcer flare-ups. In addition, he does not exercise. It is not yet clear whether J. B. has a problem with alcohol. He acknowledges having one or two drinks per day, but the subject has not been pursued further. In many ways, J. B. is an ideal candidate for life-style intervention. Unfortunately, he has also made it quite clear that he is not interested in altering his health life-style at present.

Clients such as J. B. place the therapist in a quandary. Given the role that life-style habits probably play in his life, it seems questionable to ignore them. On the other hand, they are clearly not a priority in J. B.'s agenda. The decision discussed in Chapter 5 is probably the best compromise. J. B.'s major concerns (relaxation training and family issues) will be addressed first. When they are resolved, the issue of life-style will be considered again. At that point, a sufficiently strong therapeutic relationship may have been established, so that the therapist may be more persuasive in enlisting J. B.'s support in addressing life-style concerns, without alienating him. It may also be possible to continue to document the relationship between his diet and ulcer, so that a substantial body of evidence eventually emerges, which may be used to persuade J. B. to take corrective steps.

8

Cognitive Approaches to Managing Stress

Cognitive approaches to therapy derive from the phenomenological approach to psychology, which suggests that the individual's view of him- or herself and his or her world plays an essential role in determining behavior. In the case of stress and stress-related problems, the individual's view is important in a variety of contexts: (1) the individual's interpretation of those events or situations which have been labeled as stressful; (2) his or her interpretation of the consequences of the stressor; (3) his or her view of his or her own ability to cope with the stressor or stress reaction.

Beck (1976) has proposed a cognitive model of stress which addresses both the role of cognitions in the formulation of stress, and the role of stress in the formulation of cognitions. Beck's first principle in this model is that, "The construction of a situation (cognitive set) is an active, continuing process that includes successive appraisals of the external situation and the risks, costs, and gains of a particular response. When the individual's vital interests appear to be at stake, the cognitive process provides a highly selective conceptualization" (p. 258). It is the cognitive structuring of the situation, rather than the situation itself, which leads to mobilization or action, if action does in fact occur. The content of the cognitive structures will also dictate the nature of the action, whether it be the desire to attack or avoid, or some other course of action. Unfortunately, at the same time, the presence of stress creates a disruption in cognitive organization and function; thus, concentration, recall, reason and impulse control may all be impaired.

As Beck's model suggests, cognitive approaches can be used as either problem-focused or emotion-focused strategies in stress management. Used as problem-focused tools, cognitive strategies can alter the perception of stress. As emotion-focused tools, cognitive strategies can alter the subjective response to stress, or can alter coping behavior.

189

Linking Beck's conceptualization of the stress process to Lazarus and Folkman's notion of appraisal (as described in Chapter 2), cognitive techniques can be applied to maladaptive thought patterns in an effort to alter primary appraisal (the judgment of whether a situation is stressful), secondary appraisal (evaluation of coping options), or reappraisal (new appraisal based on additional coping efforts or acquisition of new information).

Beck maintains that the first step in the management of stress is the application of the above formulation. Basically, the rationale for treatment is that particular idiosyncratic cognitive patterns become hyperactive and lead to increased physiological arousal. At the same time, adaptive functioning is strained, resulting in some visible mental or psychophysiological symptoms. The aim of cognitive therapy is therefore twofold:

(1) To reduce the occurrence of the idiosyncratic thought patterns;
(2) To reinforce adaptive functioning.

COGNITIVE THERAPY: THE THEORETICAL PERSPECTIVE

There are a variety of cognitive therapy theories and techniques. The term "cognitive therapy" is a generic term, which encompasses a number of psychotherapeutic approaches which share a general theoretical perspective as well as a number of specific objectives.

According to most cognitive theories, negative, maladaptive, or absent cognitions are involved both in the development and maintenance of a psychopathological state (Rush, 1984). The individual operates from an egocentric, idiosyncratic, and (most likely) nonobjective perspective, and interprets both internal and external events from this perspective. The initial phases of therapy are directed at teaching the client to recognize, record, evaluate, and modify such maladaptive cognitions.

Underlying the identified cognitions are certain values or notions which are often derived from earlier experience and which support the maladaptive cognitions. The second phase of therapy is usually devoted to identifying and modifying the dysfunctional attitudes which give rise to the identified problematic cognitions.

In some ways, cognitive therapy is similiar to dynamic or analytic therapy. Both types of therapy attempt to uncover dysfunctional thought patterns, often rooted in childhood experience, which lead to faulty coping in adulthood. The repressed wishes and fears that analysts identify are similar to the personal hidden agendas of which cognitive therapists speak. There are, however, some fundamental differences as well.

In cognitive therapy, agendas and coping styles are viewed as interactional—that is, the product of the combination of the individual and the specific situation. Thus, agendas are not necessarily pathogenic but may simply be the "normal" reflection of an accumulation of learning experiences. In order to understand the development of maladaptive coping, the role of other persons and situations must be taken into account.

In addition, in the cognitive therapies, understanding the origin of maladaptive coping styles is only the first step in altering them. Whereas analytic therapy assumes that illuminating maladaptive coping styles (or defenses) will resolve them, the cognitive therapist goes on to provide specific assistance in altering coping styles.

Below, the theories of three leading cognitive therapists, Albert Ellis, Aaron Beck, and Donald Meichenbaum, are discussed in more detail. There are some differences in their general approaches to therapy, as well as in the specific techniques employed in therapy by each of these three authors. As will become evident, the work of Beck and Ellis emphasizes the reduction of idiosyncratic thought patterns; the work of Meichenbaum concentrates on the reinforcement of adaptive functioning. In spite of these differences, however, there are a number of common features shared by these variants of cognitive therapy:

(1) In all cognitive therapies, cognitions are believed to play a central mediating role in the occurrence of stress and stress reactions. Cognitions form the link between emotions and behaviors. Cognitions serve to maintain consistent patterns of behavior, whether or not the patterns of behavior are adaptive.

(2) Psychopathology is thought to be the product of distorted information processing. Therapy is aimed at correcting these distortions.

(3) Cognitions or thoughts which are believed to be faulty are challenged in some systematic fashion.

(4) Therapy tends to be active-directive, with the therapist providing specific instruction and direction, including extensive use of homework assignments.

Albert Ellis: Rational-Emotive Therapy

Albert Ellis is a former analyst who also became interested in learning theory. His "rational approach" to therapy grew out of his assumptions about the nature of human beings and their emotional well-being. Ellis works from the premise that human beings are uniquely rational, and that irrational or illogical thinking results in psychological disturbance.

As a therapy, Rational-Emotive Therapy (RET) can be described with an A-B-C-D-E framework, wherein

A: is an *activating* experience or event; something happens.

B: there is a *belief*, B, about the event A, which leads to—

C: the *consequence*, which may be emotional or behavioral.

D: to overcome irrational beliefs, RET employs scientific questioning and challenging techniques such as *Disputing, Debating, Discrimination*, and *Defining*.

E: the individual acquires a new *effect* or philosophy, which helps him or her to think more rationally and constructively.

Ellis (1962) actually identifies the 11 ideas or beliefs which he considers to be irrational and senseless, yet integral to Western society, which result in psychological disturbance. These are:

1. It is essential that a person be loved or approved by virtually everyone in the community.
2. A person must be perfectly competent, adequate, and achieving to be considered worthwhile.
3. Some people are bad, wicked, or villainous, and therefore should be blamed or punished.
4. It is a terrible catastrophe when things are not as a person wants them to be.
5. Unhappiness is caused by outside circumstances and a person has no control over the feeling.
6. Dangerous or fearsome things are cause for great concern and their possibility must be continually dwelt upon.
7. It is easier to avoid certain difficulties and self-responsibilities than to face them.
8. A person should be dependent on others and should have someone strong on whom to rely.
9. Past experiences and events are the determinants of present behavior; the influence of the past cannot be eradicated.

10. A person should be quite upset over other people's problems and disturbances.
11. There is always a right or perfect solution to every problem, and it must be found or the results will be catastrophic.

The first step in RET is to demonstrate to clients that the relevant assumptions are, in fact, illogical, and to help clients understand how these ideas developed and how they relate to emotional disturbance. This step is not unique to RET, as most approaches do this. However, RET proceeds from this point to show clients that they maintain their disturbance by thinking illogically. Therefore, clients are directed to change their thinking and abandon irrational ideas.

Finally, clients are encouraged to adopt a generally more rational philosophy of living, so that they will be less apt to subscribe to other irrational ideas and beliefs (Patterson, 1986).

The general approach of RET is that of active, directive teaching. The role of the therapist is to reeducate the client by demonstrating the origin of the disturbance and contradicting the illogical position that the client holds. The therapist may confront, command, cajole, persuade, reason logically, argue, order, and interpret. In any case, the goal is to teach the client to think logically, and the goal is achieved through an active didactic exchange.

One of the distinguishing features of RET, according to Ellis (1987), is the attention devoted to absolutistic, dogmatic, and grandiose thinking. Ellis suggests that other cognitive therapies are accurate—as far as they go. But while all cognitive therapies (including RET) accept the role that illogical thinking plays in psychological disturbance, only RET stresses the role of absolutistic thinking. Ellis maintains that it is the shoulds, oughts, and musts which make the difference between mild discomfort and major psychological disturbance. He makes an essential distinction between preference statements such as "I prefer to have x" (which suggests that although x would be desirable, I can survive without it), and demand statements such as "I must have x" (which suggests, "I can't stand it! It is unbearable and I am worthless if I do not have x!!"). Although he acknowledges that either of these statements might lead to disappointment, it is only the latter which has serious mental health consequences. RET focuses on uncovering and remediating demand statements and their underlying beliefs.

There remain, of course, many questions about RET and its efficacy. Beliefs are poorly defined, with no particular definition being commonly accepted. The line between preference and demand is equally poorly defined. Outcome research is lacking. As the theory and practice of RET have changed over time, earlier studies of effectiveness are not meaningful. As is the case with almost any therapy, it is not clear which parts of the theoretical structure actually contribute to effectiveness. Some therapists also object to the highly directive, forceful, and perhaps abrasive nature of the therapy.

Nevertheless, RET seems to be effective, at least with some clients. It may be most appropriate for clients who visibly display the type of "mustabatory" beliefs that Ellis discusses. The hard-line approach may be effective for resistant clients who hold potentially self-injurious beliefs (possibly Type A individuals).

Aaron Beck: Cognitive Therapy

Like Ellis, Aaron Beck comes from a background of psychoanalysis, coupled with an interest in behavior therapy. He is also a physician by training. Beck's approach to therapy originates to some extent from his rejection of all three of his areas of training. He disagrees with the psychoanalytic emphasis on the unconscious as the source of emotional disturbance. He considers behavior therapy's concern only with overt behavior as unduly limited. He also rejects the traditional psychiatric wisdom that physiological or chemical processes are the cause of emotional disturbances. Beck's cognitive therapy is based on the common sense notion that what people think and say about themselves is relevant, important, and determines emotions and behavior.

The defining feature of Beck's therapy is his attention to what he calls "automatic thoughts." Beck (1976) maintains that while a person thinks or acts, there is a continual stream of self-evaluating "speech" occurring, often outside of the immediate awareness of the individual. These thoughts tend to be rapid and automatic, often self-evaluatory and anticipatory, rather than related specifically to content. Thus, while on the one hand the individual may be thinking and talking about a recent experience, he or she may at the same time be thinking, "This is really going to bore them; I wish I could tell a story better; why can't I learn to keep my mouth shut?" In addition, these thoughts tend to occur prior to experiencing a given emotion. In the above example, for instance, the individual will first experience the critical thoughts, and then will experience anxiety.

According to Beck, automatic thoughts are specific and discrete rather than vague. They seem plausible to the individual even though they may actually be unreasonable. The type of automatic thought may be peculiar to the individual client, or to clients with the same diagnosis (i.e., all depressed clients may have similar automatic thoughts). In addition, there may be too many such thoughts, leading to self-consciousness and inhibition; or conversely, there may be a deficit of self-monitoring, leading to impulsiveness.

Very often, automatic thoughts share two characteristics:

Personalization. Objective judgments tend to be replaced by egocentric views. The individual is apt to interpret all events as applying to him- or herself. He or she may interpret irrelevant effects as being self-directed (e.g., assuming that a frown on the face of a stranger is a reflection on his or her personal appearance or behavior). Another form of personalization is found in the tendency to compare oneself with other people—usually inappropriately and unflatteringly.

Polarized Thinking. In this case, the individual may be prone to think in extremes in situations which impinge upon sensitive areas. This characteristic has also been called dichotomous thinking. Events are viewed as either all good or all bad, always or never, with no intermediate ground apparent. Other errors in thinking due to polarization are selective abstraction (taking a detail out of context and missing the overall significance), arbitrary inference (jumping to conclusions with insufficient evidence), and overgeneralization (unjustified generalization on the basis of a single incident).

Beck contends that automatic thoughts occur within a system of rules, a program by which the individual deciphers and evaluates his or her own experience and regulates his or her behavior. Although individuals may not be aware of their own rules, Beck suggests that each individual (and indeed each diagnostic category) has rules by which the content of automatic thoughts are determined. For example, the above-mentioned automatic thoughts about telling a story poorly may derive from the rule, "If I am not witty and clever at all times in interacting with others, I am making a fool of myself." According to Beck's Law of Rules, rules will cause a person to act consistently in similar situations, but the behavior will not necessarily be appropriate, since rules tend to be unconditional and absolute.

In the case of a stressed client, Beck suggests that anxiety may result from an overactive "alarm system," indicative of excess concern about the possibility of danger. In contrast to "normal" individuals, who will show greater confidence and less anxiety as their experience with stressful situations increases, the highly anxious individual will become worse with successive confrontations. Once the anxious individual has developed a "rule" that a certain situation is stressful, successive exposures to that situation may simply reactivate the "danger" rule and the accompanying cognitions. Similarly, individuals who experience "psychosomatic" disorders are those who are prone to excess emotional upset due to cognitive interpretations of certain problem areas, but who, at the same time, are genetically programmed to react in a particular physiological system.

Like Ellis, Beck states that the goal of therapy is to correct faulty assumptions and the resultant distress by whatever techniques seem to work. He advocates a less forceful and more epistemiological approach to aid the client in identifying automatic thoughts and rules, collecting data or otherwise testing the reality of those assumptions, and challenging and replacing such assumptions. Specific techniques are discussed later in this chapter (see "Cognitive Therapy: The Process").

Donald Meichenbaum: Cognitive Behavior
Therapy and Stress Inoculation Training

Unlike Beck and Ellis, Donald Meichenbaum's background is primarily behavioral, and his training is in psychology, not medicine. His cognitive behavior modification approach represents an attempt to link the clinical concerns of cognitive-semantic therapists like Beck and Ellis with the technology of behavior therapy. Specifically, Meichenbaum is concerned with the role of cognitive events in determining and changing behavior (Meichenbaum, 1977).

Meichenbaum's work on cognitive behavior modification originally drew on Luria's (1961) three-stage model to explain the manner in which verbal control brings about the initiation and inhibition of behavior in children. In the first stage, verbal behavior of others—usually adults—directs a child's behavior. In the second stage, the child's own overt speech becomes a regulator of behavior. Finally, the child's inner or covert speech becomes self-governing. Adults tend to follow the same sequence in learning a new behavior or skill. They follow the directions of others; they give themselves directions, perhaps aloud; finally, the directions become covert and are condensed, made less complete, and eventually fade out. The cognitive behavior in the third stage is what Meichenbaum refers to as internal dialogue or internal speech. The premise of cognitive behavior modification is that by modifying the directive internal speech of an individual, one can change behavior.

Meichenbaum's theory was initially developed within the context of managing behavior of cognitively impulsive hyperactive children. Having observed that such children make less use of self-regulatory speech than do other children, that they do not analyze experience in cognitively mediated terms, and that they do not formulate and internalize rules of behavior to the same extent, Meichenbaum and his colleagues began programs of self-instructional training. Essentially, children were taught by modeling to "think out loud" as a means of monitoring and controlling performance. The cognitive skills employed in this process included:

1. Problem identification: "What is it that I have to do?"
2. Focusing attention and guiding the response: "Do it carefully; draw the line here."
3. Self-reinforcement: "Good, that's fine."
4. Self-evaluative coping skills and error-correcting options: "That's OK, one error isn't too bad. Keep going" (Meichenbaum, 1977).

Thus, whereas Beck and Ellis tend to focus on the *presence* of maladaptive assumptions and beliefs, Meichenbaum focuses on the *absence* of specific adaptive cognitive responses.

Based on his self-instructional principles, Meichenbaum has developed a primarily cognitive strategy for responding to stress. His Stress Inoculation Training (SIT) is a three-phase therapy directed at altering cognitive response to stress and at maximizing cognitive coping. He focuses less on cognitive interpretation of stressors.

The first phase of SIT is educational; its purpose is to provide the client with a conceptual framework for understanding the response to stress. Emphasis is placed on creating a connection between self-statements while experiencing arousal and the resultant behavior. The second phase of therapy, the rehearsal phase, involves the teaching of a variety of coping skills for dealing with stressors. Although specific behavioral and physiological skills such as relaxation training are included in this phase, the emphasis is on cognitive coping. Since Meichenbaum regards all behavior as being cognitively mediated, strategies which might otherwise be considered behavioral or physiological in nature become derivatives of cognitive behavior.

SIT assumes that both maladaptive and adaptive responses are mediated by self-statements. Like interpersonal instructions, self-instructions monitor, direct, and adjust the behavior of the individual. In any given stressful circumstance, the purpose of self-instructions is to encourage the individual to analyze the problem in a systematic way. They allow the individual to:

1. assess the reality of the situation
2. control negative thoughts
3. acknowledge, use, and relabel arousal
4. prepare to confront the stressor
5. cope with the reaction to the stressor
6. evaluate performance and self-reinforce

The third and final stage, application training, involves exposure to stressful situations and application of the coping skills which have been learned. Initially, less significant stressors are addressed and handled. Once these are mastered, more difficult situations are approached.

It is in this final stage that the inoculation or immunization model is employed. In medicine, the individual is inoculated against a disease by being exposed to smaller doses of a closely related antigen. This exposure results in the formulation of antibodies. When the antigen of the disease itself is encountered, resistance has already been established through the presence of these antibodies.

In the case of SIT, exposure during training to less stressful events parallels the exposure to vaccines in the inoculation process. Some initial resistance is already in place within the individual, since some sense of mastery occurs with the successful coping experience. Major stressors are therefore handled more easily and more successfully.

Meichenbaum's approach is much more behavioral than either Beck's or Ellis's. Although Meichenbaum does attempt to have clients become aware of negative self-statements, the emphasis in treatment is on developing and employing specific problem-solving and coping skills. These skills are learned by using standard behavioral procedures such as modeling, rehearsal, reinforcement, shaping, and self-monitoring.

COGNITIVE THERAPY: THE PROCESS

Rush (1984) has identified five specific objectives in cognitive therapy. First, the client must become aware of the view that he or she takes of situations, particularly those situations identified as stressful. In order to progress to subsequent stages of therapy, the client must first be able to separate out what is objective, measurable "truth," as opposed to his or her subjective interpretation of the situation.

Once the client is able to distinguish between the objective and subjective components of a situation, he or she can then learn to assess, reality test, and adjust subjective views. The client may be asked to collect specific data in the form of a diary or frequency count in order to identify and quantify problematic thoughts. In this second step, clients often become aware of stereotyped perceptions of certain situations, and may learn to correct them.

Generalizing from this knowledge, clients may learn to identify the underlying assumptions and beliefs which they operate from in a variety of situations. These underlying assumptions are not conscious thoughts but rather represent guiding principles or premises from which the individual tends to operate. This is the third step.

In the fourth step, the client actively adopts and practices specific cognitive and behavioral responses to both anticipated and unexpected stresses.

Therapy concludes with the generalization of new underlying assumptions and the application of these new assumptions to stressful circumstances.

Depending upon the specific orientation within cognitive therapy of the individual therapist, the relative importance of these steps may vary. Ellis tends to emphasize the role of underlying assumptions which may affect a variety of different situations. Beck talks a great deal about reality testing. Meichenbaum stresses the creation of new ways of exerting cognitive control over behavior. An individual therapist may well adjust the focus and emphasis depending upon the needs of the individual client and the nature of the stressor or stress reaction.

Similarly, the exact techniques which will be utilized to effect change will also vary depending upon orientation, client needs, and the nature of the problem. Some of the more common techniques of cognitive change are described below.

Problem Solving. Obvious as it may seem, many people need formal tuition in the process of problem solving. Stressed clients may have a poor conceptualization of exactly what the problem at hand is, and may only see one possible solution. D'Zurrilla and Goldfried (1971) suggest a model of problem solving which includes the following steps:

(1) Establishing general orientation: the client must accept the existence of problems in general as a normal part of life, be able to recognize them, and be prepared to work on them.
(2) Problem definition and formulation: the client must define operationally all aspects of the problem in a specific and compre-

hensive fashion, and be able to formulate or classify aspects of the problem in a way that separates relevant from irrelevant information, and that identifies goals and issues.

(3) Generation of alternatives: resisting the tendency to either act impulsively or do nothing, the client should generate a variety of possible solutions, without censorship, and encouraging creativity. Quantity is important.

(4) Decision making: the utility of each alternative is assessed so that the client can select the most suitable alternative for his or her own circumstances.

(5) Verification: once an alternative has been selected and enacted, the actual outcome is assessed so that strategies can be either confirmed or altered as necessary.

Generally, problem solving is conceptualized as a form of self-control training, so that the client first learns to solve problems in general, then applies knowledge of this skill to specific problems.

Hypothesis Testing. The process of hypothesis testing in any context refers to the generation of a statement of belief ("the world is round"), prescription of a method to test the hypothesis (try to sail around it), and the collection of data (six ships left, five came back). In cognitive therapy, the hypotheses formulated generally relate to the existence of automatic thoughts or illogical assumptions. Thus, the therapist might propose the hypothesis, "Your automatic response to any encounter with another person is 'he likes me, he likes me not.' " The method of assessment might be to observe how often the client wonders about other people's reactions to him or her. The data collected will indicate whether the hypothesis should be confirmed, denied, or modified. As in any "scientific" procedure, the researcher (or therapist in this case) must ensure that sufficient knowledge is gained before generating the hypothesis so as to maximize the likelihood of the hypothesis being confirmed. The therapist who repeatedly poses erroneous hypotheses will soon lose credibility.

Self-Monitoring. Self-monitoring strategies are described in Chapter 4. These are frequently used as homework assignments to identify and assess specific cognitions, particularly in conjunction with hypothesis testing.

Cognitive Challenges. Many potentially destructive cognitions, particularly absolutistic ones, can be challenged logically by providing evidence from the client's own history which contradicts the belief in question. The therapist may propose such challenges from his or her knowledge of the client ("You say that you have always been a failure at work, yet you told me last time that you received a promotion and raise after only three months on the job"). The client may also issue challenges, either logically or through data collection. Generally, the source of the challenges is initially the therapist, with the client gradually assuming responsibility for issuing his or her own challenges.

Generating Alternatives to Automatic Irrational Thoughts. Once automatic thoughts or irrational ideas are identified and challenged, the client needs to generate specific alternative thoughts which are reasonable, nonjudgmental, task-related, and (hopefully) positive. This is often accomplished by picking apart each component of the undesirable cognition and replacing it with a more desirable cognition. For example, the idea that "I am a failure at everything that I do" may be replaced with the more desirable and less absolute "Although I did not do well in situation X, I have succeeded before and will probably succeed again."

Self-Instruction. When cognitions are used to control and direct behavior in an adaptive fashion, these cognitions become self-instructions. Thus, the client may verbalize (overtly or covertly) directions about how to carry out the behavior in question, and may simultaneously self-reinforce, approve, and adjust behavior on an ongoing basis. Self-instructions are particularly useful for tasks which are perceived as difficult, regardless of whether the difficulty stems from a property of the task itself (i.e., it is a new or complex task) or from a reaction to the task (i.e., in approaching a phobic object). Self-instructions are generally specific, directive, and reinforcing to the individual. Examples are presented in Table 8–1.

Attribution and Reattribution. An underlying theme in cognitive therapy is that clients often make inaccurate or unhelpful attributions regarding their particular role in a situation. Thus a client may fail to accept credit for a personal success ("It was just luck") or conversely may accept responsibility for events outside of his or her control ("It's my fault that the team lost"). Forsterling (1985, 1986) suggests that retraining in causal attribution results in changes in cognitive and behavioral functioning. In general, reattribution focuses on encouraging clients to attribute problem behaviors to causes which are nonpejorative and personally controllable. For example, students who attribute academic failure to lack of

TABLE 8–1
Self-Instructional Statements Used in Stress Management

Preparing for the Stressor

What is it that I have to do?
Create a plan. I just need a strategy to deal with it.
It's ok to feel a bit uptight. That's normal.
What can I do to help?
Let's get on with it—worrying won't help.

Confronting and Handling the Stressor

One step at a time.
Relax, things are under control. I can handle it.
Just follow the plan. I can do it.
This nervousness is ok. Just use my coping skills.
Look for the good side. Where am I making progress?

Evaluating Coping Efforts

There, that wasn't so bad.
Whew, I did it. I'm proud of myself.
It didn't work as I had hoped. That's ok. I'll try again.
I handled it well. I'm pleased.
That was better. Next time it'll be even better than that.

Adapted with permission from D. Meichenbaum (1985), *Stress in-oculation training*, pp. 72–73. Elmsford, NY: Pergamon Press.

effort are more likely to improve grades than are students who make attributions to either personal inability or impossible professors. Kelley (1967) suggests three variables critical to attribution formation:

1. *Consensus.* Would everyone else agree with your conclusion about this attribution (i.e., do other students find this professor impossible)?
2. *Consistency.* Is this always the case (i.e., is the professor always impossible or just on this one assignment)?
3. *Covariation.* If you change one of the behaviors in question in this attribution, do the results change (i.e., if you work harder, do your grades improve)?

Forsterling (1980) suggests classifying attributions in a 2 × 2 matrix of internal/external by stable/unstable. He contends that no one of these four possible attributional types is inherently better than the others, but that each may be useful in some circumstances.

As demonstrated in Figure 8–1, each of the four cells of this matrix represents a different attribution, depending upon the attributional style of the individual. If, for example, the situation is perceived as being variable over time (unstable), and outside the control of the individual (external), then the client is likely to attribute the outcome to luck.

Techniques to Control or Suppress Thoughts. There are a number of both cognitive and behavioral techniques which are designed simply to control or eliminate persistent undesirable thoughts. These techniques do not challenge or alter the identified thoughts. Such approaches may be useful for obsessive or ruminative thoughts which may have already been challenged, but which remain nevertheless. Shelton and Levy (1981) mention the following techniques:

1. *Thought stopping.* The client is asked to produce the unwanted thought voluntarily, usually out loud, and then the therapist yells, "Stop!", causing the verbalization to cease. The client is then asked to say "stop" whenever the unwanted thought occurs. Eventually, the "stop" is produced subvocally (Stern, 1970).

2. *Implosion (or flooding in fantasy).* The client is required to experience the distressing thought over and over until such time as it no longer results in any emotional arousal. This may be done either by repeating the thought out loud, or by describing the content of the thought, depending upon the specific thought involved. Repetition may be effective for primarily verbal thoughts; description may be more effective for recurring visual images.

	Internal	External
Stable	Ability	Task Difficulty
Unstable	Effort	Luck

Figure 8–1. Classification of attributional style and attributions.

3. Punishment. The client receives some form of mild punishment whenever the thoughts occur. In a laboratory or clinic setting, the therapist may administer a mild electric shock. As a self-control procedure, the client may snap an elastic band on his or her wrist, or take a whiff of smelling salts.

4. Redirecting thoughts. The client is asked to redirect the problematic thoughts to a certain place (e.g., a particular chair) or to a particular time (e.g., only worry for one half hour before dinner).

5. Changing the environment. The client is asked to leave the room or change his or her activity when the thoughts occur.

6. Aversive tasks. The client is asked to engage in an aversive task (such as scrubbing the floor) when the thoughts occur.

7. Delaying the thoughts. The client is to put off thinking about the problem area for a specified period of time (e.g., to delay for one half hour before thinking about it).

ISSUES AND PROBLEMS

Although cognitive therapy now claims almost as many adherents among therapists as dynamic therapy and eclecticism, there remain a number of unresolved questions about both the mechanism and efficacy of change. The problems are particularly evident in the context of stress management. The bulk of the literature on cognitive therapy has been conducted on depressed subjects (if clinical populations are employed at all). Only Meichenbaum's cognitive behavior modification techniques have been explicitly assessed on stressed individuals. It is not at all clear, therefore, how much of the existing literature on efficaciousness applies to the field of stress management.

Is cognitive therapy effective at all? Miller and Berman (1983) reviewed 48 studies assessing the efficacy of cognitive therapy and concluded that cognitive therapy does indeed seem to work better than an absence of any treatment. There did not appear to be strong evidence for the superiority of cognitive therapy over other forms of psychotherapy, including behavior therapy. Clients treated with cognitive therapy did tend to have slightly higher reports of improvement on self-report measures, as compared to clients who had participated in other forms of therapy. However, independent ratings of these clients did not show a corresponding difference. Evidence from this review also did not support the hypothesis of differential effectiveness for various diagnostic groups. In other words, there was no evidence that cognitive therapy was superior to other psychotherapies for some particular diagnostic groups but not for others.

More recent studies have confirmed these impressions. Several studies have assessed the differential effectiveness of cognitive therapy versus behavior therapy in depressed or anxious individuals, but have failed to find significant differences between approaches (cf. Rehm, Kaslow, & Rabin, 1987; Lindsay et al., 1987; Durham & Turvey, 1987).

An interesting study by Marchione, Michelson, Greenwald, and Dancu (1987) raises the possibility that cognitive therapy may have a slightly different—if not superior—effect, compared to other therapies. Using several different combinations of cognitive therapy and behavior therapy techniques, these authors were able to demonstrate a general superiority of combined techniques over individual techniques. In addition, different techniques tended to enhance performance on different outcome measures. Studies such as these tend to support the clinical tendency to use multifaceted approaches. These findings may also reaffirm the importance of selecting interventions according to individual client needs, rather than according to preestablished protocols.

In general, the outcome research evaluating cognitive therapy remains equivocal. One of the reasons for this may lie in the difficulty of defining exactly what cognitive therapy is. The three types of therapy described in this chapter obviously have some similarities, but also have some distinct differences. Reviews such as Miller and Berman's (1983) include all such variants. Authors such as Kendall (1984) caution against construing cognitive therapy as a single-minded approach. Although theoretical arguments are evident in the literature (cf. Ellis, 1987; Marzillier, 1987), virtually no work has assessed empirical differences in outcome among the different types of cognitive therapy. To compound the situation further, if one accepts Meichenbaum's notion of the role of cognitions in mediating behavior, then all behavioral techniques become cognitive. Consider, for example, the study by Michelson, Mavissakalian, and Marchione (1985), in which graduated exposure and progressive deep muscle relaxation are described and assessed as cognitive-behavioral treatments. In the absence of agreement about what constitutes cognitive therapy, it is difficult to assess effectiveness.

Regardless of the answers to questions about therapeutic effectiveness, there are also questions about the validity of some of the theoretical assumptions underlying cognitive therapy.

One of the underlying themes in cognitive therapy is that psychopathology is a product of a distorted or unrealistic assessment of oneself and one's personal situation. Taylor and Brown (1988) point out quite convincingly, however, that it is actually mental health which is a product of unrealistic perceptions. Normal "healthy" cognitions tend to be characterized by overly positive self-evaluations, exaggerated perceptions of control or mastery, and unrealistic optimism about one's own future. A realistic and accurate appraisal of one's own situation may well encourage rather than defeat depression. (One is reminded of the age-old axiom, "You don't have an inferiority complex; you are just inferior.") The thoughts of depressed individuals may be pessimistic and negative, but not irrational or untrue (Beidel & Turner, 1986).

There are also questions about the relationship between cognitions and emotions. It is difficult to determine which, of cognition, emotion, and physiological arousal, occurs first in any given situation. Although Beck and Ellis maintain that cognitions precede emotions, attribution theorists suggest that physiological arousal is first perceived as emotion, then given cognitive meaning. Emotion thus assumes a kind of signaling function (Kendall, 1984). Meichenbaum (1985) cautions against viewing cognitions as antecedents to other psychological or physiological processes. Rather, he suggests that cognitions should be viewed as one of several entry points into a process which contains a number of interrelated parts (including emotions, physiological reactions, behavior, and social consequences). Clearly, one cannot assume that cognitions always predict and precipitate emotional responses.

Finally, there are inconsistencies between cognitive theory and cognitive therapy. It seems apparent that cognitive processes such as attention and perception can be altered by application of learning-theory-based behavioral techniques. It is not clear whether specific "cognitive" techniques do the job any better or any faster. This confusion is attributable in part to the disagreement about whether cognitions are a behavior much like other behaviors, only private, or whether they are in some way distinct and separate phenomena. If cognitive activities do indeed follow established laws of learning, then it is questionable whether the creation of a "new" theory of cognitive behavior will actually increase understanding of maladaptive behavior (Beidel & Turner, 1986).

All of these issues argue in favor of the inclusion of cognitive therapy in a multifacted behavioral framework. Kendall (1984) cites some evidence that individuals who score high on self-control measures may do better with cognitive approaches. Logically, the therapist might suggest cognitive therapy for those clients who show evidence of self-defeating or stress-producing cognitions, or who have demonstrated a relationship between cognitive content and subsequent behavior. Cognitive techniques will probably be most usefully employed with those individuals who demonstrate personal suitability for such approaches, as indicated by a thorough assessment of symptoms. Below, cognitive approaches to each of the three continuing case studies are described. In each instance, the need clearly exists for some cognitive intervention, yet there are also some distinct differences in the needs of each client. For Cathy, Meichenbaum's self-instructional approach is most useful. In Jean's case, Beck's cognitive therapy seems most appropriate. For J. B., who is somewhat resistant to the idea of personal change, a more forceful approach such as Ellis's may be necessary.

CASE STUDIES

Cathy

According to the preestablished plan for Cathy's group, the fifth session of the series was entitled "Talk Sense to Yourself," and focused on employing self-instructional techniques in stressful situations. Like most members of the group, Cathy had identified academic pressures as being most salient at this point in her life. The group leader asked the participants to identify the exact aspects of their studies which were most problematic, and the consensus was that exam pressure was a major problem. After continued discussion, the group members were able to identify three aspects of this problem to deal with: apprehension prior to exams, anxiety during the exam itself, and anticipation of exam results (after the exam was completed but before results were received).

The group leader divided the group into three sections, each of which was to deal with one aspect of the problem. Cathy elected to join the group oriented toward dealing with apprehension prior to the exam. Each section was asked to generate two lists. First, they were to try to identify the stress-engendering thoughts that they usually experienced prior to an exam. Second, they were to create positive self-statements which would aid in decreasing the level of anxiety experienced. The first list included the following:

- "If I fail this exam, it's all over."
- "I'll bet everyone else knows more than I do."
- "It's going to be awful."
- "Everyone says this professor's exams are terrible."
- "I'm so stupid; I don't know how I ever got this far."
- "I don't understand any of this material!"

- "Why did I ever decide to take this course anyhow?"
- "Maybe I just won't show up."
- "If I could just concentrate, I'd be better off!"
- "My mind has turned to mush—I can't even look at all this material."
- "There's so much material to learn; I'll never get through it all."
- "My study habits are the pits."

Under the guidance of the group leader, the members listed positive self-statements directed at four areas:

1. *Problem Identification.*

   - "My job is to study and do my best; don't get upset about it."
   - "Don't get into a lather about it. I'll try to organize the material I need to know."
   - "It's just an exam. I'll do my best and that's all I can expect."
   - "I've gotten this far; I'm sure I can prepare for and take this exam just like I have many others."

2. *Focusing Attention.*

   - "My goal for the next hour is to read this chapter. I'll just concentrate on this."
   - "Just pay attention and keep working. That's the best thing to do."
   - "OK, I've finished that part. What's next?"
   - "I can't let my mind wander. Keep on track!"

3. *Self-reinforcement.*

   - "I'm right on schedule. Keep at it."
   - "Good, I've finished that part."
   - "It's hard not to panic, but so far, so good."
   - "OK, I seem to be getting a handle on this stuff. Keep going."

4. *Self-evaluation.*

   - "It's not going too badly, but there's still a lot to go."
   - "My attention seems to be wandering, but maybe if I have a break, I can get back to it."

- "Most of this stuff seems to be falling in place, but I think this section needs a bit more work."
- "I seem to be following my schedule, but I had better keep at it."

Once each of the three sections of the group had had time to work through the assigned scenario, the group reconvened as a whole, and discussed the findings of each session. As a group, they discussed the various emotions which were generated from both the adaptive and nonadaptive self-statements, and also discussed how they might apply this knowledge in specific situations.

Jean

The baseline measures which Jean completed indicated that she was having a great deal of difficulty with role expectations, as well as with specific expectations of herself. Jean was able to state clearly that she felt that her primary obligations were to her family, including both her children and her parents. Nevertheless, she also felt a great deal of resentment over these obligations. On the one hand, Jean stated that she enjoyed her job, and wanted to advance her career. On the other hand, she frequently felt guilty about these desires, and tried to convince herself (and others) that she was only working because of financial need.

Jean did complain of feeling guilty very often, so she was asked to keep a continuing diary of the times when she felt guilty. The feelings seemed to occur most often when Jean was involved in activities which did not involve her family, or when she was consciously angry at the demands placed on her by her family. When asked to record the thoughts that accompanied these incidents, she noted the following typical thoughts:

- "If I were a better mother, I wouldn't resent the kids for making all these requests."
- "If I weren't so tired from work, I'm sure I would be more patient with the kids."
- "My parents probably think I'm awful because I haven't had them over for dinner this week."
- "Maybe I should never have had children; I'm just not willing to sacrifice enough for them."
- "I bet my mother never felt like this."
- "How come I can't be like all the other mothers who can keep house, work, and raise their kids with no trouble?"

- "If I ever let my family obligations interfere with my job, I'll be in big trouble."

It seemed clear that Jean expected herself to be perfect at all times in all roles that she played. Thus, her thinking is typically polarized; Jean thinks that if she is not the perfect parent/worker/daughter at all times, then she is worthless. Jean herself was able to agree that these were expectations that she had of herself; furthermore, she felt that they were reasonable expectations and was surprised to find them being questioned. Over the course of several weeks, Jean was given several homework assignments, directed at assessing the validity of some of her beliefs.

First, Jean was to speak to her mother about some of her feelings. Although Jean was reluctant to expose her own thoughts, she was able to ask her mother how it was for her when she had young children. Jean was surprised to hear her mother speak of her own frustration; she had wanted some activity outside the home, but had believed that her absences would be too hard on the children. Jean's mother actually expressed admiration for the job that Jean was doing of working and raising children. Jean's mother also spoke of her own strained relationship with her mother, and how she had never felt that she measured up to her mother's standards.

Jean reported that she had realized that some of her assumptions had not been supported by her "data collection." She was able to challenge her beliefs about needing to be at home all the time, and her conflicts about her desire to hold a job. The next time that Jean noted herself having self-critical thoughts about her lack of patience with the children, she was able to say, "Everyone runs out of patience now and then. If I were home all day with the children, I might be even less patient." She was also able to state that, "Once every two weeks is a reasonable period of time to have my parents over."

Jean was indeed relieved to have found support from her mother on some of her concerns, but she asked the therapist what would have happened if her mother had expressed the opposite opinion. When the therapist turned the question back to Jean, she hesitated, and responded, "I can't imagine how awful it would be!" When the therapist asked what was the worst thing that could possibly happen, Jean paused, then replied, "Well, I'm a big girl now. I guess I would have to learn to get along without my mother's approval."

Jean and the therapist continued to record and challenge Jean's thoughts about her role conflicts. Two somewhat different lines of reasoning were used to help her challenge the automatic and repetitive criticisms which she directed at herself. First, Jean was asked to continue talking to a variety of other women who had children, to gain some appreciation of the wide range of opinions and behaviors which can be viewed as "normal." Jean had spent so many years condemning her own behavior that she rarely spoke to other mothers, and thus had somewhat lost sight of the support that she could gain from others. Second, Jean learned to note and contradict self-deprecating thoughts when they occurred. In one session, she reported the following spontaneous thoughts from the previous week, as well as her rebuttals to them:

"If we eat fast food one more time this week, my children will probably be taken away!" was replaced by "This may not be the most nutritious food in the world, but ordering out gives me time to sit and talk with the kids."

"If I say I can't work late again tonight, the boss will be furious" was replaced by "It is unfortunate that I can't work more overtime, but I am sure the boss realizes that I have other time commitments."

"I forgot to call my mother this morning. She must think I am awful" was replaced by "I must apologize for forgetting to call my mother, but these things do happen."

After several weeks of systematic recording and challenging, Jean and the therapist were able to identify a pattern to her thoughts, as well as to note the current of the underlying "rules" which Jean has imposed upon herself. Once these became apparent, they spent some time discussing and delineating Jean's priorities, for the present time, and for her future. She had some difficulty both setting priorities and admitting certain priorities to the therapist, since some conflicted with her impression of what she "should" do. However, once these were clarified, Jean was ready to begin looking at her own daily schedule, in order to manage her time more effectively.

J. B.

As noted in his plan in Chapter 5, J. B. was reluctant to deal with any of the material relating to the expectations or beliefs underlying his driven behavior and his family conflicts. Thus, this section is actually chronologically out of order for this case, since the behavioral changes to be described in the following chapter will be dealt with by J. B. in therapy before any consideration is given to cognitive interventions. As will be described in the next chapter, J. B. was amenable to working on communication skills within his family, and to having a look at his use of leisure time. He remained ambivalent about delving further into his belief structure. The therapist considered confronting him in a fairly directive and pointed manner about his beliefs, but was somewhat reluctant to do so, for several reasons. J. B. was clearly a man who was used to being in control, and who liked to be in control. For the therapist to unilaterally usurp this control would, in all probability, lead to termination of therapy. Since the other aspects of therapy had progressed relatively well, it would seem unfortunate to terminate on a negative note. Furthermore, the therapist had noted a slight softening in J. B.'s position in regard to his general expectations. Although he still did not choose to challenge his beliefs openly, he did appear to be reflecting on this. Therefore, the therapist decided to present J. B. with some of his observations, as well as some suggestions as to where therapy might progress, then to leave the client with the option to pursue these observations in the future. The therapist did feel that J. B. would benefit from (and actually enjoy) the debating and disputing of an RET approach, but only if the client himself initiated the move in this direction.

In the course of working on family interactions, the therapist had observed that J. B.'s behavior seemed to be governed by several irrational beliefs like those identified by Ellis. These included the following:

- With regard to the behavior of his son, J. B. seemed to impose the standard, "A person must be perfectly competent, adequate, and achieving to be considered worthwhile." The therapist pointed out that since his son was aware of that standard, one he could not possibly meet, he easily gave up trying.
- The therapist also noted J. B.'s tendency to slot all people into the categories of "good" or "bad," with the latter being responsible for most of the evils of the world. Both J. B.'s wife and son were hesitant to bring home friends or to include J. B. in social activities, for fear that he would "pass judgment" on others.
- Finally, J. B. refused to take responsibility for his own emotions, and viewed himself as having no control over his happiness, which he believed was controlled by circumstances outside of himself. Thus, his moods varied tremendously, which was another source of great concern to his family.

In the final sessions of therapy, the therapist made these observations to J. B., while at the same time acknowledging that J. B. did not see things in the same fashion. The therapist did suggest to J. B., however, that he might want to think about the relationship between these beliefs and his identified problems. The therapist offered to assist J. B. in looking further at these beliefs, and in exploring their role in his life—but only if J. B. initiated the discussion. Once again, J. B. defensively maintained that he was confident that the therapy that he had undergone so far would be sufficient to remedy his distress. He reiterated that although he was able to grasp the impact of his acute episodes of stress and his life-style on his ulcer flare-ups, he did not see how his personal beliefs could make any difference in his condition. In spite of further efforts of the therapist to clarify the causal connection, J. B. declined the offer, and therapy terminated—albeit on a relatively positive note.

9

Behavioral Strategies for Managing Stress

The purpose of the present chapter is to examine the mechanisms for altering the behaviors that are related to stress—that is, how people act, and what they do (or don't do) that causes stress, or that occurs as a result of stress.

In the broadest sense, virtually any human activity (including cognitive and physiological activity) can be considered a behavior. For the purposes of this chapter, however, behavior is defined in a somewhat narrower fashion, as observable human activity. This is largely a distinction of convenience, since cognitive and physiological activities have been dealt with elsewhere.

The relationship between stress and behavior is bidirectional; some behaviors produce stress, whereas others occur in response to stress. The same behavior may play either role. Failing to complete an assignment at work on time, for example, may be a stressor for the employee. It may result in harsh words from the boss, self-deprecation, and increased time pressures. On the other hand, failure to complete an assignment may also represent a response to stress. The employee whose spouse has just absconded with a third party may fail to function as efficiently as usual, and may not complete his or her work promptly. In this case, sympathy, concern, and a temporarily reduced work load may (or may not!) accompany the behavior. In the first example, the required intervention may be skill training in time management and organization. This would probably not be the treatment of choice in the second case.

In stress management, an important step in altering specific behaviors is to determine the role of the specific behavior in the stress process. Is the behavior a stressor? Is it part of the response to stress? If the behavior is part of the stress response, it may be more appropriate to determine if the stressor which is producing this response can be altered. If this is the case, alteration of the behavioral response may not be necessary. It is not always the case that the stressor can be altered, however; in cases in which it is not possible to alter the stressor, the behavioral response may need direct alteration. Depending upon the function of the behavior in question, behavior change may be a problem-focused or an emotion-focused stress management technique.

A simplistic view of stress-related behaviors might identify those obvious and serious behaviors which provoke a strong stress reaction. The nature of stress-related behaviors is more complex than this would suggest. Behaviors to be targeted in stress management can be loosely categorized into three types.

BEHAVIORAL EXCESSES, DEFICITS, AND ASSETS

The first category includes behavioral excesses. These are behaviors which occur too much. "Too much" may be indicative of excesses in frequency (the behavior occurs too often); duration (the behavior lasts too long); intensity (the behavior is too strong); or quality (the behavior is simply not "normal" or socially acceptable). Behaviors which occur in excess may of course exhibit more than one of these characteristics. A common behavioral excess in a stressed client is an unduly strong emotional reaction to a minor event; frequently, aggressive behavior is displayed. The client may react too intensely, perhaps in an inappropriate fashion (e.g., throwing things). A chronically stressed individual might display such an excess too often, or may continue to react for a long time.

The second category includes those behaviors which are notable by their absence. A behavioral deficit is evident when a desirable behavior fails to occur with sufficient frequency, for a proper duration, with adequate intensity, in an appropriate manner, under socially expected conditions. Deficits in social skills and assertiveness are common behavioral deficits which are related to stress. Other behavioral deficits encountered in stressed clients include the inability to manage time efficiently, and the inability to use leisure time effectively.

The third category of stress-related behavior includes behavioral assets. In contrast to excesses and deficits, behavioral assets are not problem behaviors, but rather, positive behavioral attributes which either reduce stress or moderate the stress response. In the treatment of the stressed client, it is advantageous to identify and reinforce behavioral assets, both to ensure their continued performance and to encourage their generalization.

Regardless of the exact nature of the behaviors identified, the general strategies for change are the same. In stress management programs, it is most likely that self-management procedures will be employed, rather than externally controlled contingency management approaches (unless the therapist is dealing with an institutionalized population). The stress therapist usually does not have direct access to the target behaviors, which generally occur outside the therapeutic situation. Stressful behaviors are frequently linked to cognitive or covert activities, which are in any case inaccessible to direct observation. Therefore, the need for self-management of behavior is partly a matter of necessity. But in addition, the purpose of stress management is not simply to modify or eliminate specific behaviors, but also to introduce a set of generalizable skills and coping strategies which the client can employ in future situations. As a result, self-management techniques are the most useful and most appropriate behavior change techniques to be used in stress management.

Below, the general principles of self-management or self-directed behavior change are described. In addition, three types of behavior which are very often important in stress management are also described; these include assertiveness, time management, and using leisure time effectively.

SELF-MANAGEMENT

Self-management approaches to behavior change are directed at providing clients with a framework for assessing and changing their own behavior, through implementation of a series of behavioral strategies. In contrast to other behavioral approaches which involve passive conditioning, self-management approaches require the client to carry out the tasks of monitoring, measuring, shaping, and reinforcing behavior, tasks which are carried out by the therapist in other therapist-implemented behavioral programs. In essence, the client receives a crash course in the experimental analysis of behavior (Rimm & Masters, 1979).

The Theory of Self-Regulation

The practice of self-management builds on the premise that when an individual needs to acquire new behaviors, or when habitual behaviors are no longer effective, the process of self-regulation comes into play (Kanfer & Goldstein, 1986). The self-regulation process, as described by Kanfer (1970, 1971; Kanfer & Hagerman, 1981) comprises three stages; these are presented in Figure 9–1. The first stage is self-monitoring. In

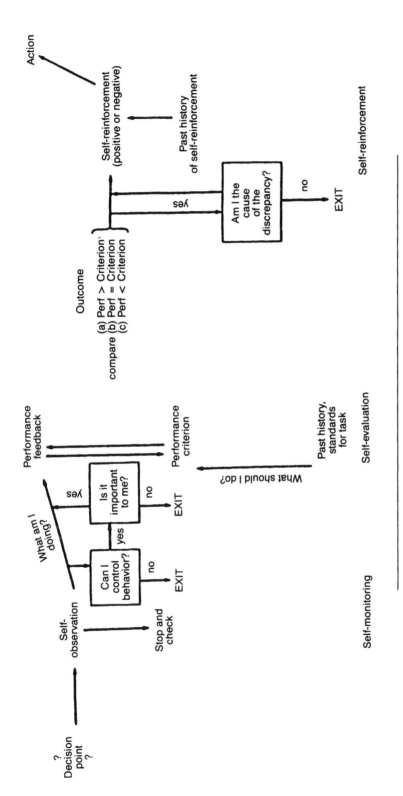

Figure 9–1. A model of self-regulation. Reprinted with permission from F. H. Kanfer and A. P. Goldstein (1986), *Helping people change: A textbook of methods* (3rd edition). New York: Pergamon Press.

this stage, the individual begins to attend to his or her own behavior, monitoring or assessing qualitative or quantitative aspects of that behavior. The individual may monitor the frequency and duration of the behavior, or he or she may attend to the quality of the behavior, or the circumstances surrounding the behavior. As the process of self-regulation begins, the individual faces a number of decisions. First, is the behavior in question under the individual's control? More specifically, does the individual perceive that he or she can control the behavior? If the client doubts his or her own efficacy, the self-regulation process does not come into play. In addition, the individual must address the importance of the behavior in question. As Kanfer and Goldstein (1986) point out, trivial behaviors are generally not the focus of self-regulatory activity. The process of change is difficult and time-consuming. Whether the individual is engaging in the process of self-regulation spontaneously or as a part of therapy, the benefit of the change must be weighed against the work of changing.

The manner in which an individual monitors his or her behavior will reflect that individual's beliefs about acceptable behavior. Most individuals have formulated expectations of the appropriate frequency, duration, or other characteristic for the specified behavior. It is these preconceived rules or standards which the individual will use both to determine the units of self-monitoring and to compare with his or her own behavior, in the second stage of self-regulation.

The second stage in the self-regulation process is self-evaluation. Once an individual has determined that a behavior is controllable and important, and he or she has monitored the behavior in some way, he or she will compare his or her own behavior to his or her personal standard. Further action is likely to be based on the perception of the fit of personal behavior to personal standards. In order for the individual to arrive at a satisfactory evaluation, two criteria must be met. First, self-monitoring must be accurate and specific. Second, the standards must be reasonable and appropriate.

Finally, in the third stage, the individual reacts to the results of the self-evaluation. This stage is called the self-reinforcement stage, and its primary purpose is to motivate change. If the individual's assessment is that his or her own behavior meets or exceeds his or her own standard, then self-reinforcement occurs. Failure to meet the established standard leads the individual to address the source of the discrepancy. If it is felt to lie within the individual, then he or she is motivated to initiate a new response, and the whole self-regulatory process begins again.

The Structure of Self-Management

Kanfer and his colleagues (Kanfer & Grimm, 1980; Kanfer & Gold-stein, 1986; Schefft & Kanfer, 1987) have described the process involved in the therapeutic utilization of the self-management process. This process gives systematic attention to the context in which treatment occurs, and specifies seven stages in the process. Kanfer's conceptualization is particularly well suited for use within the stress management framework. The focus of Kanfer's approach is the creation of a structure and environment within which behavior change can occur. Its emphasis is proactive and participatory, as is the emphasis of stress management in general. Kanfer's approach permits the client to adopt a problem-solving orientation which can be applied to any problem behavior.

The seven phases of this process include:

1. role structuring and creating a therapeutic alliance;
2. developing a commitment for change;
3. conducting a behavioral analysis;
4. negotiating treatment objectives;
5. executing treatment and maintaining motivation;
5. monitoring and evaluating progress;
7. programming for generalization.

These steps mirror the abstract process of self-regulation (Kanfer & Grimm, 1980), inserting it into the context of therapy. The therapeutic relationship, as denoted in phases 1 and 2 of this process, have already been addressed in Chapters 1 and 5 of this book. At this point in stress management, the alliance is established, and initial commitment, in the form of a general contract, has been developed and formalized. In the five remaining phases of self-management, the behavior change process is emphasized.

Behavioral Analysis. The process of behavioral analysis, which includes self-monitoring, was begun in Chapter 4, in conjunction with the preliminary assessment of stress. Prior to determining the general goals of therapy (i.e., the contract), those behaviors targeted for change were identified and defined. At this point, the work of describing the network of variables affecting the controlling the target behaviors begins. The typical format for such an analysis is the A-B-C format, in which the antecedents (A) and consequences (C) of the behavior (B) are noted, in addition to the behavior itself.

Identifying antecedents requires the client to address the "when, where, how, who, why" questions about the behavior. By recording the antecedents of several different occurrences of the same behavior, the therapist and client should be able to determine the factors which control or precipitate the behavior. Modifying behavior is often a matter of modifying the antecedents or consequences first. The need for thorough assessment is obvious; results of this analysis dictate subsequent intervention.

In spite of the apparent simplicity of making A-B-C observations, it is not always possible to identify consistent or meaningful antecedents or consequences. In situations in which the As and Cs are not readily apparent, it may be that the behavior in question is part of a longer chain of antecedents, behaviors, and consequences. The consequence of one behavior might well be the antecedent of another behavior. Identifying the most significant antecedent or consequence of a behavior may require analysis (and therefore monitoring) of a longer behavioral chain.

Monitoring behavioral excesses and behavioral assets tends to follow the prescribed A-B-C method more easily than does monitoring behavioral deficits. When the behavior in question is one which tends *not* to occur, direct observation and recording of that behavior may yield little information to analyze. In such cases, it may be more useful to monitor problem situations or competing behaviors, either in addition to or instead of the behavior itself.

Negotiating Treatment Objectives. The final result of a behavioral analysis should be a thorough understanding of exactly what the behavior is, what provokes the behavior, what maintains the behavior, and what would be a reasonable goal for change. Whereas a general target as stated in the initial contract (Chapter 5) might state "to work at using leisure time more effectively," the behavioral analysis should yield a goal more akin to "increase the personal discretionary time I have from 20 minutes to one hour daily by restructuring household duties." In addition to stipulating goals, the negotiated objectives should specify the period of time required to meet the goals, and the methods to be employed. As described below, behavior change can occur as a result of altering antecedents and consequences, as well as altering the behavior itself. Altering antecedents or consequences often requires involvement of "significant others" in the process—a prospect which does not suit every client (nor every "other"). Decisions about which strategies and which participants will be involved, and for how long, are all part of the negotiation.

Executing Treatment. Just as there are three elements of the A-B-C process, so are there three points at which change can occur.

1. Altering antecedents. In cases in which a clear A-B relationship exists, and in which antecedents are under the control of the client, behavior can be changed by altering the antecedents themselves. The nature of the A-B relationship will determine the type of change to be employed. Antecedents may be changed through environmental manipulation, skill training, simple avoidance, altering behavioral chains, or asserting cognitive control. Generally, alteration of antecedents is a problem-focused stress management strategy. The antecedent is in fact the stressor; alteration of the stressor leads to a change in the behavioral aspect of the stress response. (This is not to suggest that behaviors are always part of the stress reaction in general. Inappropriate behavior may well be a stressor itself, provoking a stress reaction in the client.)

Consider, for example, the problem behavior of biting one's fingernails under stress. Behavioral analysis may suggest that this behavior occurs most frequently during and immediately after negative encounters with the boss. There are numerous ways in which the antecedent could be altered:

- relocate one's desk so that encounters with the boss will occur as infrequently as possible (environmental manipulation);
- learn to deal with the boss differently (skill acquisition);
- leave the room whenever one sees the boss coming (avoidance);
- determine and alter the cause of negative interactions with the boss (altering the behavioral chain);
- convince oneself that these negative encounters with the boss are meaningless (cognitive control).

In some situations, antecedent control is not feasible. The client may have no control over the antecedent, or there may be many antecedents (as is likely to be the case in nail biting). A second option is to alter the consequences of the behavior.

2. Altering consequences. Behavior which is positively reinforced tends to recur, whereas behavior which is ignored or punished tends not to recur. In cases in which an undesirable behavior is followed by a positive consequence, one simple means of altering the behavior is to remove the positive consequence. This process (extinction) leads to the gradual fading and eventual elimination of the target behavior. Unfortunately, some behaviors are maintained for a long time after the cessation of positive reinforcement, by virtue of habit strength. For some behaviors, the consequences are integral to the behavior itself, and thus cannot be separated out. In some cases, the existing positive consequences can be realigned to occur in conjunction with the absence of the target behavior, rather than with the presence of that behavior. Similarly, a new positive consequence can be introduced, to occur in conjunction with the desirable outcome. (These relationships between behavior and consequence will of course be reversed in the case of behavioral deficits—that is, the presence of the behavior will be reinforced and the absence will not.)

The manipulation of consequences requires that the client be able to identify positive and negative reinforcers. The range of items which can be reinforcing in general is endless. Material possessions, money, activities, attention, privileges, fantasies, and indulgences can all be reinforcing. There is almost nothing, however, which is universally reinforcing. The key is to match individuals with reinforcers.

When manipulating the consequences of a behavior, the therapist and client must also consider the frequency of the behavior (and therefore of the consequence). Frequent behaviors require either small reinforcers or infrequent reinforcement. The rate at which a behavior is reinforced (called the reinforcement schedule) also has implications for the maintenance of behavior. A full discussion of reinforcement schedules is beyond the scope of this chapter. It is worth noting, however, that although continuous reinforcement (i.e., reinforcing the behavior every time it occurs) does alter behavior quickly, its cessation results in the rapid elimination of that behavior. For behaviors which are to be maintained or generalized, less frequent reinforcement is more effective. Thus, the behavior in question might be reinforced after every fifth time it occurs, or after every second hour of its occurrence.

In spite of the wide range of potential reinforcers, there are times in which it is difficult to identify reinforcers. Depressed individuals often complain that nothing appeals to them. Other individuals may be able to identify a variety of material items which would be reinforcing to them, but which are unavailable or unaffordable. Still others may be able to identify reinforcers, but they may already have as much access to these as they want. In cases such as these, reinforcement can be created within the context of the Premack Principle. This principle was first articulated by Premack (1965) and later applied to self-management strategies by Danaher (1974). It states that one way to increase the frequency of a low-frequency (desirable) behavior is to make the occurrence of another high-frequency behavior contingent on the performance of the low-frequency behavior (Watson & Tharp, 1981).

In the case of nail biting, the following options emerge for altering consequences:

- coat the nails with a foul-tasting substance (punishment);
- for every day in which nail biting occurs, $10 must be donated to charity (response cost);
- for every day in which nail biting does not occur, $10 may be put in a wardrobe fund (positive reinforcement);
- in order to go out to lunch (a high-frequency behavior) the client must first not nail bite for one day (Premack Principle—here, not biting one's nails is a low-frequency behavior).

Just as not all behavioral antecedents lend themselves to alteration, not all consequences can be easily manipulated. Often, consequences are outside of the client's control, or difficult to identify. In some cases, therefore, direct manipulation of the behavior is indicated.

3. *Changing behaviors.* When altering antecedents or consequences is not effective, it is often because the desired behavior is not in the client's normal behavioral repertoire—that is, the client does not know how to perform the behavior, performs it poorly, or is uncomfortable performing it. When this is the case, as it frequently is when behavioral deficits are evident, direct training and modification of the behavior is indicated. One of the most obvious solutions to this dilemma is direct skills training. If the client does not know how to perform the behavior, teach him or her. The client who is stressed by having too much to do at work, for example, may benefit from specific training in additional job skills—typing faster, writing more fluently, communicating more effectively, manipulating objects in a more efficient manner. Obvious as this solution may seem, it is often overlooked. In some cases, the client may be unaware that there is a more efficient way to accomplish a task (". . . but we've always done it this way!") Stressed clients may also be reluctant to sacrifice time, which may already be at a premium, to take a course or otherwise obtain instruction. Either of these excuses can usually be countered by rational argument. It behooves the therapist to be aware, however, of the essential truth within the arguments of some clients' reluctance to change their ways. For an extremely stressed client, the additional burden of skills training may be overwhelming. The decision to take this course must be considered carefully within the context of the individual client's needs. Proper timing is important.

It is also possible and appropriate to teach some specific behaviors in the therapy setting. These are unlikely to be specific job behaviors, but may be more general interpersonal skills. They may also be related to specific problem situations. In addition, they may be behaviors which the client knows how to perform, but does not. Behaviors such as assertiveness are commonly learned in the therapy setting. There are a number of common behavioral techniques which are used to teach specific behavioral skills, or to encourage the use of behavioral skills which have been acquired but not utilized. Some of these are listed below.

1. *Shaping (or successive approximation)*. These terms refer to a procedure which allows the individual to acquire the target behavior in a gradual fashion. Initially, any behavior which shows some similarity to the desired behavior is rewarded. As time progresses, the behavior produced must become more similar to the target behavior in order to be reinforced (Rimm & Masters, 1979). Gradually, the client's behavior becomes closer to the target behavior, until eventually, the target behavior itself is achieved. If the target behavior is assertiveness, for example, any attempt toward acting assertively will be reinforced initially. At first, the client may be asked simply to identify those situations which call for assertive behavior. Next, any attempt at being assertive is reinforced. Eventually, only a proper assertive behavior merits reinforcement.

2. *Modeling*. If a client is unable to produce a particular behavior, he or she may benefit from watching another individual perform the target behavior. This may be done in person or by way of a tape or film. Generally, models who are similar to the client have the greatest effect upon the client. (This may mean that the therapist is not the most effective model for the client, since the client may feel that the therapist is much more competent in general, and the client may therefore not identify with him or her.) Modeling is frequently used to help individuals who have to cope with stressful medical procedures. The most effective model seems to be one who is able to demonstrate the use of coping strategies to deal with the stressor, rather than one who is not affected by the stressor. An individual who is fearful of undergoing surgery, for example, will benefit more from seeing a model who is also fearful but who copes with the fear, as opposed to seeing a model who is not fearful.

3. *Rehearsal*. With rehearsal, the therapist simply gives the client the opportunity to practice the target behavior outside of the problem situation. Bandura (1971) suggests that the impact of modeling will be maximized if it is followed by rehearsal. Rehearsal also tends to employ elements of shaping; the client offers his or her best approximation of the target behavior, then selective reinforcement is provided and another (hopefully better) approximation of the behavior is offered.

Although rehearsal may initially occur in the confines of the therapy session, it tends to be more beneficial and generalizes more effectively if some rehearsal is done in a natural setting.

4. *Role-playing*. For target behaviors related to interpersonal or social skills, the client and the therapist may take part in role-playing. In this procedure, the client is asked to assume the "role" of another person. He or she may be asked to play the role of a person with whom he or she normally has difficulty, while the therapist plays the client. The client may also be asked to role-play the behavior of another individual in the situation which the client finds problematic. The client may even be asked to role-play his or her own behavior in a particular situation. Role-playing combines elements of modeling, rehearsal, shaping, and desensitization.

5. *Flooding*. When the behavior which needs to be changed is an avoidance behavior, a high level of exposure to the stressful stimulus may extinguish the behavior. In flooding, the client is repeatedly exposed to the identified stressor, but is prevented from making an avoidance response. Initially, the reaction to the stressor may be extreme, but it gradually lessens as the client becomes habituated. This technique may be applied in vivo, in which case the actual stressor is present; or the exposure may be done imaginarily. Either approach is effective; the latter is often more practical.

Flooding has the disadvantage of being an aversive technique. It is preferable to select a positive technique such as modeling if it is appropriate. Flooding and modeling appear to be about equally effective (Rimm & Masters, 1979).

6. *Negative practice*. When the problem is one of behavioral excess or inappropriate behavior, practicing the undesirable behavior repeatedly seems to lead to its extinction. Although negative practice seems contrary to common sense, it appears that the fatigue, boredom, and (perhaps) disgust that accompany forced negative practice are effective negative consequences. Rapid smoking, mentioned in Chapter 7, is a negative practice technique.

7. *Reinforcing incompatible behaviors*. This principle, which underlies the technique of systematic desensitization, suggests that one way to eliminate a behavior is to perform an incompatible behavior. The nail biter, for example, cannot bite his or her nails and knit at the same time.

8. *Self-monitoring*. Although self-monitoring was originally conceptualized as an assessment technique, it has emerged as an effective behavior change technique as well. When the client is required to attend closely to his or her behavior in order to record it, behavior change is likely (Kanfer & Goldstein, 1986). Self-monitoring is most effective within the self-

regulation context, in which the individual has standards against which to compare, and in which some reinforcement for change occurs.

These are only a few of the many behavioral change methods in the literature. Those described above are among those most frequently used in conjunction with self-management of stress problems. Details of these procedures and others can be found in texts of behavior therapy such as Kanfer and Goldstein (1986) and Rimm and Masters (1979).

Monitoring and Evaluating Progress. At regular predetermined intervals in therapy, the client and therapist should assess progress. This practice allows adjustment of procedures, reformulation of goals, and reinforcement of change. It is often useful to repeat some of the initial assessment strategies to demonstrate change (or lack of change). The monitoring/evaluation process actually coincides temporally with the treatment phase (Kanfer & Grimm, 1980). As each behavior change technique is employed, its quantitative or qualitative effect is assessed, so that the therapist and client are both aware of what is working, and what is not working. Throughout the entire process of behavior change, it is essential to assess and reassess the client's motivation for change, his or her commitment to change, and the relevance of the established goals. Failure to approach or achieve the target behaviors can be attributable to a variety of causes. The most obvious of these is selection of inappropriate behavior change methods—but this is only one of many possible sources of difficulty. It is important to consider all of the potential sources of treatment failure, in order to avoid premature abandonment of the selected behavior change technique. At times, a client may lose interest or motivation. In multistage procedures, clients may experience difficulty with only one aspect of the procedure. Sometimes apparent treatment failures may be attributable to improper execution of the selected technique, rather than to improper selection of techniques.

Finally, the therapist needs to be aware of the impact that changing life circumstances may have on the treatment goals. Target behaviors may become less relevant or less desirable if the circumstances surrounding the behavior change. (For example, the motivation to become assertive with one's family may change if one's spouse leaves.)

The process of behavior change does not always follow a smooth course. By reviewing and monitoring progress on a regular basis, the therapist and client can address problems and questions as they arise, thus maximizing the potential for therapeutic success.

Treatment Generalization. The process of behavior change culminates in the transfer of skills learned in therapy to use in the daily life and natural setting of the client. One way in which generalization outside the therapy situation can be encouraged is through use of systematic assignments to practice the target behavior in specific situations. Use of such "homework" assignments is a fairly standard procedure in behavior therapy. The most effective means of generalization, however, is to ensure that the client learns the rules and principles that govern a behavior, rather than simply learning to perform a target behavior. By employing variety in practice situations and by emphasizing general principles of behavior change, the therapist can maximize the possibility of transfer of skills to new situations.

Generalization also requires emphasis on the connection between the client's own effort and the improvement or achievement of goals. In order for the client to invoke new behavioral skills in new situations, he or she must be convinced that his or her own efforts were responsible for the observed changes. If the client is confident that he or she has acquired a new set of behavioral skills, that he or she understands the principles underlying the behavior change, and that he or she controls the circumstances surrounding the behavior, then the client is likely to employ both the new behavioral skills and the learned principles outside of the therapy situation.

These steps outline the general procedure and basic principles involved in changing any behavior. As noted, almost any behavior can be related to stress. There are, however, several types of problematic behavior which often occur in stressed clients. These are described briefly below.

ASSERTIVENESS

Assertiveness (or assertion) training refers to the teaching of social interaction skills which are direct and straightforward, but which are also considerate of the feelings of others (Rimm & Masters, 1979). Although there is no commonly accepted definition of assertive behavior, Jakubowski and Lange (1978) suggest that, "Acting assertively means standing up for your assertive rights and expressing what you believe, feel and want, in direct, honest, appropriate ways that respect the rights of the other person" (p. 2). For several reasons, assertiveness training is often a component of stress management programs.

First, it is generally accepted that behaving in an assertive manner results in an increased feeling of well-being in the client. More specifically, some authors (Wolpe, 1958; Salter, 1949) maintain that assertive behavior is incompatible with anxiety, in much the same way that relaxation is incompatible with anxiety. Wolpe (1958) suggests that assertive behavior can therefore be used to combat anxiety within the model of reciprocal inhibition. In the context of stress management, assertive behavior can be used to counter the anxiety engendered by stress.

Second, assertive behavior is useful in stress management because of its potential to increase the client's control over his or her environment. Stress can frequently be reduced through such simple assertive acts as saying no, asking for help, expressing one's own opinion, or identifying a problem. When a stressed client needs to perform one of these behaviors and cannot, stress increases. When the behavior is performed in an aggressive fashion, without regard for the feelings of others, stress increases. When the problems are addressed in a direct but nonthreatening manner—an assertive manner—the potential for constructive change is maximized, and stress is reduced.

Third, performance of assertive behaviors requires that the client become aware of and accept a variety of personal rights. The failure to accept personal rights is often a contributing factor in stress problems. The client who believes that he or she does not have the right to say no, ask for help, or change his or her mind will interpret more situations as stressful than will the client who acknowledges these rights.

Assertiveness is a behavior, not a personality trait. It is a specific behavior, related to situational variables. Assertive behavior in any individual situation is not apt to be a good predictor of assertive behavior in another unrelated situation. Because of the specific nature of assertive behavior, it is an ideal target for most behavioral change techniques.

There is no general consensus about the specific content of a program of assertiveness training. There are, however, some elements which are common to almost all assertiveness training programs. Most programs begin by identifying the types of situations which are problematic for the client. Whether the problems are most evident in family, work, social, or other situations, training is likely to be geared to remediating difficulties in the specific situations identified. At the same time, the therapist attempts to discover whether the lack of assertive behavior is attributable to skill deficiency, faulty cognitive appraisal, or anxiety.

The bulk of assertiveness training is oriented toward the remediation of behavioral skills deficits. The behavioral technique most commonly employed in assertiveness training is rehearsal. This technique requires that the client and therapist rehearse or act out the identified problematic interactions. In this way, the client is able to practice the desired response and receive feedback about his or her performance. At the same time, the client can examine the potential effect of a change in his or her behavior on the behavior of others involved in the interaction. Such practice may also include role reversal, in which the therapist assumes the role of the client, and the client assumes the role of the other person in the interaction. In addition to perfecting assertiveness skills, the repetition of the desired behavior also allows the client to diminish his or her level of anxiety in regard to that specific situation. Assertive behavior skills are often taught in groups, in which the potential for experience and feedback is greater.

Most assertiveness training programs also include some attention to cognitive appraisal, and acceptance of personal rights related to assertive behavior.

Details of assertiveness techniques and training programs are available in such sources as Jakubowski and Lange (1978) and Alberti and Emmons (1982). Assertiveness training programs are offered by a variety of professionals, in a variety of settings. One advantage of this availability is that the stress therapist may be able to encourage the client to take an assertiveness course at a local community college, women's center, or other agency, while the therapist focuses on another problem, or works on applying (rather than teaching) assertiveness skills. The advantages and disadvantages of "farming out" part of the stress management therapy have been discussed already, particularly in Chapter 6. These advantages and disadvantages must be evaluated in relation to the individual client. Nevertheless, the therapist who does a great deal of stress management work would be well advised to be aware of the local options for assertiveness training programs.

TIME MANAGEMENT

Although stress problems can be the result of either too much or too little stress, the former situation is far more common than the latter. For many overstressed clients, the problem is one of overload; there is simply too much to be done in too little time. For these clients, time management may be an effective stress management tool.

The concept of time management refers to the use of organizational techniques to aid in employing one's time in the most efficient and effective manner possible. Time management techniques developed largely from the area of business management rather than from within the mental health or counseling area. As a result, much of the literature in this field is oriented toward executive and management personnel. There is also a significant industry producing "packaged" programs of time management, including books, seminars, forms, and systems. Thus, time management materials are readily available commercially. What is not as readily available is outcome research on the effectiveness of various techniques or programs. It is therefore essential that the therapist select techniques carefully, and evaluate them on a regular basis.

The basic premise of most time management programs is that wise use of time requires a clear statement of priorities, with most time devoted to high priority items. Regardless of whether time is a problem at work, at home, or in general, time is used most effectively when priorities are clearly identified. For this reason, the first step in most time management programs is to identify the relative importance of the various tasks competing for time.

In a general sense, deciding priorities requires that the client review all the different roles and responsibilities, and attempt to assign an order of priority to them. Is work more important than family? Does the value of returning to school part-time outweigh the value of social activities in the evening? Until the client can identify some general direction and hierarchy of importance in his or her life in general, it is not possible to organize time within the day. Once general priorities are clear, Lakein (1973) suggests that specific demands can be dealt with by assigning each demand a priority rating of "A" (high priority), "B" (moderate priority), or "C" (low priority). He further suggests that all the "As" should be addressed before time is devoted to lower priority items.

Determining priorities may seem an obvious step, but it is often more complicated than it might appear on the surface. Sometimes priorities are not clear. The client may need to consult with coworkers and supervisors or with family members to clarify priorities. Often the client feels that *all* tasks are priorities. Yet if time is a problem, some differentiation must be made. Which of the three projects is most important to the company? Does the family prefer gourmet meals or clean floors? The desires or priorities of others should not necessarily override individual priorities, but input from others can provide clarification in ambiguous circumstances.

Even when priorities are obvious, they can easily be overlooked by the client. It is easy to forget that attending to the children outweighs mopping the floors, or that beginning a major report is more valuable than completing the filing. The act of identifying and recording priorities can help to overcome these difficulties.

This advice sounds simple, yet it is often difficult to implement. High priority items are often long, complicated, and involved projects, whereas low priority items may be brief and straightforward. The tendency is often to deal with the latter first, since it is easy to accomplish many low priority items in a fraction of the time necessary to accomplish one "A" item. Unfortunately, this approach generally leads to frustration, as the important tasks never get done. Lakein (1973) recommends breaking down large, important tasks into smaller chunks which can be managed more easily. Finding time to do the spring-cleaning all at once may be difficult, since it is such a large and time-consuming project. However, if the task is subdivided (e.g., clean the bedroom closet, wash the bedroom baseboards, send the bedroom curtains for cleaning, and so forth) each small part can be taken on individually, and accomplished in a briefer period of time.

Once priorities have been established, specific goals are set and plans to achieve them are developed. Some of the more common techniques used in time management include:

Task analysis. Large, time-consuming tasks are broken down into small units that are more easily accomplished.

Daily planning. Time is routinely put aside at the start or end of each day, to list, organize, and prioritize that day's (or next day's) activities. When constructing such lists, one should take into account how much time is actually available during a given day.

Time restructuring. Attempts can be made to create larger chunks of time during the day. One hour is infinitely more useful than six 10-minute periods. Reorganization can help create larger chunks of time.

Identifying time wasters. Taylor (1981) lists 56 common time wasters, including such items as procrastination, poor control of meetings, idle talk with coworkers, frequent telephone interruptions, rewriting letters and memos, poor listening skills, and perfectionism. The first step in getting rid of time wasters is to identify them.

Delegation. Whether to coworkers or family members, many tasks can be assigned to others.

Saying no. Many people find it difficult to turn down an assignment, even when it is clear that they cannot carry it out. Assertiveness training may help.

Avoiding perfectionism. Lakein (1973) points out that there are very few things worth doing perfectly. One should identify these few things and do them perfectly; other things should be done adequately.

Time analysis. Keeping a time log for a week or two will tell exactly where time is going, and where changes can be made.

Scheduling efficiently. Most individuals have a particular time of day when they are most effective. Creative endeavors and "A" activities should be slotted into the most productive time of day.

Time management is a process rather than a discrete skill. Like most self-management approaches, it relies on the acquisition of general principles by the client, principles which can be applied as needed over time. Efficient time management can reduce some of the stress engendered by work overload. What time management cannot do is put more hours in the day or increase the length of the week. There is a danger of creating unrealistic expectations when talking about time management. The ideally organized, efficient, controlled, unflappable person who *always* schedules, plans, and structures his or her time perfectly and to the minute probably does not exist. If this person did exist, he or she would probably not be much fun. Some time wasting—in the form of recreation, socializing, and personal indulgence—is essential to human functioning. What time management can do is allow one to be organized and efficient more often, and to use the available time more effectively.

LEISURE ACTIVITIES

Leisure activity is traditionally defined as "a state characterized by meaningful and nonutilitarian activity" (Neulinger, 1974, p. 3). It is the characteristic of meaningfulness which makes leisure activity important in stress management. However, leisure activity is an area which is frequently overlooked in the lives of stressed clients, primarily because of its nonutilitarian nature. Because leisure activity is nonutilitarian, many clients view it as dispensable, or—at best—a low priority activity. For understressed clients, the problem is reversed. Making good use of excess leisure time can be equally problematic.

The function of leisure activity in stress management is to assist in achieving balance in the client's life—balance between eustress and distress, balance between too much and too little stress.

Selection of leisure activities is often governed by the principle of optimal incongruity. Leisure activities are to assist the individual in attaining an optimal level of arousal and stimulation. The notion of incongruity suggests that individuals who are overstressed, who participate in many energetic, challenging, and tiring activities will select restorative leisure pursuits—activities which are quiet and nonenergetic, but pleasant. Restorative leisure activities allow the individual to compensate for high levels of arousal in other aspects of life. Conversely, in an understimulated individual, leisure activities may serve a diversionary function; a high-energy, challenging, and competitive activity can provide the stimulation and excitement which might otherwise be lacking in the individual's life (Iso-Ahola, 1980).

Witt and Bishop (1970) examined the motivating forces behind individuals' selection of leisure activities. They found that the major motivating forces were: (1) the need for additional stimulation; (2) catharsis, the need to release emotional tension and anxiety; and (3) compensation, the need to compensate for unattained goals in other aspects of life. Hollender (1977) also identified escape as an important motivational factor.

The implications of these observations for stress management are clear. Depending upon what else is happening in the client's life, leisure activities can be selected to help achieve the proper balance and quality of stress for the client.

Discussion of leisure activity often overlaps with the topics of time management and cognitive interventions. The overstressed client may need to convince him- or herself that leisure activity is a legitimate use of time; he or she may also need assistance in organizing the time to carry out leisure activities. The understressed individual may need to be convinced that nonutilitarian activity can be meaningful; he or she may also need to manage time effectively to arrive at the optimal level of stimulation.

CASE STUDIES

Cathy

Within Cathy's group, some time was dedicated to both time management and assertiveness. (In view of the small number of group sessions scheduled, no time was allotted for formal discussion of self-management principles in general.)

In the time management session, each group member was first asked to list all his or her goals for the next year (a two-minute time limit was imposed on this activity). Cathy was surprised to find this a difficult task, and was forced to acknowledge that she largely worried about day-to-day concerns, rather than long-range plans. The group leader discussed the importance of clear personal goals, in order to utilize time more efficiently.

The group members were also asked to list everything that they had done on the previous day, and how much time each activity took. Most group members were surprised at how little of the day they were able to account for. The group members were then encouraged to compare their stated goals with how their time was actually spent. Again, the inconsistencies between goals and time usage were discussed.

The session concluded with distribution of a time management reading list.

In another session, assertiveness was first defined by the group leader. He then demonstrated a number of possible responses to interpersonal interactions, and group members were asked to categorize the responses as passive, aggressive, or assertive. Once the group members had an idea of the concept of assertiveness, each member was asked to identify a situation which was problematic for him or her, and then to practice an assertive response. For this exercise, the group was subdivided into units of three.

Finally, each participant was asked to identify one thing that prevents him or her from acting assertively. A brief discussion of personal rights ensued.

Cathy was surprised to find that her initial reluctance to act assertively seemed to be influenced largely by her belief (developed in childhood) that this type of behavior is "selfish" and unladylike. This was a feeling shared by several of the group members, who were then able to counter with arguments against these ideas.

Jean

Within the behavioral sphere, Jean had expressed interest in learning how to manage her many time commitments better. Her basic concern is how to balance the demands from work, from her children, from her household responsibilities, and from her own personal needs. Jean had a great deal of difficulty identifying her priorities among all these various demands. She was able to acknowledge that housework was probably the least important of the lot, but admitted that she found it very difficult to ignore the housework when it was not done properly. She was also able to define work as being a priority only within working hours. The major remaining problem was to find a balance between the need for time for her own personal needs, and time to spend with the children. Jean's immediate time management goals were therefore:

1. To turn down any and all requests for overtime work. Jean acknowledged that there were few times that such requests were true emergencies, and that better organization at work on her own part as well as that of her coworkers could minimize the emergencies.

2. To determine reasonable allotments of time for herself, for the kids, and for housework.

Jean was asked if she thought that assertiveness training would help her to avoid extra work at the office, but she declined the offer, stating that she felt that she could be assertive if she made up her mind to do so.

Since the two highest priorities were her personal needs and those of the kids, Jean began work on a schedule to plan meaningful activities in these areas. She confessed that when she gets home from work, she is usually too tired to think of something to do with the kids, so they often end up watching TV together. After reviewing the types of things that she likes to do with the children, Jean decided to try to implement a regular once-a-week picnic time with the children. She was encouraged to delegate to the children the task of preparing a picnic supper every Tuesday, so that they could leave as soon as Jean was home from work. Jean expressed some concern about the nutritional soundness of a meal prepared by her sons, but was able to acknowledge that for this one meal, the time spent together was a higher priority than was the nutritional adequacy. Jean agreed to try this activity for four weeks, at which time she and the children would review the success of the activity.

Jean also mentioned that she found the unkempt state of the house to be particularly annoying when she got home from work. Thus, she frequently did some housework while making dinner. Jean would be in the kitchen working while the children watched TV. She agreed to reschedule all housework until after the children were in bed. Jean stated that she generally liked to have a bit of quiet time after coming home from work, yet she felt that she should be spending this time with the kids. Again, a compromise was proposed, in which she would watch TV with the kids after work. This activity gave Jean the opportunity to sit and relax, but also to share an activity with the children.

Jean also wanted to schedule some time for herself, but generally found that she simply ran out of hours in the day to do the things that she enjoyed. When she was asked how she found time for herself, she stated that once the kids were taken care of and the housework was done, she tried to knit, read, or do exercises, but more often than not, bedtime came before she had accomplished these goals. Referring back to priorities that she had determined earlier, Jean agreed that personal time should be more important than housework. She agreed to schedule one 45-minute period during each evening in which she could participate in an activity of her own choosing.

Jean reported back after a few weeks that the picnic evenings with her children were working well. She was surprised to find that the boys

quite enjoyed making dinner. As a result, Jean and her sons are considering having a second evening every week in which the boys make
dinner—this time, to be eaten at home (with supervision as needed).
Jean was very pleased about this development, as it was a way to incorporate essential work with time with the children.

Jean has had some difficulty refraining from doing housework during
her own personal time in the evening. She finds it difficult to tolerate
untidiness. As a result, she has decided to spend one half hour tidying
the room in which she is going to be for the evening, then to engage in
her leisure pursuits. She was amused to report that she found herself
cleaning with much more enthusiasm, since she knew that her activity
would be rewarded by "time off."

There were several other problems within the time management area
which Jean was interested in addressing. These included learning to
manage the time before work and school better, deciding what to do
with her limited vacation time from work, and getting some time for
social activities outside the home. Jean and the therapist agreed to address these concerns once the changes she had already made had had a
chance to gel.

J. B.

J. B. had expressed interest in dealing with the issue of family conflict,
particularly with his teenaged son. As a first step in the process, he was
asked to keep a diary identifying the antecedents and consequences of
these arguments. J. B. kept such a diary for two weeks. He found that
arguments were most likely to occur on days on which he was particularly tired, or when he had just returned from being out of town. There
seemed to be little substance to the arguments; they argued over petty
matters such as hairstyles, dress, and his son's tendency to be secretive.
J. B. acknowledged that he really did not have very strong feelings about
these issues, and he was not sure why they argued about them. The
arguments almost invariably occurred between 5 and 7 P.M. It was somewhat more difficult to identify consequences of these interactions. J. B.
tended to have a strained relationship with his son, at best, so these
encounters did not have a strikingly negative effect on the relationship.
However, they did help to maintain his stress. As noted earlier, they also
contributed to J. B.'s ulcer problems.

J. B. and the therapist concluded that the arguments were probably
not isolated behaviors, but rather, part of a long and complex chain of
behaviors, partly related to J. B.'s tired state and lower tolerance at the

time, and partly related to the lack of a meaningful relationship between J. B. and his son.

Although it was not noted in the diary, J. B. mentioned that usually his wife and son avoided him immediately following one of these arguments, so he had some time to himself at that point; he usually read the paper and watched the news. Although he felt a bit guilty about this, he rather enjoyed the break between work and dinner.

The therapist suggested to J. B. that he try both to alter the whole after-work chain of behavior, and that he develop a more positive relationship with his son, perhaps stemming from an activity that they might both enjoy. After some discussion, it was decided that J. B. would try to go on a brief bicycle ride after work each day, to help him relax and to act as a transition time. (Coincidentally, this also helped address J. B.'s concern about his use of leisure time.) In addition, J. B. would encourage his son to accompany him on bike rides, on those days when J. B. was not unduly stressed. J. B. expressed some concern about how reliably he might be able to carry out this behavior, but agreed to try it for three weeks.

Epilogue

Cathy

At the conclusion of the group, Cathy and the other group members were asked to complete an evaluation of the program. Cathy stated that she considered the educational component of the program to have been the most useful part for her. Cathy felt that through the group she had been able to develop an overall understanding of the nature and effects of stress, and of the many solutions available for stress-related problems. Like many of the other group members, Cathy also felt that the coverage of most interventions was too brief. Though she did not feel confident enough to make any substantial changes in her own life, she did feel able to single out potential problem areas.

Cathy's assessment of her group program is fairly typical of the observations of many individuals who participate in such programs. They serve a primary didactic, educational, and preventative purpose. They are generally inadequate for actually inducing change, yet they typically enable participants to identify problems and to determine what (if any) work remains to be done. As it turns out, Cathy did not think it necessary to proceed any further at present. However, it is not at all unusual for individuals in groups or workshops to use these programs as a first step in seeking individual help. For individuals with no experience in the mental health system, groups and workshops provide a relatively non-threatening mode of access to this system. Therapists who carry out groups or workshops in stress management may find that they are approached afterwards by individuals seeking individual therapy. Therefore, it is wise to be prepared for such requests, and to be able to provide or arrange follow-up.

Jean

Jean continued in weekly therapy for just over six months, and accomplished much of what she had set out to do. She was able to achieve significant changes in terms of attitudes and cognitions. Once Jean was able to appreciate the role of appraisal in stress, and her own biases in appraisal, change had come rapidly. Her ability to challenge some of her longstanding beliefs about work and family, and about her own self-worth, enabled her to effect change in other areas. Time management became much less of a problem as Jean's priorities were clarified. In fact, the ability to issue and respond to cognitive challenges was the foundation for change in many areas of Jean's life. Much of Jean's behavior had been influenced by her maladaptive cognitions. By acquiring the skills to reinterpret and reappraise the situations around her, Jean was able to reduce her stress level significantly, yet without creating a great deal of upheaval in her life. Jean did not change jobs, hire household help, or become estranged from her parents—but the amount of stress experienced in all these areas was reduced either directly or indirectly because of her reinterpretation of these stressors. Thus, even without direct physiological interventions, many of Jean's somatic symptoms lessened. Certainly her mood was significantly improved.

The logical outcome of Jean's changing perceptions was her decision that she might better spend time taking an exercise class rather than continuing in therapy. This decision was supported by her therapist. Jean enrolled in a yoga program at the community recreation center.

Over the following six months, Jean intermittently contacted her therapist to discuss specific issues. During this time, the relationship served a primarily supportive function for Jean, reinforcing the gains that she was making.

Jean's course of therapy was remarkably successful. A number of factors probably contributed to that success. Jean was ready for change, and obviously capable of participating in therapy. She was distressed enough to be motivated, yet not so distressed as to be immobilized. Her particular problems were directly attributable to stress, and consequently responded well to an integrated stress management perspective. As Jean had had no previous experience in therapy, she was able to participate with few preconceived ideas. Finally, the therapist had been able to conceptualize Jean's problems in a credible manner, select appropriate interventions, and carry them out effectively. The program worked well.

J. B.

J. B.'s program of therapy met with some success, as measured by the reduction in level of discomfort caused by his ulcer. However, further work could have been done, had J. B. been so inclined. J. B.'s attempts to spend more time with his son were not terribly successful. The high level of tension between J. B. and his son tended to make the bicycling trips seem a bit contrived, and as a result both often avoided them. After this failure, J. B. was reluctant to pursue the idea of family issues any further.

Looking back at J. B.'s original plan (Figure 5–4), one can see that he was reasonably successful in learning a relaxation type; he made a slight gain in the area of using leisure time effectively; and he did not deal with life-style issues or family issues to any significant extent. Cognitive issues, as noted in Chapters 5 and 8, were really never even considered by J. B.

On the surface, J. B.'s course of treatment seems unsatisfactory, or at least incomplete. It is interesting to note that J. B. felt much more positive about the outcome of therapy than did the therapist. J. B.'s original intent had been: to learn a bit more about the relationship between his ulcer and stress; to learn a relaxation technique; and to decrease ulcer symptoms. In fact he had achieved these goals. Although the therapist remained convinced that much more work could be done, J. B. was not convinced that this was necessary. In retrospect, the therapist might have been wiser to have been more conservative in establishing the plan originally. On the other hand, at least J. B. now knows what treatment options are open to him.

Cathy, Jean, and J. B.—three different individuals who followed different courses to deal with stress, and achieved different levels of change. Is there actually a common denominator? Can all three of these cases be appropriately subsumed under the heading "stress management"? The problems were different and the solutions were different, but the conceptualization was the same. And conceptualization is, in fact, the essential and unique component that turns "therapy" into "stress management."

The conceptualization of stress as a taxing relationship between the individual and his or her environment permits focus on both changing problems and dealing with emotions. In other words, this conceptualization allows for both action and coping. Though it includes attention to the dynamics and intrapsychic functioning of the individual, it is not limited to these areas. It is a comprehensive approach to therapy, one in which the component parts are integrated into a coherent framework. It is the formulation of issues and the development of an operational definition of stress within the therapeutic relationship that gives stress management its identity.

References

Alberti, R., & Emmons, M. (1982). *Your perfect right: A guide to assertive behavior.* (4th ed.). San Luis Obispo, CA: Impact.

Alexander, F. (1950). *Psychosomatic medicine: Its principles and application.* New York: Norton.

Alexander, F., French, T., & Pollack G. (Eds.). (1968). *Psychosomatic specificity* (Vol. I). Chicago: University of Chicago Press.

Allan, C. A., & Cooke, D. J. (1985). Stressful life events and alcohol misuse in women: A critical review. *Journal of Studies in Alcohol, 46,* 147–152.

Allen, R. J., & Hyde, D. (1980). *Investigations in stress control.* Minneapolis: Burgess.

Anderson, G. E. (1972). *College schedule of recent experience.* Unpublished master's thesis, North Dakota State University.

Andres, R. (1980). Influence of obesity on longevity in the aged. In C. Borek, C. M. Fenoglio, & D. W. King (Eds.). *Aging, cancer and cell membranes.* Stuttgart: Thieme Verlag.

Antonovsky, A. (1982). *Health, stress and coping.* San Francisco: Jossey-Bass.

Armstrong, B., & Doll, R. (1974). Bladder cancer mortality in England and Wales in relation to cigarette smoking and saccharin consumption. *British Journal of Preventive and Social Medicine, 28,* 233–240.

Asterita, M. F. (1985). *The physiology of stress.* New York: Human Sciences Press.

Bakal, D. A. (1979). *Psychology and medicine: Psychobiological dimensions of health and illness.* New York: Springer.

Bandura, A. (1971). Psychotherapy based on modelling principles. In A. E. Bergin & S. L. Garfield (Eds.). *Handbook of psychotherapy and behavior change* (pp. 111–136). New York: Wiley.

Barnett, R. C., Biener, L., & Baruch, G. K. (1987). *Gender and stress.* New York: The Free Press.

Barrett, D. E., & Radke-Yarrow, M. (1985). Effects of nutritional supplementation on children's responses to novel, frustrating and competitive situations. *American Journal of Clinical Nutrition, 42* (July), 102–120.

Basmajian, H. V. (1979). *Biofeedback—Principles and practice for clinicians.* Baltimore: Williams & Wilkins.

Beatty, J. (1982). Biofeedback in the treatment of migraine: Simple relaxation or specific effects? In L. White and B. Tursky (Eds.), *Clinical biofeedback: Efficacy and mechanisms* (pp. 211–221). New York: Guilford Press.

Beck, A. T. (1976). *Cognitive therapy and the emotional disorders.* New York: Times-Mirror.

Beidel, D. C., & Turner, S. M. (1986). A critique of the theoretical bases of cognitive-behavioral theories and therapies. *Clinical Psychology Review, 6,* 177–197.

Bell, R. A., Keeley, K. A., Clements, R. D., Warheit, G. J., & Holzer, C. E. (1976). Alcoholism, life events and psychiatric improvement. *Annals of the New York Academy of Sciences, 273,* 467–480.

Benson, H. (1975). *The relaxation response.* New York: Morrow.

Benson, H., Kotch, J., Crassweller, K., & Greenwood, M. (1977). Historical and clinical considerations of the relaxation response. *American Scientist, 65,* 441–445.

242

Benson, H., & Wallace, R. K. (1972). Decreased drug abuse with transcendental meditation: A study of 1,862 subjects. In C. J. Zarafonetis (Ed.), *Drug abuse: Proceedings of the international conference* (pp. 369–376). Philadelphia: Lea & Febiger.

Berdanier, C. D. (1987). The many faces of stress. *Nutrition Today, 22*(2), 12–17.

Bernstein, D., & Borkovec, T. (1973). *Progressive relaxation training: A manual for the helping professions.* Champaign, IL: Research Press.

Bernstein, D., & Given, B. (1984). Progressive relaxation: Abbreviated methods. In R. L. Woolfolk & P. Lehrer (Eds.) *Principles and practice of stress management* (pp. 43–69). New York: Guilford Press.

Billings, A. G., & Moos, R. H. (1981). The role of coping responses and social resources in attenuating the stress of life events. *Journal of Behavioral Medicine, 4,* 138–157.

Blanchard, E. B., & Andrasik, F. (1985). *Management of chronic headaches: A psychological approach.* New York: Pergamon Press.

Blanchard, E. B., Andrasik, F., Neff, D., Arena, J., Ahles, T., Jurish, S., Pallmayer, T., Saunders, N., Teders, S., Barron, K., & Rodichok, L. (1982). Biofeedback and relaxation training with three kinds of headache: Treatment effects and their prediction. *Journal of Consulting and Clinical Psychology, 50,* 562–575.

Bloom, B. L. (1985). *Stressful life event theory and research implications for primary prevention.* Rockville, MD: U.S. Department of Health and Human Services, National Institute of Mental Health.

Bloomfield, H. H., Cain, M. P., & Jaffe, D. T. (1976). *Transcendental meditation: Discovering inner energy and overcoming stress.* London: George Allen & Unwin.

Borkovec, T. D. (1979). Pseudo(experimental)-insomnia and idiopathic (objective) insomnia: Theoretical and therapeutic issues. *Advances in Behavior Research and Therapy,* (2), 27–55.

Braunwald, E., Isselbacher, K., Petersdorf, R., Wilson, J., Martin, J., & Fauci, A. (1987). *Harrison's principles of internal medicine.* New York: McGraw-Hill.

Brickman, P., Rabinowitz, V. C., Karuza, J., Jr., Coates, D., Cohn, E., & Kidder, L. (1982). Models of helping and coping. *American Psychologist, 37*(4), 368–384.

Brooks, G. R., & Richardson, F. C. (1980). Emotional skills training: A treatment program for duodenal ulcer. *Behavior Therapy, 11,* 198–207.

Brownell, K. D. (1982a). The addictive disorders. In C. M. Franks, G. T. Wilson, P. C. Kendall, & K. D. Brownell (Eds), *Annual Review of Behavior Therapy: Theory and Practice* (Vol. 8, pp. 208–272). New York: Guilford Press.

Brownell, K. D. (1982b). Behavioral medicine. In C. M. Franks, G. T. Wilson, P. C. Kendall, & K. D. Brownell (Eds), *Annual Review of Behavior Therapy: Theory and Practice* (Vol. 8, pp. 156–207). New York: Guilford Press.

Brownell, K. D. (1982c). Obesity: Understanding and treating a serious, prevalent and refractory disorder. *Journal of Consulting and Clinical Psychology, 50*(6), 820–840.

Brownell, K. D. (1984). The management of chronic pain. In G. T. Wilson, C. M. Franks, K. Brownell, & P. C. Kendall (Eds.), *Annual Review of Behavior Therapy* (Vol. 9, pp. 191–210). New York: Guilford Press.

Budzynski, T. H., & Stoya, J. M. (1969). An instrument for producing deep muscle relaxation by means of analogue information feedback. *Journal of Applied Behavior Analysis, 2,* 231–237.

Burkitt, D., Walker, A., & Painter, N. (1974). Dietary fiber and disease. *Journal of the American Medical Association, 229,* 1068.

Burns, D. D. (1980). *Feeling good.* New York: New American Library.

Campbell, A. (1975). *Transcendental meditation and the nature of enlightenment.* New York: Harper & Row.

Cannon, W. B. (1929). *Bodily changes in pain, hunger, fear and rage.* New York: Appleton-Century-Crofts.

Carrington, P. (1978). *Clinically standardized meditation.* Kendall Park, N.J.: Pace Educational Systems.

Carrington, P., Collings, G. H., Jr., Benson, H., Robinson, H., Wood, L. W., Lehrer, P. M., Woolfolk, R. L., & Cole, J. W. (1980). The use of meditation-relaxation techniques for the management of stress in a working population. *Journal of Occupational Medicine, 22,* 221–231.

Cautela, J. R., & Upper, D. (1976). The behavioral inventory battery: The use of self-report measures in behavioral analysis and therapy. In M. Hersen & A. S. Bellack (Eds.), *Behavioral assessment: A practical handbook* (pp. 77–109). New York: Pergamon Press.

Chapman, G. E., & Greenwood, C. E. (1987). Diet, brain and behavior: Implications for stress management. *Nutrition Quarterly, 11*(1), 9–13.

Charlesworth, E., & Nathan, R. (1984). *Stress management.* New York: Ballantine.

Chobanian, A. (1983). Hypertension. *Clinical Symposia, 35*(1).

Cleary, P. D. (1987). Gender differences in stress-related disorders. In R. C. Barnett, L. Biener, & G. K. Baruch (Eds.). *Gender and stress* (pp. 39–74). New York: The Free Press.

Cluss, P., & Fireman, P. (1985). Recent trends in asthma research. *Annals of Behavioral Medicine, 7*(4), 11–16.

Cohen, F. (1980). Personality, stress and the development of physical illness. In G. Stone, F. Cohen, & N. Adler (Eds.). *Health psychology—A handbook.* San Francisco: Jossey-Bass.

Cohen, S. (1983). *The alcoholism problems: Selected issues.* New York: Haworth Press.

Cohen, S. (1986). Contrasting the hassles scale and the perceived stress scale: Who's really measuring appraised stress? *American Psychologist, 41,* 716.

Coleman, V. (1978). *Stress Control.* London: Pan Books.

Confer, C. N., & Appley, M. H. (1964). *Motivation: Theory and research.* New York: Wiley.

Corcoran, K., & Fischer, J. (1987). *Measures for clinical practice: A sourcebook.* New York: The Free Press.

Cotton, D. H. G. (1986). *The health belief model and health lifestyle behavior: Application and analysis of a conceptual framework.* Unpublished doctoral dissertation, Queen's University, Kingston, Ontario, Canada.

Cotton, D. H. G. (1988). *The health belief model and cigarette smoking: Analysis of a conceptual framework.* Paper presented at the Annual Convention of the American Psychological Association, Atlanta, GA.

Creed, F. (1985). Life events and physical illness. *Journal of Psychosomatic Research, 29,* 113–123.

Danaher, B. G. (1974) Theoretical foundations and clinical applications of the Premack Principle: Review and critique. *Behavior Therapy, 5,* 307–324.

Davis, M., Eshelman, E., & McKay, M. (1982). *The relaxation and stress reduction workbook.* Oakland, CA: New Harbinger.

Dawber, T. (1975). *Risk factors for atherosclerotic disease.* Kalamazoo, MI: The Upjohn Company.

Derogatis, L. R. (1983). *BSI Administration and Procedures: Manual I.* Towson, MD: Clinical Psychometric Research.

Derogatis, L. R., & Cleary, P. A. (1977a). Confirmation of the dimensional structure of the SCL-90: A study in construct validation. *Journal of Clinical Psychology, 33,* 981–989.

Derogatis, L. R., & Cleary, P. A. (1977b). Factorial invariance across gender for the primary symptom dimensions of the SCL-90. *British Journal of Social & Clinical Psychology, 16,* 347–356.

Derogatis, L. R., Lipman, R. S., Rickels, K., Uhlenhuth, E. H., & Covi, L. (1974). The Hopkins Symptom Checklist (HSCL): A self-report symptom inventory. *Behavioral Science, 19,* 1–15.

Deutsch, J. (1986). Calling on freeze on "stress wars": There is hope of adaptation outcomes. *American Psychologist, 41,* 713–714.

Diagnostic and statistical manual of mental disorders (3rd Ed.-Revised.). (1987). Washington, DC: American Psychiatric Association.

Dohrenwend, B. S., & Dohrenwend, B. P. (1981a). Life stress and illness: Formulation of the issues. In B. S. Dohrenwend & B. P. Dohrenwend (Eds.), *Stressful life events and their contexts* (pp. 1–27). Canton, MA: Neale Watson.

Dohrenwend, B. S., & Dohrenwend, B. P. (1981b). Life stress and psychopathology. In D. A. Regier & G. Allen (Eds.), *Risk factor analysis in the major mental health disorders* (pp. 131–141). Washington, DC: U. S. Government Printing Office.

Dohrenwend, B. S., Dohrenwend, B. P., Dodson, M., & Shrout, P. E. (1984). Symptoms, hassles, social supports and life events: Problem of confounded measures. *Journal of Abnormal Psychology, 93*, 223–236.

Dohrenwend, B. P., Krasnoff, L., Askensay, A. R. et al. (1978). Exemplification of a method for scaling life events: The PERI life events scale. *Journal of Health and Social Behavior, 19*, 205–229.

Dohrenwend, B. P., & Shrout, P. E. (1985). "Hassles" in the conceptualization and measurement of life stress variables. *American Psychologist, 40*, 780–785.

Dohrenwend, B. P., & Shrout, P. E. (1986). Reply to Deutsch and Green. *American Psychologist, 41*, 716–718.

Durham, R. C., & Turvey, A. A. (1987). Cognitive therapy versus behavior therapy in the treatment of chronic general anxiety. *Behavior Research and Therapy, 25*(3), 229–234.

D'Zurilla, T. J., & Goldfried, M. R. (1971). Problem solving and behavior modification. *Journal of Abnormal Psychology, 78*(1), 107–126.

Eaton, T., Peterson, M., & Davis, J. (1976). *Psychiatry.* Flushing, NY: Medical Examination Publishing.

Edwards, M. (1987). How does stress affect nutrition? *Nutrition Quarterly, 11*(1), 3–7.

Elliot, G. R., & Eisdorfer, C. (1982). *Stress and human health.* New York: Springer.

Ellis, A. (1962). *Reason and emotion in psychotherapy.* Secaucus, NJ: Citadel Press.

Ellis, A. (1987). A sadly neglected cognitive element in depression. *Cognitive Therapy and Research, 11*(1), 121–146.

Estes, N. J., & Heineman, M. E. (1986). *Alcoholism: Developments, consequences and interventions.* St. Louis: C. V. Mosby.

Farber, P. D., Khavari, K. A., & Douglas, F. M. (1980). A factor analytic study of reasons for drinking: Empirical validation of positive and negative reinforcement dimensions. *Journal of Consulting and Clinical Psychology, 48*, 780–781.

Folkins, C. H., & Sime, W. E. (1981). Physical fitness training and mental health. *American Psychologist, 36*(4), 373–389.

Folkman, S., & Lazarus, S. (1980). An analysis of coping in a middle-aged community sample. *Journal of Health and Social Behavior, 21*, 219–239.

Follick, M. J., Ahern, D. K., Ahanasio, V., & Riley, J. F. (1985). Chronic pain programs: Current aims, strategies and needs. *Annals of Behavioral Medicine, 7*(3), 17–20.

Folkman, S. & Lazarus, R. S. (1985). If it changes it must be a process: A study of emotion and coping in three stages of a college examination. *Journal of Personality and Social Psychology, 48*, 150–170.

Fordyce, W. E. (1976). *Behavioral methods for clinical pain and illness.* St. Louis: Mosby.

Forsterling, F. (1980). Attributional aspects of cognitive behavior modification: A theoretical approach and suggestions for technique. *Cognitive Therapy and Research, 4*, 27–37.

Forsterling, F. (1986). Attributional conceptions in clinical psychology. *American Psychologist, 41*(3), 275–285.

Freis, E. (1976). Salt, volume, and prevention of hypertension. *Circulation, 53*, 589–595.

French, A. P., Tupin, J., Wright, L., Drummer, J. (1981). Psychological changes with a simple relaxation method. *Psychosomatics, 9*, 794–801.

Freudenberger, H. J., & North, G. (1985). *Women's burnout.* New York: Doubleday.

Friedman, H. S., & Booth-Kewley, S. (1987). The "disease-prone personality." *American Psychologist, 42*, 539–555.

Friedman, M., & Rosenman, R. (1974). *Type A behavior and your heart.* Greenwich, CT: Fawcett.

Fuller, G. D. (1977). *Biofeedback: Methods and procedures in clinical practice.* San Francisco: Biofeedback Institute of San Francisco.

Gambrill, E. D. & Richey, C. A. (1975). An assertion inventory for use in assessment and research. *Behavior Therapy, 6,* 550–561.

Glueck, B. C., & Stroebel, C. F. (1975). Biofeedback and meditation in the treatment of psychiatric illness. *Comprehensive Psychiatry, 16,* 303–321.

Goldberg, R. J. (1982). Anxiety reduction by self-regulation: Theory, practice and evaluation. *Annals of Internal Medicine, 96,* 483–487.

Goldfried, M., & Trier, C. (1974). Effectiveness of relaxation as an action coping skill. *Journal of Abnormal Psychology, 83,* 348–355.

Goleman, D. (1977). *The varieties of the meditative experience.* New York: Irvington.

Green, B. L. (1986). On the confounding of "hassles" stress and outcome. *American Psychologist, 41,* 714–715.

Green, J., & Shellenberger, R. (1986). Biofeedback research and the ghost in the box: A reply to Roberts. *American Psychologist, 41*(9), 1003–1005.

Greenberg, J. S. (1987). *Comprehensive stress management* (2nd ed.). Dubuque, IA: Brown.

Guyton, A. C. (1981). *Textbook of medical physiology* (6th ed.). Philadelphia: Saunders.

Hadaway, P., Beyerstein, B., & Kimball, M. (1986). Addiction as an adaptive response: Is smoking a functional behavior? *Journal of Drug Issues, 16*(3), 371–390.

Hall, S. M., Tunstall, C. D., Rugg, D. L., Jones, R. T., & Benowitz, N. L. (1985). Nicotine gum and behavioral treatment in smoking cessation. *Journal of Consulting and Clinical Psychology, 53*(2), 256–258.

Hamburg, B. A., Lipsett, L. F., Inoff, G. E., & Drash, A. L. (1979). *Behavioral and psychosocial issues in diabetes.* U. S. Department of Health and Human Services, Public Health Service, National Institute of Health: NIH Publications.

Harris, D., & Guten, S. (1979). Health-protective behavior: An exploratory study. *Journal of Health and Social Behavior, 20,* 17–29.

Hartman, L. M. (1984). Cognitive components of anxiety. *Journal of Clinical Psychology, 40,* 137–139.

Hastings, A. C., Fadiman, F., & Gordon, J. S. (1981). *Health for the whole person.* Boulder, CO: Westview Press.

Hauri, P. (1981). Treating psychophysiological insomnia with biofeedback. *Archives of General Psychiatry, 38,* 752–758.

Herman, C. P., & Polivy, J. (1980). Restrained eating. In A. B. Stunkard (Ed.). *Obesity* (pp. 208–225). Philadelphia: Saunders.

Hersen, M., & Bellack, A. S. (Eds.). (1976). *Behavioral assessment: A practical handbook.* New York: Peragamon Press.

Hersen, M., & Bellack, A. S. (Eds.). (1981). *Behavioral assessment: A practical handbook* (2nd ed.). New York: Pergamon Press.

Hinkle, L. E. (1974). The concept of "stress" in the biological and social sciences. *International Journal of Psychiatric Medicine, 5,* 355–357.

Hodges, W. F., & Felling, F. B. (1970). Types of stressful situations and their relation to trait anxiety and sex. *Journal of Consulting and Clinical Psychology, 34,* 333–337.

Hoffman, J. W., Benson, H., Arns, P. A., Stainbrook, G. L., Landsberg, L., Young, J. B., & Gill, A. (1982). Reduced sympathetic nervous system responsivity associated with the relaxation response. *Science, 215,* 190–192.

Holahan, C. K., Holahan, C. J., & Belk, S. S. (1984). Adjustment in aging: The roles of life stress, hassles and self-efficacy. *Health Psychology, 3,* 315–328.

Hollender, J. (1977). Motivational dimensions of the camping experience. *Journal of Leisure Research, 9,* 133–141.

Hollon, S. D., & Bemis, K. M. (1981). Self report and the assessment of cognitive functions. In M. Hersen & A. S. Bellack (Eds.). *Behavioral assessment: A practical handbook* (2nd ed., pp. 125–174). New York: Pergamon Press.

Hollon, S. D., & Kendall, P. C. (1980). Cognitive self-statements in depression: Development of an automatic thoughts questionnaire. *Cognitive Therapy and Research, 4,* 383–395.

Holmes, D. S., & McGilley, B. M. (1987). Influence of a brief aerobic training program on heart and subjective response to a psychologic stressor. *Psychosomatic Medicine, 49,* 366–374.

Holmes, T. H., & Masuda, M. 1974. Life change and illness susceptibility. In B. S. Dohrenwend & B. P. Dohrenwend (Eds.), *Stressful Life Events: Their nature and effects* (pp. 45–72). New York: Wiley.

Holmes, T. H., & Rahe, R. H. (1967). The social readjustment rating scale. *Journal of Psychosomatic Research, 11,* 213–218.

Horowitz, M., Schaefer, C., Hiroto, D., et al. (1977). Life events questionnaire for measuring presumptive stress. *Psychosomatic Medicine, 39,* 413–431.

Horowitz, M., Wilner, N., & Alvarez, W. (1979). Impact of event scale: A measure of subjective stress. *Psychosomatic Medicine, 41,* 209–218.

Hughes, J. R., Casal, D. C., & Leon, A. S. (1986). Psychological effects of exercise: A randomized cross-over trial. *Journal of Psychosomatic Research, 30*(3), 355–360.

Institute of Medicine, National Academy of Sciences. (1982). *Frontiers of Research in Biobehavioral Sciences.* Washington, DC: National Academy Press.

International Committee on Autogenic Therapy. (1961). *ICAT regulations. Proceedings in the third world congress of psychiatry* (Vol. 3). Montreal: University of Toronto and McGill University Press.

Iso-Ahola, S. (1980). *The social psychology of leisure and recreation.* Dubuque, IA: Brown.

Jacobson, E. (1938). *Progressive relaxation* (2nd ed.). Chicago: University of Chicago Press.

Jacobson, E. (1964). *Self operations control.* Chicago: National Foundation for Progressive Relaxation.

Jacobson, E. (1976). *You must relax* (5th ed.). New York: McGraw-Hill.

Jakubowski, P., & Lange, A. J. (1978). *The assertive option: Your rights and responsibilities.* Champaign, IL: Research Press.

Jeffrey, R. W. (1987). Behavioral treatment of obesity. *Annals of Behavioral Medicine, 9*(1), 20–24.

Johnston, C. (1970). *The book of the spiritual man: An interpretation.* London: Stewart & Watkins.

Kales, A., & Kales, J. (1984). *Evaluation and treatment of insomnia.* New York: Oxford University Press.

Kamarck, M. S., & Lichtenstein, E. (1985). Current trends in clinic-based smoking control. *Annals of Behavioral Medicine, 7*(2), 19–23.

Kanfer, F. H. (1970). Self-regulation: Research, issues and speculations. In C. Neuringer and J. L. Michaels (Eds.), *Behavior modification in clinical psychology* (pp. 178–220). New York: Appleton-Century-Crofts.

Kanfer, F. H. (1971). The maintenance of behavior by self-generated stimuli and reinforcement. In A. Jacob and L. B. Sachs (Eds.), *The psychology of private events* (pp. 46–71). New York: Academic Press.

Kanfer, F. H., & Goldstein, A. P. (Eds.). (1986). *Helping people change: A textbook of methods* (3rd ed.). New York: Pergamon Press.

Kanfer, F. H., & Grimm, L. G. (1980). Managing clinical change: A process model of therapy. *Behavior Modification, 4,* 419–444.

Kanfer, F. H., & Hagerman, S. (1981). The role of self-regulation. In L. P. Rehm (Ed.), *Behavior therapy for depression: Present status and future directions* (pp. 143–148). New York: Academic Press.

Kannas, L. (1981). The dimensions of health behavior among young men in Finland. *International Journal of Health Education, 24,* 146–155.

Kannel, W. (1971). Current status of the epidemiology of brain infarction associated with occlusive arterial disease. *Stroke, 2,* 295–318.

Kanner, A. D., Coyne, J. C., Schaefer, C., & Lazarus, R. S. (1981). Comparison of two modes of stress measurement: Daily hassles and uplifts versus major life events. *Journal of Behavioral Medicine, 4*, 1–39.

Kaplin, R. (1984). The connection between clinical health promotion and health status. *American Psychologist, 39*, 755–765.

Kazdin, A. E. (1980). *Behavior modification in applied settings* (rev. ed.). Homewood, IL: The Dorsey Press.

Keable, D. (1985a). Relaxation training techniques: A review. Part one: What is relaxation? *British Journal of Occupational Therapy, 48*(4), 99–102.

Keable, D. (1985b). Relaxation training techniques: A review. Part two: How effective is relaxation training? *British Journal of Occupational Therapy, 48*(7), 201–204.

Kelley, H. H. (1967). Attribution theory in social psychology. In D. Levine (Ed.), *Nebraska Symposium on Motivation* (pp. 192–238). Lincoln: University of Nebraska Press.

Kendall, P. C. (1984). Cognitive processes and procedures in behavior therapy. In C. M. Franks, A. Wilson, P. C. Kendall, & K. D. Brownell, *Annual Review of Behavior Therapy* (Vol. 10, pp. 123–163). New York: Guilford Press.

Kiester, E. (Ed.) (1982). *New family medical guide.* Des Moines, IA: Meredith.

Killen, J. D., Maccoby, N., & Taylor, C. B. (1984). Nicotine gum and self-regulation training in smoking relapse prevention. *Behavior Therapy, 15*, 234–248.

King, N. J. (1980). Abbreviated Progressive Relaxation. In M. Hersen, R. M. Eisler, & P. M. Miller (Eds.), *Progress in behavior modification* (pp. 150–161). New York: Academic Press.

Knapp, T. J., Downs, D. L., & Alperson, J. R. (1976). Behavior therapy for insomnia: A review. *Behavior Therapy, 7*, 614–625.

Kobasa, S. C. (1979). Stressful life events, personality & health: An inquiry into hardiness. *Journal of Personality and Social Psychology, 37*, 1—11.

Kobasa, S. C., Maddi, S. R., & Kahn, S. (1982). Hardiness and health: A prospective study. *Journal of Personality and Social Psychology, 42*(1), 168–177.

Kobasa, S. C., Maddi, S. R., & Puccetti, M. L. (1982). Personality and exercise as buffers in the stress-illness relationship. *Journal of Behavioral Medicine, 5*, 391–404.

Krantz, D. S., Grunberg, N. E., & Baum, A. (1985). Health psychology. *Annual review of psychology, 36*, 349–383.

Lachman, S. (1972). *Psychosomatic disorders: A behavioristic interpretation.* New York: Wiley.

Lakein, A. (1973). *How to get control of your time and your life.* New York: New American Library.

Lalonde, M. (1974). *A new perspective on the health of Canadians.* Ottawa: Health and Welfare Canada.

Langlie, J. (1979). Interrelationships among preventive health behaviors: A test of competing hypotheses. *Public Health Reports, 94*, 216–225.

Lavallee, Y. J., LaMontagne, Y., Annable, L., & Tetreault, L. (1977). Effects of EMG feedback, diazepam and their combination on chronic anxiety. *Journal of Psychosomatic Research, 21*, 65–71.

Lazarus, R. S. (1984). Puzzles in the study of daily hassles. *Journal of Behavioral Medicine, 7*, 375–389.

Lazarus, R. S., & DeLongis, A. (1983). Psychological stress and coping in aging. *American Psychologist, 38*, 245–254.

Lazarus, R. S., DeLongis, A., Folkman, S., & Gruen, R. (1985). Stress and adaptation outcomes: The problem of confounded measures. *American Psychologist, 40*, 770–779.

Lazarus, R. S., & Folkman, S. (1984). *Stress, appraisal and coping.* New York: Springer.

Lazarus, R. S., & Folkman, S. (1986a). Reply to Cohen. *American Psychologist, 41*, 718–719.

Lazarus, R. S., & Folkman, S. (1986b). Reply to Deutsch and Green. *American Psychologist, 41*, 715–716.

Lazarus, R. S., Kanner, A., & Cohen, J. B. (1980). Emotions: A cognitive-phenomenological analysis. In R. Plutchik & H. Kellerman (Eds.), *Theories of emotion* (pp. 189–217). New York: Academic Press.

Le Bouef, A., & Lodge, J. A. (1980). A comparison of frontalis EMG feedback training and progressive relaxation in the treatment of chronic anxiety. *British Journal of Psychiatry, 137*, 279–284.

Lefcourt, H. (1981). *Research with the locus of control construct.* (vol. I). New York: Academic Press.

Lehrer, P. M. (1982). How to relax and how not to relax: A re-evaluation of the work of Edmund Jacobson. *Behavior Research and Therapy, 20*, 417–428.

Lehrer, P. M., Atthowe, J. M., & Weber, E. S. P. (1980). Effects of progressive relaxation and autogenic training on anxiety and physiological measures, with some data on hypnotizability. In F. D. McGuigan, W. Sime, & J. M. Wallace (Eds.), *Stress and tension control.* New York: Plenum Press.

Lehrer, P. M., and Woolfolk, R. L. (1984). Are stress reduction techniques interchangeable, or do they have specific effects? A review of the comparative empirical literature. In R. L. Woolfolk and P. M. Lehrer (Eds.), *Principles and practice of stress management* (pp. 404–477). New York: Guilford Press.

Lehrer, P. M., Woolfolk, R. L., Rooney, A. J., McCann, B., & Carrington, P. (1983). Progressive relaxation and meditation: A study of psychophysical and therapeutic differences between two techniques. *Behavior Research and Therapy, 21*, 651–652.

Leon, G. R., & Roth, L. (1977). Obesity: Psychological causes, correlations, speculation. *Psychological Bulletin, 84*, 117–193.

Leventhal, H., & Cleary, P. D. (1980). The smoking problem: A review of the research and theory in behavioral risk modification. *Psychological Bulletin, 88*(2), 370–405.

Lewis, C. E., Biglan, A., & Steinbock, E. (1978). Self-administered relaxation training and money deposits in the treatment of recurrent anxiety. *Journal of Consulting and Clinical Psychology, 46*, 1274–1283.

Lichtenstein, E. (1982). The smoking problem: A behavioral perspective. *Journal of Consulting and Clinical Psychology, 50*(6), 804–819.

Lindsay, W. R., Gamsu, C. V., McLaughlin, E., Hood, E. M., and Espie, C. A. (1987). A controlled trial of treatments for generalized anxiety. *British Journal of Clinical Psychology, 26*, 3–15.

Luria, A. R. (1961). *The role of speech in the regulation of normal and abnormal behaviour.* Ed. by J. Tizard. New York: Pergamon Press.

Luthe, W. (1977). *Introduction to the methods of autogenic therapy.* Denver, CO: Biofeedback Society of America.

Luthe, W., & Schultz, J. H. (1969). *Autogenic therapy* (Vols. 1–6). New York: Grune & Stratton.

MacDonald, A. P., & Games, R. G. (1972). Ellis' irrational values. *Rational Living, 7*, 25–28.

MacDonald, W. S. (1977). Emotional life of college students. Cited in D. L. Watson & R. G. Tharp, *Self-directed behavior: Self modification for personal adjustment* (3rd ed., p. 64). (1981). Monterey, CA: Brooks/Cole.

Marchione, K. E., Michelson, L., Greenwald, M., & Dancu, C. (1987). Cognitive behavioral treatment of agoraphobia. *Behavior Research and Therapy, 25*(5), 319–328.

Marcinek, M. (1980). Hypertension: What it does to the body. *American Journal of Nursing, 80*(5), 928–932.

Martin, J. E., & Dubbert, P. M. (1982a). Exercise and health: The adherence problem. *Behavioral Medicine Update, 4*(1), 16–24.

Martin, J. E., & Dubbert, P. M. (1982b.) Exercise applications and promotion in behavioral medicine: Current status and future directions. *Journal of Consulting and Clinical Psychology, 50*(6), 1004–1017.

Martin, J. E., Dubbert, P. M., Katell, A. D., Thompson, J. K., Raczynski, J. R., Lake, M., Smith, P. O., Webster, J. S., Sikora, T., & Cohen, R. E. (1984). Behavioral control of exercise in sedentary adults: Studies 1 through 6. *Journal of Consulting and Clinical Psychology, 52*, 795–811.

Marziali, E. A., & Pilkonis, P. A. (1986). The measurement of subjective response to stressful life events. *Journal of Human Stress*, Spring, 5–11.

250 *Stress Management: An Integrated Approach to Therapy*

Marzillier, J. (1987). A sadly neglected cognitive element in depression: A reply to Ellis. *Cognitive Therapy and Research, 11*(1), 147–152.

Mathews, A. M. (1982). *Anxiety and its management.* Unpublished manuscript, St. George's Hospital Medical School, London.

McCaffrey, R., & Blanchard, E. B. (1985). Stress management approaches to the treatment of essential hypertension. *Annals of Behavioral Medicine, 7*(1), 5–12.

McCann, I. L., & Holmes, D. S. (1984). Influence of aerobic exercise on depression. *Journal of Personality and Social Psychology, 46*(5), 1142–1147.

McCormick, I. A. (1984). A simple version of the Rathus assertiveness schedule. *Behavior Assessment, 7*, 95–99.

McGovern, H. (1986). Comment on Roberts's criticism of biofeedback. *American Psychologist, 41*, (9), 1007.

McKinney, M. E., & White, H. (1985). Dietary habits and blood chemistry levels of the stress-prone individual: The hot reactor. *Comprehensive Therapy, 11*(8), 21–28.

Meichenbaum, D. (1976). A cognitive-behavior modification approach to assessment. In M. Hersen & A. S. Bellack (Eds.), *Behavioral assessment: A practical handbook* (pp. 143–171). New York: Pergamon Press.

Meichenbaum, D. (1977). *Cognitive-behavior modification: An integrative approach.* New York: Plenum Press.

Meichenbaum, D. (1985). *Stress inoculation training.* New York: Pergamon Press.

Michelson, L., Mavissakalian, M., & Marchione, K. (1985). Cognitive and behavioral treatments of agoraphobia: Clinical, behavioral and psychophysiological outcomes. *Journal of Consulting and Clinical Psychology, 53*(6), 913–925.

Miller, R. C., & Berman, J. S. (1983). The efficacy of cognitive behavior therapies: A quantitative review of the research evidence. *Psychological Bulletin, 94*(1), 39–53.

Miller, S. M., & Kirsch, N. (1987). Sex differences in cognitive coping with stress. In R. C. Barnett, L. Biener, & G. K. Baruch, (Eds.), *Gender and stress* (pp. 278–307). New York: The Free Press.

Mitchell, C. M. & Drossman, D. A. (1987). The irritable bowel syndrome: Understanding and treating a biopsychosocial illness disorder. *Annals of Behavioral Medicine, 9*(3), 13–18.

Monroe, S. M. (1983). Major and minor life events as predictors of psychological distress: Further issues and findings. *Journal of Behavioral Medicine, 6*, 189–205.

Morganstern, K. P. (1976). Behavioral interviewing: The initial stages of assessment. In M. Hersen & A. S. Bellack (Eds.), *Behavioral assessment: A practical handbook* (pp. 51–76). New York: Pergamon Press.

Morganstern, K. P., & Tevlin, N. E. (1981). Behavioral interviewing. In M. Hersen & A. S. Bellack (Eds.), *Behavioral assessment: A practical handbook* (2nd ed., pp. 71–100). New York: Pergamon Press.

Mostofsky, D. I., & Balaschak, B. A. (1977). Psychological control of seizures. *Psychological Bulletin, 84*(4), 723–750.

Murray, D. J. (1983). *A history of Western psychology.* Englewood Cliffs, NJ: Prentice-Hall.

Neulinger, J. (1974). *The psychology of leisure.* Springfield, IL: Thomas.

Nigl, A., & Jackson, B. (1979). EMG biofeedback as an adjunct to standard psychiatric treatment. *Journal of Clinical Psychiatry, 40*, 433–436.

Norman, R. M. (1985). Studies of the interrelationships amongst health behaviours. *Canadian Journal of Public Health, 76*(6), 407–410.

Norris, P. (1986). On the status of biofeedback and clinical practice. *American Psychologist, 41*(9), 1009–1010.

Norris, P., & Fahrion, S. (1984). Autogenic biofeedback in psychophysiological therapy and stress management. In R. L. Woolfolk & P. Lehrer (Eds.), *Principles and practice of stress management* (pp. 220–254). New York: Guilford Press.

Nunnally, J. C. (1967). *Psychometric Theory.* New York: McGraw-Hill.

Oldridge, N. B. (1979). Compliance of post myocardial infarction patients to exercise programs. *Medicine & Science in Sports, 4*, 373–375.

Oldridge, N. B., Wicks, J. R., Hanley, C., Sutton, J. R., & Jones, N. L. (1978). Noncompliance in an exercise rehabilitation program for men who have suffered a myocardial infarction. *Canadian Medical Association Journal, 118*, 361–364.

O'Neill, D. (1955). *Modern trends in psychosomatic medicine*. London: Butterworth.

Paffenberger, R., Hale, W., Brand, K., & Hype, R. (1977). Work-energy level, personal characteristics and fatal heart attack: A birth cohort effect. *American Journal of Epidemiology, 105*, 200–213.

Patel, C. M. (1973). Yoga and biofeedback in the management of hypertension. *Lancet, ii*, 1053–1055.

Patel, C. (1984). Yogic therapy. In R. L. Woolfolk & P. Lehrer (Eds.), *Principles and practice of stress management* (pp. 70–107). New York: Guilford Press.

Patterson, C. H. (1986). *Theories of counselling and psychotherapy* (4th ed.). New York: Harper & Row.

Pilkonis, P. A., Imber, S. D., & Rubinsky, P. (1985). Dimensions of life stress in psychiatric patients. *Journal of Human Stress, Spring*, 5–11.

Pinkerton, S., Hughes, H., & Wenrich, W. W. (1982). *Behavioral medicine: Clinical applications*. New York: Wiley.

Polefrone, J., & Manuck, S. (1987). Gender differences in cardiovascular and neuroendocrine response to stressors. In R. C. Barnett, L. Biener, & G. K. Baruch, (Eds.), *Gender and stress* (pp. 13–38). New York: The Free Press.

Prager-Decker, I. J. (1979). The relative efficacy of progressive relaxation, EMG biofeedback and music for reducing stress arousal of internally versus externally controlled individuals. *Dissertation Abstracts International, 39*, 3177B.

Premack, D. (1965). Reinforcement theory. In D. Levine (Ed.), *Nebraska Symposium on Motivation*. Lincoln: University of Nebraska Press, pp. 123–180.

Raskin, M., Johnson, G., Rondesvedt, J. W. (1973). Chronic anxiety treated by feedback-induced muscle relaxation: A pilot study. *Archives of General Psychiatry, 28*, 263–266.

Rathus, S. A. (1973). A 30-term schedule for assessing assertive behavior. *Behavior Therapy, 4*, 398–406.

Rehm, L. P., Kaslow, N. J., & Rabin, A. S. (1987). Cognitive and behavioral targets in a self-control therapy program for depression. *Journal of Consulting and Clinical Psychology, 55*(1), 60–67.

Report of the Inter-Society Commission for Heart Disease Resources. (1972). Primary prevention of the atherosclerotic diseases. *Circulation, 42*, 1–44.

Richmond, J. (1979). *Health people: The Surgeon General's report on health promotion and disease prevention*. Washington, DC: U.S. Government Printing Office.

Rimm, D. C., & Masters, J. C. (1979). *Behavior therapy: Techniques and empirical findings*. New York: Academic Press.

Roberts, A. H. (1985). Biofeedback: research training and clinical roles. *American Psychologist, 40*(8), 938–941.

Rogers, M. P., Dubey, D., & Reich, P. (1979). The influence of the psyche and the brain on immunity and disease susceptibility: A critical review. *Psychosomatic Medicine, 41*, 147–164.

Rosenthal, T. L., & Rosenthal, R. H. (1983). Stress causes, measurement and management. In K. D. Craig and R. J. McMahon (Eds.), *Advances in clinical behavior therapy* (pp. 3–26). New York: Brunner/Mazel.

Roskies, E., Seraganian, P., Oseasohn, R., Hanley, A., et al. (1986). The Montreal Type A Intervention Project: Major Findings. *Health Psychology, 5*(1), 45–69.

Roth, D. L., & Holmes, D. S. (1985). Influence of physical fitness in determining the impact of stressful life events on physical and psychologic health. *Psychosomatic Medicine, 47*(2), 164–173.

Roth, D. L., & Holmes, D. S. (1987). Influence of aerobic exercise training and relaxation training on physical and psychologic health following stressful life events. *Psychosomatic Medicine, 49,* 355–365.

Ruderman, A. J. (1986). Dietary restraint: A theoretical and empirical review, *Psychological Bulletin, 99*(2), 247–262.

Runkel, P. J., & McGrath, J. E. (1972). *Research on Human Behavior.* New York: Holt, Rinehart & Winston.

Rush, A. J. (1984). Cognitive therapy. In T. B. Karasu (Ed.), *The psychiatric therapies* (pp. 397–414). Washington, DC: American Psychiatric Association.

Russell, M. A., & Jarvis, M. J. (1985). *Theoretical background and clinical use of nicotine chewing gum.* National Institute on Drug Abuse: Research Monograph Series, Monograph 53, 110–130.

Salter, A. (1949). *Conditioned reflex therapy.* New York: Farrar, Straus & Giroux.

Sanne, H., (1973). Exercise tolerance and physical training of non-selected patients after myocardial infarction. *Acta Medica Scandinavica,* Suppl. 551, 5–27.

Sarason, I. G., Johnson, J. H., & Siegal, J. M. (1978). Assessing the impact of life changes: Development of the Life Experiences Survey. *Journal of Consulting and Clinical Psychology, 46,* 932–946.

Schefft, B. K., & Kanfer, F. H. (1987). The utility of a process model in therapy: A comparative study of treatment effects. *Behavior Therapy, 18,* 113–134.

Schwartz, G. E., Blanchard, E. B., & Neff, D. F. (1986). Behavioral treatment of irritable bowel syndrome: a one year follow-up study. *Biofeedback and Self-Regulation, 11*(3), 189–198.

Schwartz, G. E., Davidson, R. J., & Goleman, D. T. (1978). Patterning of cognitive and somatic processes in self-regulation of anxiety: Effects of meditation versus exercise. *Psychosomatic Medicine, 40,* 321–328.

Schwartz, R. (1982). Cognitive-behavior modification: A conceptual review. *Clinical Psychology Review, 2,* 267–293.

Selye, H. (1956). *The stress of life.* New York: McGraw-Hill.

Shellenberger, R., & Green, J. (1986). *From the ghost in the box to successful biofeedback training.* Greeley, CO: Health Psychology Publications.

Shelton, J. L., & Levy, R. L. (1981). *Behavioral assignments and treatment compliance.* Champaign, IL: Research Press.

Shiffman, S. (1986). A cluster analytic classification of smoking relapse episodes. *Addictive Behaviors, 11*(3), 295–307.

Shopland, D. R., & Brown, C. (1985). Changes in cigarette smoking prevalence in the U.S.: 1955 to 1983. *Annals of Behavioral Medicine, 7*(2), 5–8.

Shorkey, C. T., & Whiteman, V. L. (1977). Development of the Rational Behavior Inventory: Initial validity and reliability. *Educational and Psychological Measurement, 37,* 527–534.

Shulman, Lawrence. (1979). *The skills of helping.* Itasca, IL: Peacock.

Silver, B. V., & Blanchard, E. B. (1979). Biofeedback and relaxation training in the treatment of psychophysiological disorders: Or, are the machines really necessary? *Annals of Behavioral Medicine, 1,* 217–239.

Sinyor, D., Golden, M., Steinert, Y., & Seraganian, P. (1986). Experimental manipulation of aerobic fitness and response to psychosocial stress: Heart rate and self-report measures. *Psychosomatic Medicine, 48*(5), 324–337.

Sinyor, D., Schwartz, S. G., Peronnet, F., Brisson, G., & Seraganian, P. (1983). Aerobic fitness level and reactivity to psychosocial stress: Physiological, biochemical and subjective measures. *Psychosomatic Medicine, 45,* 205–217.

Slater, E., & Roth, M. (1977). *Clinical psychiatry.* London: Bailliere Tindall.

Sloane, R. B., Staples, F. R., Cristol, A. H., Yorkston, N. J., & Whipple, K. (1975). *Psychotherapy versus behavior therapy.* Cambridge, MA: Harvard University Press.

Smith, J. C. (1986). Meditation, biofeedback, and the relaxation controversy: A cognitive behavioral perspective. *American Psychologist, 41*(9), 1007–1009.

Smith, J. C. (1985). *Relaxation dynamics: Nine world approaches to self-relaxation*. Champaign, IL: Research Press.

Snow, W. G. (1977). *The physiological and subjective effects of several brief relaxation training procedures*. Unpublished doctoral dissertation, York University, Canada.

Spaulding, W. (1976). The psychosomatic approach in medicine. In Z. Lipowski, D. Lipsitt, & P. Whybrow (Eds.), *Psychosomatic Medicine* (pp. 457–469). New York: Oxford University Press.

Staples, R. J. (1978). A comparison of EMG feedback training and progressive relaxation training of hospitalized psychiatric patients. *Dissertation Abstracts International, 38*(12-B), 6176–6177.

Staples, R. J., Coursey, R., & Smith, B. (1976). *A comparison of EMG biofeedback, autogenic and progressive training as relaxation techniques*. Paper presented at the annual meeting of the Biofeedback Research Society, Monterey, CA.

Stern, R. S. (1970). Treatment of a case of obsessional neurosis using thought-stopping technique. *British Journal of Psychiatry, 117*, 441–442.

Stone, E. M. (Ed.). (1988). *American psychiatric glossary*. Washington, D.C.: American Psychiatric Press.

Stoyva, J. M. (1979). Guidelines in the training of general relaxation. In J. V. Basmajian (Ed.). *Biofeedback: Principles and practice for clinicians*. Baltimore: Williams & Wilkins.

Surawy, C., & Cox, J. (1987). Smoking under natural conditions: A diary study. *Personality and Individual Differences, 8*(1), 33–41.

Surwit, R. S. (1982). Biofeedback and the behavioral treatment of Raynaud's Disease. In L. White & B. Tursky (Eds.), *Clinical biofeedback efficacy and mechanisms* (pp. 222–231). New York: Guilford Press.

Surwit, R. S., & Keefe, F. J. (1978). Frontalis EMG feedback training: An electronic panacea? *Behavior Therapy, 9*, 779–792.

Tapp, J., & Goldenthal, P. (1982). A factor analytic study of health habits. *Preventive Medicine, 11*, 724–728.

Targan, S., Britvan, L., & Dorey, F. (1981). Activation of human NKCC by moderate exercise: Increase frequency of NK cells with enhanced capability of effector-target lytic interactions. *Clinical and Experimental Immunology, 45*, 352–360.

Taylor, H. L. (1981). *Making time work for you*. Don Mills, Ontario: General Publishing Co. Ltd.

Taylor, S. E., & Brown, J. D. (1988). Illusion and well-being: A social psychological perspective on mental health. *Psychological Bulletin, 103*(2), 193–210.

Tennant, C., Langeluddecke, P., & Byrne, D. (1985). The concept of stress. *Australian and New Zealand Journal of Psychiatry, 19*(2), 113–118.

Toomin, M. (1974). GSR biofeedback techniques in psychotherapy. *Proceedings of the Biofeedback Research Society*, Colorado Springs.

Turk, D. C., Sobel, H. J., Follick, M. J., & Youkilis, H. D. (1980). A sequential criterion analysis for assessing coping with chronic illness. *Journal of Human Stress*, June, 35–40.

Turner, J. A. (1978). *A comparison of muscle relaxation, meditation, and self-relaxation in anxious patients*. Unpublished master's thesis, Somerville College, Oxford University.

Turner, J. A., & Chapman, C. R. (1982). Psychological interventions for chronic pain: A critical review: I. Relaxation training and biofeedback. *Pain, 12*, 1–21.

Vishnudevananda, Swami. (1960). *The complete illustrated book of yoga*. New York: The Julian Press.

Wallace, R. K. (1970). Physiological effects of transcendental meditation. *Science, 167*, 1751–1754.

Wallace, R. K., & Benson, H. (1972). The physiology of meditation. *Scientific American, 226*, 84–90.

Wallace, R. K., Benson, H., & Wilson, G. (1971). A wakeful hypometabolic physiological state. *American Journal of Physiology, 221*, 795–799.

Watson, D. D., & Tharp, R. G. (1981). *Self-directed behavior: Self-modification for personal adjustment* (3rd ed.). Monterey, California: Brooks/Cole.

Weinberger, M., Hiner, S. L., & Tierney, W. M. (1987). In support of hassles as a measure of stress in predicting health outcomes. *Journal of Behavioral Medicine, 10,* 19–31.

Weissman, A. N. (1980). Assessing depressogenic attitudes: A validation study. Paper presented at the 51st Annual Meeting of the Eastern Psychological Association, Hartford, CT.

White, S., & Tursky, B. (1986). Commentary on Roberts. *American Psychologist, 41*(9), 1005–1007.

Whitehead, W. E., & Bosmajian, L. S. (1982). Behavioral medicine approaches to gastrointestinal disorders. *Journal of Consulting and Clinical Psychology, 50*(6), 972–983.

Wilhelmsen, L., Sanne, H., Elmfeldt, D., Grimby, G., Tibblin, G., & Wedel, H. S. (1975). Controlled trial of physical training after myocardial infarction. *Preventive Medicine, 4,* 491–508.

Williams, A., & Wechsler, H. (1972). Interrelationships of preventive actions in health and other areas. *Health Services Reports, 87,* 969–976.

Williams, B. J., Martin, S., & Foreyt, J. P. (1976) *Obesity: Approaches to dietary management.* New York: Brunner/Mazel.

Witt, P. A., & Bishop, D. W. (1970). Situational antecedents to leisure behavior. *Journal of Leisure Research, 2,* 64–77.

Wolpe, J. (1958). *Psychotherapy by reciprocal inhibition.* Stanford, CA: Stanford University Press.

Wolpe, J., & Lang, P. J. (1964). A fear survey schedule for use in behavior therapy. *Behavior Research and Therapy, 2,* 27–30.

Woodson, P. P., Buzzi, R., Nil, R., & Bättig, K. (1986). Effects of smoking on vegetative reactivity to noise in women. *Psychophysiology, 23*(3), 272–282.

Woolfolk, R. L., & Lehrer, P. (Eds.). (1984). *Principles and practice of stress management.* New York: Guilford Press.

Wyngaarden, J., & Smith, L. (Eds.). (1985). *Cecil textbook of medicine.* Philadelphia: Saunders.

Zales, M. R. (Ed.). (1985). *Stress in health and disease.* New York: Brunner/Mazel.

Zarcone, V. (1981). Differential diagnosis of sleep disorders. *Behavioral Medicine Update, 3*(2), 9–11.

Zebroff, K. (1975). *Beauty through yoga.* Vancouver: Fforber.

Zung, W. K. (1971). A rating instrument for anxiety disorders. *Psychosomatics, 12,* 371–379.

Zuroff, D. C., & Schwartz, J. C. (1978). Effects of transcendental meditation and muscle relaxation on trait anxiety, maladjustment, locus of control and drug use. *Journal of Consulting and Clinical Psychology, 46,* 264–271.

Name Index

Subject Index

,